PEACE FOR PALESTINE

PEACE
FOR
PALESTINE

First Lost Opportunity

Elmer Berger

University Press of Florida

Gainesville
Tallahassee
Tampa
Boca Raton
Pensacola
Orlando
Miami
Jacksonville

An earlier version of this book was
published in *The Palestine Yearbook of International Law* 5 (1989).

Library of Congress Cataloging-in-
Publication data appear on the last
printed page of the book.

The University Press of Florida is
the scholarly publishing agency
for the State University System of
Florida, comprised of Florida
A & M University, Florida Atlantic
University, Florida International
University, Florida State
University, University of Central
Florida, University of Florida,
University of North Florida,
University of South Florida, and
University of West Florida.

University Press of Florida
15 Northwest 15th Street
Gainesville, FL 32611

For Roselle,

*who will know and remember
all the reasons*

CONTENTS

MAPS

FOREWORD

Rabbi Elmer Berger is not usually thought of as a Middle East scholar but rather as an activist, an avowed anti-Zionist who for the past half century has been in the vanguard of one of the most unpopular and generally misunderstood ideological movements in America. The very name of the most recent organization he established at the request of some of his associates, American Jewish Alternatives to Zionism (AJAZ), has made him anathema to many whose closed minds prevent them from examining, even critically, the message Rabbi Berger has sought to bring to American Jews. Because his name is so closely associated with this unpopular cause, many "know," without examining any of his works, that Elmer Berger is not, indeed, cannot be a scholar. This book refutes that perception. It demonstrates the extent to which Dr. Berger is capable of examining one of the most controversial issues of our times with honesty, objectivity, insightfulness, and empathy, even with those whose views are at variance with his.

I have known Elmer Berger for the past thirty-five years and although we often disagree, I have always found that he is prepared, willing, and even eager to become familiar with diverse perspectives on controversial issues, including the Arab-Israeli conflict. His work in this volume is evidence of his eagerness to search out the truth, insofar as there *is* a "truth" in this very controversial dispute. This is a work of genuine discovery that uses both the methods and sources of first-rate scholarship.

It is a valuable addition to the "new thinking" about the Middle East that many Israeli scholars such as Benny Morris, Avi Shlaim, Simha Flapan, Tom Segev, etc. have begun in recent years, and it adds to and complements their work. Unfortunately, as we know from the efforts made to publish this volume, there are many who will refute its contribution without so much as a glance at its first page because it was written by Elmer Berger. The loss is theirs. Who will gain are those, like Berger himself, with an open mind and a willingness to become familiar with new perspectives on an ancient controversy.

Don Peretz,
Professor of Political Science,
SUNY–Binghamton

PREFACE

Recently declassified documents from Israeli and Zionist archives provide fresh insights into the early years of the ongoing dispute over the future political conformation of Palestine, Israel, and the Palestinian people. The following volume analyzes those documents that cover the 1948–49 armistice negotiations between Israel and the then-belligerent Arab states. Also included are relevant UN resolutions and U.S. attitudes and policies cited from the volumes of *Foreign Relations of the United States* for those years. There are also references to such recent works as Simha Flapan's *The Birth of Israel*, Benny Morris's *The Birth of the Arab Refugee Problem, 1947-49*, Avi Shlaim's *Collusion Across the Jordan*, and Yehoshafat Harkabi's *Israel's Fateful Hour*.

The recorded frustrations of Dr. Ralphe Bunche, the UN's acting mediator for the bargaining sessions, provide fresh insights on the negotiating strategies of several parties. The inadequate preparedness of the Arab participants and their contrast with the well-informed Israeli diplomats, the disagreements among the Arab states, and a conspiracy with Israel abetted by one of those states, all contributed to the failure of the negotiations to lead to a durable peace. The Israeli government documents[1] had been classified for more than three decades. They may now be accepted as the authoritative Israeli record and are therefore an important—and new—historical source.

Before proceeding to analyze and interpret this material it is appropriate to compliment the editor of the published volumes. In fact, the work of the editors appears to have been so conscientious that there is no simple reading of the finished product. It is often necessary to shuttle back and forth among the 1,000 pages to comprehend fully the context in which many of the documents should be read. They are not literarily appealing works. Despite the editors' best efforts there is no clearly marked trail through this minefield of information. This present volume is an attempt to plow a furrow through this field of information that has remained only inadequately explored, if not almost entirely ignored, by historians of the problem of Palestine.[2] Given the four decades of failure of all parties to find the comprehensive peace toward which these negotiations for the first armistices were intended to lead, some clues to a more efficacious approach may be found in these historic records.

Accounts of the diplomatic efforts concerning Palestine have suffered from fragmented, episodic, and disconnected historical review. Of the several parties involved, one has benefited most from the omissions. I hope that this present analysis will serve serious observers of the prolonged conflict over Palestine as a guide to the applicable international law and to the attitudes and negotiating policies of the parties. Such new insights should help determine which party bears the heaviest responsibility for the failure to "chart the road to a peace for Palestine," to quote the hope so solemnly expressed by Dr. Bunche when he inaugurated the negotiations on the island of Rhodes over forty years ago (*M. V.*, p. 13).

Acknowledgments

I am indebted to many for much of what I know—or think I know—about the seemingly intractable problem of Palestine/Israel and the Palestinians. The list includes people from many walks of life, those of high stations and average citizens, and individuals from many countries, ethnic backgrounds, and religious preferences. Here, it is possible to identify only a few who, in my more than four decades of study and activism, have appeared to me *personally* to be most helpful, insightful, and responsible.

Directly responsible for the initiative of this volume is Dr. Anis F. Kassem, a leading Palestinian intellectual and legal authority. It was he who asked me to study and interpret the Israeli and American primary sources that provide much of the documentation for this work. I am grateful to Professors Fred J. Khouri and Don Peretz for their critical reading of the manuscript and their many constructive recommendations. Special thanks go to Ms. Angela Goodner-Piazza for constructive editing of the "Notes" and for preparation of the final typescript. I owe my elementary knowledge of the principles of international law to a long-time friendship and collaboration with Professor Emeritus Dr. W. T. Mallison, Jr. Special thanks, too, to Ann Leggett who perceptively captured the spirit I tried to convey in writing by her jacket illustration of the children—future citizens of the state-principals involved in the diplomacies reviewed and analyzed.

Finally, I find the few words permissible here inadequate to express my profound gratitude to the men and women who, for more than four decades, have encouraged me with their active support to continue my concentration on and my public expression of an essentially unconventional viewpoint about what many believe to be the central problem in the Middle East.

I hope all these—and others who will read this book—will find it a helpful contribution toward solving the many vexatious problems still obstructing the road to peace in one of the world's most challenging and potentially explosive areas.

chapter 1

ORIGINAL SINS AND
PRESENT MOTIVES

The "Sacred Rite"—Classified Documents

The substantive issues in the armistice negotiations were not new in 1948–49. Nor were they generated by the first Arab-Israeli war. Their origins are found in visible form in the first two decades of the twentieth century. They acquired status as a subject of international diplomacy in 1917 with the issuance of the Balfour Declaration and later, during the Paris Peace Conference of 1919. The increasing importance of the entire Middle East, not least economically, has added intellectual spice to the expanding knowledge of the area—including accounts of how present circumstances there came to pass.

Now, nearly three-quarters of a century after the events recorded in previously classified documents, it would be foolish to try to deny that this present historical survey enjoys the infinite wisdom of 20/20 hindsight. This readily offered confession invites a comment that is applicable to the conduct of the current crop of wheelers and dealers in diplomacy. If they are haunted by fear of judgments of their handiwork to be made twenty years after completion, let them take a second look at the sanctimony with which they randomly employ the near-universal, bureaucratic practice of "classified documents" and the feigned horror with which they contemplate "leaks." Most of that game is designed to protect the players more than the audience, who, in a free society, are the people with a "right to know."

A classic example of this irreverent proposition is the so-called Pentagon Papers, published in 1971 by the *New York Times* and other major American newspapers. These leaked documents were appropriately subtitled, "The Secret History of the Vietnam War." After the first few installments (there were estimated to be 2.5 million words in forty-seven volumes) were made available to the American people, the U.S. government attempted to stop the publishing, claiming that "the national defense interests of the United States and the nation's security will suffer immediate and irreparable harm." On June 30, 1971, by a vote of six to three, the U.S. Supreme Court denied the government's petition to terminate publication of the balance of the documents.[1]

"The proof of the pudding was in the eating." The scare words used by the government to terminate publication proved to be as ill founded as most of the cerebrations of the decision makers contained in the leaked documents. The greatest damage done by the disclosures was the unscheduled deflation of the demigods who had greased the skids for American involvement in its most hurtful war. They had guessed wrong more often than they had deliberately reasoned their way through the facts to realistic conclusions. They had fabricated clever camouflages to make bad—and sometimes illegal—judgments look plausible, or legal. It has been well put that the "eyes only," "top secret" classifications on these documents served, in the main, to cover momentarily the fallacies, the "goofs" of those who were committing the nation's resources of life and material goods to a project badly conceived from the beginning and consequently badly executed up to and including its demeaning and tragic end.

If now—more than forty years later—an evaluation of the 1948–49 negotiations of the first armistice agreements in the Palestine conflict appears to offer harsh judgments on the motives and ultimate purposes of the negotiators, they have only themselves to blame. And if now, with historic perspective and new evidence, it is possible to speculate on those earlier motives and objectives, it is justifiable to do so if the exercise provides some clues to the persistence of the conflict and suggests to those now engaged in the search for the elusive peace some new and radical shift away from the flawed earlier policies and postures. By demythologizing and deflating some of the propagandized versions that have distorted much of Palestinian history for so long,[2] this account of the armistice negotiations will serve its intended purpose. Essentially, this study will attempt to show why the armistices were so short lived and why, in fact, they nurtured future wars instead of leading the parties on the first step of the thousand-mile journey to peace.[3]

The Israeli documents may not always do justice to the Arab viewpoint. If there are organized Arab archives no doubt they would suggest nuances, perhaps even fundamental perspectives and motives different from the Israeli records used as the principal sources here.

chapter 2

HISTORY, SOURCES, LAW

On November 29, 1947, the General Assembly of the United Nations, by a narrow margin, voted to *recommend* the partition of Palestine into a so-called Jewish state and an Arab state, with the city of Jerusalem to be established as a *corpus separatum* administered by the Trusteeship Council "on behalf of the United Nations."[1] The two recommended states were to join in an "economic union." The Security Council was charged with responsibility for implementation of the plan. If "an attempt to alter by force the settlement envisaged" by the partition recommendation occurred, the Security Council was to determine, "in accordance with Article 39 of the Charter," if it constituted "a threat to or breach of the peace or an act of aggression."

A commission was established (Part I, B, "Steps Preparatory to Independence") to "carry out measures for the establishment of the frontiers" of the two recommended states and the City of Jerusalem along "the general lines" of the General Assembly's partition "recommendations." For a variety of reasons, the commission "never left New York."[2]

The adoption of the partition recommendation triggered immediate conflict in Palestine between Arabs and Zionists in places like Jerusalem, Haifa, Tel Aviv, Jaffa, and other "areas where Arabs and Jews lived in close proximity."[3] The Palestinian Arabs were understandably motivated by opposition to the partition of their country. This resistance should not be confused with the intervention of armies of the Arab

League states after May 15, 1948, when the British had decided to evacuate the last of their occupying troops. Just after 10:00 A.M. Eastern Standard Time on May 14, "one hour before the mandate was to end," representatives of "the Jewish Community of Eretz-Israel [Land of Israel] and of the Zionist Movement" declared "the Establishment of a Jewish State in Eretz-Israel, to be known as the State of Israel."[4]

The community fighting that erupted with the UN's vote was not a new phenomenon. Palestinian Arab resistance to Zionism had existed since about 1920, when knowledge of the Balfour Declaration became widespread in the Middle East. Even during the mandate, irregular Zionist forces in the form of armed Zionist settlements accompanied the Zionist movement's policy to stake out "facts on the ground," to put territorial flesh on the skeleton promise of a "national home for the Jewish people." In fact, civil war had existed in Palestine almost continuously for more than a quarter century before the May 15 declaration of establishment of the Zionist state. The civil war character of hostilities continued until May 15, 1948, when the armies of Egypt, Transjordan, Iraq, Syria, and Lebanon moved to provide assistance to the Palestinian Arabs who were no match, either in funds, equipment, or numbers, for the Zionist forces. And if the Palestinian Arabs jumped the gun at the end of the mandate and were more aggressive than the better-organized Zionist forces in late 1947/early 1948, Zionist irregulars were not far behind. The Irgun Zvai Leumi expanded its attacks and improved the organization of its guerrilla warfare at about the same time.[5]

The declaration of the establishment of Israel on May 15, 1948, escalated the civil war into an international conflict. The United Nations belatedly took notice of the expanding violence and responded with a number of resolutions. Their titles reflect the expanding violence and increasing urgency of finding an alternative to the conflict. On March 5, 1948, the Security Council adopted Resolution No. 42 "Appealing for Prevention or Reduction of Disorders in Palestine." Resolution No. 43 (1948) was adopted on April 1, "Calling for a Truce Between the Arab and Jewish Communities of Palestine." Note that the principals identified in the resolution are referred to as "communities of *Palestine*." There was, as yet, no declared Arab state intervention. On the same date, Security Council Resolution No. 44 requested "the Secretary-General to Convoke a Special Session of the General Assembly to Consider the Future Government of Palestine." The session convened on April 20. The United States offered a proposal to supersede the partition recommendation by referring the problem of Palestine to the Trusteeship Council to establish a "temporary trusteeship."[6]

On April 17, 1948, Security Council Resolution No. 46 called for "a Cessation of Military Activities in Palestine." The principals specifically charged with this responsibility were the United Kingdom (still officially the mandatory power), the Jewish Agency, and the Arab Higher Committee. The absence of any Arab state is of historical importance. On April 23, Security Council Resolution No. 48 established a truce commission to supervise implementation of the truce called for in Resolution No. 46. On May 14, the General Assembly (in a special session) adopted Resolution No. 186 (S-2) asking for a UN mediator in Palestine and called on "all Governments, organizations and persons" to observe the truce called for in the resolution of the Security Council. Section III of the resolution relieved the Palestine Commission of the responsibilities detailed in the partition resolution (*UN Res.*, pp. 14–15). The addition of the words "all Governments" to this resolution reflected the then-current international character of the hostilities. Security Council Resolution No. 49 of May 22 called for a "Cease-Fire in Palestine and a Truce in Jerusalem."

On May 29, Security Council Resolution No. 50 again called on "all Governments and authorities concerned" to order a cessation of all acts of armed force for a period of four weeks. Other measures were called for, all concerned with the effort to end the fighting and to prohibit the importation of war matériel or fighting personnel from outside sources. Count Folke Bernadotte, the UN mediator, was charged with supervising the provisions of this resolution. Putting teeth into this action, at least rhetorically, paragraph 11 called for action under Chapter VII of the charter for any violation of the resolution involving "aggression," or a "threat to" or "breach of the peace." Another cease-fire was ordered and the mediator was given three days to bring about compliance of the belligerents. Special attention was given the situation in Jerusalem, where "an immediate and unconditional cease-fire" was ordered. Bernadotte was also charged to "bring about the demilitarization" of the city, "without prejudice" to its future political status and "to assure the protection of and access to Holy Places, religious buildings and sites in Palestine." Resolution No. 54 states that "subject to further decision by the Security Council or the General Assembly, the truce still remains in force . . . until a peaceful adjustment of the future situation of Palestine is reached." (The full texts of Security Council Resolution Nos. 42–56 are found in *UN Res.*, pp. 125–28.)

On August 19, Security Council Resolution No. 56 established guidelines for the mediator's efforts to attain and supervise a truce. Two subparagraphs became important—and contentious—issues in the armistice negotiations: 2(d) No party is permitted to violate the truce on the ground that it is undertaking reprisals or retaliations against the other party; 2(e) No party is entitled to gain military or political advantage through violation of the truce.

An important geopolitical fact, with bearing on the future negotiations for armistices to replace the fragile truces, is that between the first and second truce, Israel "seized some 780 square miles of territory from the Arabs on nearly all fronts." Most of these areas had been allocated by the partition proposal to the Arab state. On the other hand, once the second truce came into effect, the Arabs held parts of eastern Galilee and most of the Negev, both of which the partition had designated as Israeli territory. And both belligerents occupied parts of Jerusalem contrary to the November 29 partition plan.[7]

In addition to his efforts to gain all belligerents' immediate compliance with provisions of the truce, Bernadotte had been strenuously engaged attempting to implement General Assembly Resolution No. 186 (S-2) of May 14, 1948. On September 16, from Beirut, Bernadotte sent the UN secretary-general a progress report, destined to play a very important role in future diplomacy about Palestine. What came to be known unofficially as the Bernadotte Plan held to the broad outlines of the November 29, 1947, partition proposal. It envisaged two states. It eliminated the recommendation for economic union. "Political and economic union," Bernadotte concluded, may be "desirable," but "the time is certainly not now propitious for the effectuation of any such scheme." And "Jerusalem, because of its religious and international significance and the complexity of interests involved, should be accorded special and separate treatment."[8]

Bernadotte also recommended several significant boundary changes that departed from the November plan. (1) Most of the Negev, which the partition plan had assigned the Jewish State, should be defined as Arab territory. (2) Lydda and Ramleh (in the so-called Triangle) should be "in Arab territory," but the boundary should skirt those Arab cities, giving Israel part of the Triangle area that had been designated in the

November recommendation as part of the Arab state. (3) "Galilee should be defined as Jewish territory." The original partition plan had assigned western Galilee to Arab territory.[9]

These territorial alterations, Bernadotte stated, were motivated by "the principle of geographical homogeneity and integration." He cautioned against any plan to establish frontiers "rigidly controlled by the territorial arrangements envisaged in the resolution of 29th November."[10]

The proposals were "flatly rejected . . . by both parties," and, after June 27, Bernadotte did not press them. As an alternative to agreement by the parties he recommended a "technical boundaries commission appointed by and responsible to the United Nations"[11] to determine the frontiers between the two states. But in the armistice negotiations Bernadotte's territorial proposals became some of the stickiest points for establishing armistice lines.

Bernadotte was greatly concerned with the human problem of the Palestinians who had been displaced. He recommended a formula composed of two basic components: the right of the refugees "to return to their homes in Jewish-controlled territory at the earliest possible date" and "their repatriation, resettlement and economic and social rehabilitation" and "payment of adequate compensation for the property of those choosing not to return."[12]

Bernadotte also proposed the establishment of a "Palestine conciliation commission" to serve for a "limited period," acting under the authority of the United Nations. The commission was to take steps "ensuring the continuation of the peaceful adjustment of the situation in Palestine."[13]

On September 17, 1948, Bernadotte was assassinated in Jerusalem by Stern Gang terrorists. Dr. Ralph Bunche was appointed acting mediator.

The substantive thrust of these UN resolutions provides a greatly condensed legal and factual context in which Security Council Resolutions No. 61 of November 4 and No. 62 of November 16 must be interpreted. Bunche's statement opening the armistice negotiations informed the negotiators that they were to devise the means for implementing these two resolutions (*M. V.*, pp. 12–15, particularly 13). The texts of these two resolutions will be reproduced at relevant places in the following analyses of the negotiations. (The full texts are found in *UN Res.*, pp. 129, 130.)

Two other UN resolutions of 1948 had relevance to the armistice negotiations. The first, General Assembly Resolution No. 194 (III), was adopted on December 11. This resolution embodied the essential recommendations of Count Bernadotte's report of September (*UN Res.,* pp. 15–17). It avoided the murdered mediator's specific boundary recommendations for Palestine as a whole but contained detailed territorial specifics for the "Jerusalem area" and for "the Holy Places—including Nazareth—religious buildings and sites" (paras. 7 and 8). It established a conciliation commission that was, "in so far as it considers necessary, to . . . assume the functions given to the United Nations Mediator . . . by Resolution 186 (S-2) of the General Assembly of May 14, 1948" (para. 2). It retained, in paragraph 11, an almost verbatim repetition of Bernadotte's proposal for resolving the problem of the refugees. In a general way, this December 11, 1948, General Assembly resolution supplanted the November 29, 1947, partition recommendation as the blueprint for partitioning the country. Since the 1967 war, its practical, political, and geopolitical relevance has been in some doubt. There are legal scholars who hold that, under certain conditions, General Assembly resolutions constitute international law.[14] Events have overtaken much of the December 11, 1948, resolution, but there is no comprehensive replacement for it.

The other UN resolution with relevance to the armistice agreements was Security Council Resolution No. 66 of December 29, 1948 (*UN Res.,* p. 130). This action was in response to an Israeli military campaign in "southern Palestine" (the eastern and southern areas of the Negev) after the "final" truce and in violation of the armistice negotiations with Egypt. Each armistice agreement, consistent with UN resolutions, provided that termination of the fighting and fixing of the armistice lines were to be "without prejudice" to the ultimate disposition of territory or the rights of the humans affected in permanent peace agreements.

chapter 3

THE STARTING POINT—
PARIS, 1919

It is legitimate to ask which of the negotiating parties respected the intent of the Security Council that the armistices were "to facilitate the transition from the present truce to permanent peace in Palestine . . ." (*UN Res.*, pp. 129–30). Dr. Bunche, inaugurating the negotiations with the Israeli-Egyptian delegations on January 13, 1949, declared that implementation of the Security Council resolutions was the objective of the armistice-diplomacy. "We are not holding a peace conference here," he cautioned (*M. V.*, p. 13).

The Israeli documents provide no explicit answers to these questions. But some guidance for speculation is provided by a basic Zionist document of 1919. The following excerpts from the Zionist Organization's memorandum to the Supreme Council at the peace conference ending World War I deals with the Zionist-proposed boundaries for the Balfour Declaration's projected "national home for the Jewish people."

The Boundaries of Palestine
Schedule
The boundaries of Palestine shall follow the general lines set out below:

Starting on the North at a point on the Mediterranean Sea in the vicinity of Sidon and following the watersheds of the foothills of the Lebanon as far as Jisr El Karaon, thence to El Bireh, following the dividing line between the two basins of the Wadi El Korn and the Wadi Et Teim line between the Eastern and Western slopes of the Hermon, to the vicinity West of Beit Jenn, thence Eastward following the northern watersheds of the Nahr Mughaniye close to and west of the Hedjaz Railway.

In the East a line close to and West of the Hedjaz Railway terminating in the Gulf of Akaba.

In the South a frontier to be agreed upon with the Egyptian Government.

In the West the Mediterranean Sea.

The details of the delimitations, or any necessary adjustments of detail, shall be settled by a Special Commission on which there shall be Jewish representation.[1]

These Zionist territorial aspirations should be read in conjunction with map 1 and compared with the boundaries recommended for the partition in 1947 (map 2).

None of the territory beyond the borders of Palestine in map 1 had ever been considered Palestinian. In the days of the Ottoman Empire, these lands were part of Greater Syria, one of the empire's provinces, insofar as they had any definable borders at all. After World War I, the victorious Allied powers divided up the old empire. The authors of the 1919 Zionist proposal may—or may not—have been aware of these machinations. In any event, the contemporary relevance of this map is that many of the territorial objectives of the 1919 Zionist plan still appear to be important to the territorial expansionists in today's Israel. These include southern Lebanon up to the Litani River (much of this territory is now held by Israel with the help of a surrogate army as a "security zone"); the Golan Heights (until 1967 considered Syrian territory); all of the West Bank (now called in Israeli parlance Judea and Samaria); a part of the east bank of the Jordan River, to a line just barely west of the old Hedjaz Railroad; and the Gaza Strip (in 1919 considered part of Palestine).

The 1919 memorandum offered essentially economic arguments to support these territorial claims. The following excerpts are illuminating.

Boundaries

The boundaries above outlined are what we consider essential for the necessary *economic* foundation of the country. Palestine must have its natural outlets to the seas and the control of its rivers

Map 1. Territory requested by Zionists at Paris Peace Conference, 1919.

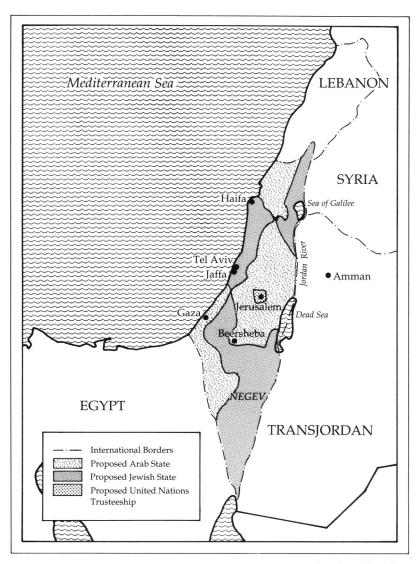

Map 2. Territorial partition proposed by UN General Assembly plan, 1947.

and *their headwaters*. . . . [The Special] Commission will bear in mind that it is highly desirable, in the interests of economical administration that the geographical area of Palestine should be as large as possible so that it may eventually contain a large and thriving population. . . .

It is, therefore, of *vital importance not only to secure all water resources already feeding the country, but also to be able to conserve and control them at their sources.*

The Hermon is Palestine's real "Father of Waters" *and cannot be severed from it* without striking at the very root of its economic life. The Hermon not only needs reforestation but also other works before it can again adequately serve as the water reservoir of the country. It must therefore be *wholly under the control of those who will most willingly as well as most adequately restore it to its maximum utility.* Some international arrangement must be made whereby the riparian rights of the people dwelling south of the Litani River may be fully protected. . . .

The fertile plains *east of the Jordan*, since the earliest Biblical times, have been linked economically and politically with the land west of the Jordan. . . . A just regard for the economic needs of Palestine and Arabia demands that *free access to the Hedjaz Railway through its length* be accorded both Governments.

An intensive development of the agriculture and other opportunities of Transjordania make it imperative that *Palestine shall have access to the Red Sea and an opportunity of developing good harbours on the Gulf of Akaba.* . . . The ports developed in the Gulf of Akaba should be free ports through which the commerce of the Hinterland may pass on the same principle which guides us in suggesting that free access be given to the Hedjaz Railway. (all emphases supplied)

There are no references here to security, and the relevance of references to biblical times must certainly raise some eyebrows in a formal political document dated 1919. Israeli strategy, in both the fighting and the armistice negotiations in 1948–49, adhered closely to the 1919 Zionist aspirations.[2] The Biltmore Program, adopted by "an extraordinary conference" of Zionists at the Biltmore Hotel in New York, on May 11, 1942 (para. 8), called for "Palestine [to] be established as a Jewish Commonwealth." The paragraph left little ambiguity about the Zionist meaning of commonwealth. It asked that "the gates of Palestine be opened; that the Jewish Agency be vested with control of immigration into Palestine and with the necessary authority for upbuilding the country, including the development of its unoccupied and uncultivated lands." The program was "endorsed in Jerusalem the following November by the Inner General Council (the supreme wartime policy-making body of the Zionist movement) [and] constituted the basis of Zionist demands in later efforts to settle the Palestine problem, first by the mandatory power and then by the United Nations."[3]

The powers to be granted the Jewish Agency—"control of immigration" and "authority for upbuilding the country, including development of its unoccupied and uncultivated lands"—are usually prerogatives of sovereignty. The Zionist proposal made no provision for the indigenous inhabitants to participate in the discussions of these crucial questions. Paragraph 5 expresses "the readiness and desire of the Jewish people for full cooperation with their Arab neighbors." But nothing substantive from the second safeguard clause of the Balfour Declaration remains in the critical paragraph 8. In sum, the Biltmore Program proposed Zionist sovereignty in all of Palestine and ignored completely even the declaration's guarantee of the vague "civil and religious rights" of Palestine's "non-Jewish communities" and "the rights and political status of Jews in any other country."

The American site of the conference signaled the shift of Zionist lobbying for great power support from London to Washington. The shift was dictated not only by the perception that England would emerge from the war with greatly diminished strength and weary of the mounting cost of colonialism, including the mandate, but that the United States would be virtually unchallenged as the dominant Western power. There were other, less apparent but equally or more important advantages recommending the transfer. England had long experience in the Middle East, and many of its people displayed the usual colonial insensitivity to the aspirations of the native Arabs. But there were also many who had cultivated strong empathy for them. Until World War II, the United States had relied on the British for the political wisdom and military presence to protect American interests in the area. There were Middle East specialists in the U.S. Foreign Service. But Americans generally were almost totally uninformed about the area and its inhabitants. Two exceptions to this assertion were a minuscule number of academic specialists and an equally small coterie of missionaries, among whom had been the founders and supporters of such institutions as the American University of Beirut.

As the years passed and Palestine's internal political problems worsened, these became virtually the only visible activists for the rights of Palestine's Arabs. In the crunch of the political struggle after the British announced termination of the mandate and as the arena of political debate moved to the United Nations, the Foreign Service specialists, for the most part, opposed partition.[4] The cold war was in full cry, and the U.S. foreign policy establishment was obsessed with stopping Communist expansion. British power in the Middle East was waning, and conventional American wisdom dictated that alienating the Arab states was no way to protect and promote U.S. geopolitical and oil interests in this area of such critical economic and strategic importance.

The British and American positions on the Palestine problem were hardly in concert. President Harry Truman had only scanty knowledge of both the tangled web of the international politics of Middle East history, on one hand, and even less familiarity with the stubborn, bitter Zionist-Arab internal feuding in Palestine. His focus was almost entirely on humanitarian solutions for the displaced Jewish victims of Hitler, whose lives, among others in Europe, had been devastated by the Nazis during the war. Truman's State Department was almost unanimously opposed to partition, fearing a violent uprising among the Arabs and permanent jeopardy to U.S. interests. But Clark Clifford, one of the president's closest personal advisors brought to Washington from Kansas City, was unmovably convinced that reelection in 1948 was crucially dependent on winning the Jewish vote in New York and other metropolitan centers. Clifford, accordingly, waged an incessant campaign with the president to persuade him to support partition. In this, Clifford had the full support of David Niles, another Missouri import, who, although no committed Zionist himself, became a political ally with Clifford urging presidential support for Zionism.

Policy makers in England were divided, largely along party lines, about solutions for the increasingly burdensome problem of Palestine in the context of continuing British interests in the Middle East. In 1947, Churchill, as the leading Conservative, had been a moderate Zionist. With the end of the war, "he became a moving spirit behind the solution of partition and its possible corollary of an independent Jewish State." But as early as 1946 he had said, "It is our duty . . . to offer to lay down the Mandate. We should . . . as soon as the war stopped, have made it clear to the United States that unless they come in and bear their share, we shall lay the whole case and burden at the foot of the United Nations organization."[5]

Churchill's opposite in the Labour party, Ernest Bevin, had become foreign secretary when Labour succeeded the Conservatives after the war. He displayed less equivocation than could be implied in the growing support for partition as an expedient for resolving the Zionist-Arab problem within Palestine. The Balfour Declaration, he declared, "was the source of all the trouble. . . . It was the greatest mistake in Britain's imperial history. . . . It did not take into account the Arabs and was really a Power Politics declaration." He became disillusioned and even bitter because he "learned the Americans would not follow his lead in resolving the Palestine issue and that President Truman would respond to the pressures and opportunism of American politics more than to the dilemmas of the British." Bevin "hoped that the United Nations might endorse the solution of a binational state."[6]

The Arabs were unified in their opposition to the proposed Jewish commonwealth. Among U.S. policy makers there were those who saw such an entity, with a constituency of Western Jews (most of whom had come from eastern and central Europe) as a potential ally against the "irresponsible, eastern" Arab regimes. The propaganda machine of the Jewish Agency and the American Jews it claimed by cooption and whose institutions it had penetrated to the point of control was up to the challenge. It proceeded to build the image of a Jewish vote. And for an American public unaware of Palestine's turbulent political history under the mandate, the propaganda campaign successfully tutored the electorate in the idea that Zionism was a blessing of enlightenment for the backward Arabs. The Department of State resisted partition. But for the most part its reasoning was confined to intragovernmental memoranda that would not be declassified until a quarter of a century later.[7] The political advisors to the president responded to special interests, domestic political pressures fueled by the propaganda. They overpowered the State Department's professional counsel and postwar U.S. influence tilted heavily to the Zionist side. The die was cast—and loaded—for the American "moral" commitment to Zionist aspirations for a Jewish state. Then—and to a large extent even now—the Arab side was no match in the propaganda and public relations game. The Palestinians' case was almost totally ignored.

The Zionist approach was essentially in the pattern of the moribund

British colonialism. Addressing an indoctrinated electorate led by uninformed politicians and with any knowledgeable expertise restricted to intragovernmental discussions, the records of which would remain classified for two decades, the proponents of the Jewish commonwealth had a virtual field day in shaping American public opinion. In the recent tragic history of Palestine, which saw Zionist political and territorial claims imposed on the country and its people, this American connection has proven to be Israel's most reliable and profitable asset.

In 1947 the Jewish state proponents came to the UN deliberations well armed. They knew what they wanted. Their terrorists in Palestine accelerated and intensified harassment of the British. Aided by the increasing public awareness of the tragedy that Hitler had inflicted on Europe, including coverage that concentrated on Europe's Jews among the millions of the Nazis' victims, Zionism enjoyed the virtually unchallenged support of American public opinion.

The General Assembly's recommendation for partition offered only a partial fulfillment of the 1919 Zionist territorial aspirations. But the Zionists were not unprepared for compromise. In 1946, they had informed the British and American governments they were prepared to accept partition of the country.[8] They proposed a territorial division different only in some details—but important details—from those incorporated in the UN partition plan. Their 1946 plan provided a corridor to the sea for the proposed Arab state, but all of Galilee was included in the Jewish state, along with the Negev and the Golan Heights. Jerusalem was to be part of the Arab territory. Map 3 makes an interesting comparison with the 1947 UN recommendation and has a bearing on the armistice negotiations following the first Arab-Israeli war.

The Jewish Agency–Zionist 1946 proposal was motivated by several pragmatic considerations. In 1946 a joint Anglo-American committee had submitted to the British and American governments a recommendation for the immediate admission into Palestine of 100,000 Jewish survivors of Hitler's savagery. This humanitarian concession to Zionism was balanced by the qualification that "Jew shall not dominate Arab and Arab shall not dominate Jew" (Recommendation No. 3).[9] In other words, there was to be a democratic political system. After this emergency admission of the 100,000, future immigration into Palestine would be determined by the majority population, differing from the exclusive control sought by the Zionists.

A second motivation for the 1946 Zionist compromise was, undoubt-

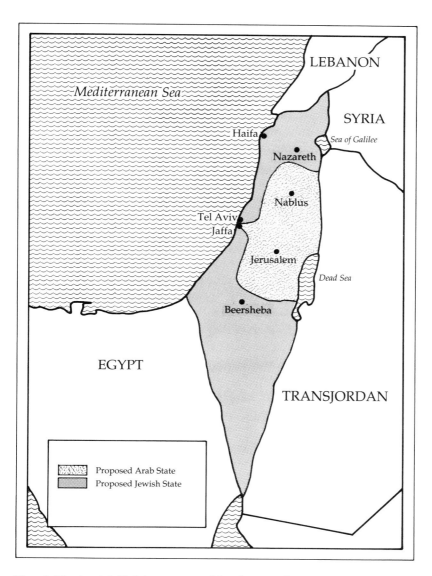

Map 3. Territorial division proposed by the Jewish Agency, 1946.

edly, growing Palestinian resistance to further Zionist development and creeping acquisition of land. The increasing resistance had evoked stronger British curbs on Zionist–Jewish Agency activity. The shape of less rosy things to come for Zionists had been revealed in the Peel Commission's partition proposal[10] in 1937 and in the McDonald White Paper[11] of 1939 following the formidable Arab revolt that lasted from 1936 to 1939. Both of these reports submitted by royal commissions to the British government contemplated severe limitations on Zionist expansion in Palestine.

A third factor influencing the Zionists' 1946 decision was increasing American involvement in the Palestine problem. The Biltmore Conference had signaled the shift of Zionist great power lobbying to Washington. But the Zionists did not yet have anything in the United States comparable to their long experience in England and the Parliamentary bloc support that they had enjoyed.

Zionism has long pursued a strategy of creeping land acquisition, of "establishing facts on the ground," to advance its ultimate goal of sovereignty as a fait accompli. "Dunam by dunam," as Ben-Gurion once put it, was a pragmatic program that the English found difficult to oppose, both because of fear of being charged as anti-Jewish and also because limitations on the acquisition of land were of questionable legitimacy under the mandate.

Also, Zionist policy makers were constantly concerned with maintaining favorable world public opinion. Minimal as knowledge of the Arabs and Arab rights may have been, it did exist and was attracting increased public attention. The expanding great power investment in and exploitation of Arab oil and rising national self-consciousness of the Arabs had begun to have more influence on great power policy than at the end of World War I.

One other consideration appears to have influenced the Zionist tactical acceptance of the territorial shrinkage recommended in the UN proposal for partition. Zionist public relations and political pressures in Western Europe and the United States had stressed the stark tragedy suffered by Jews (with little or no reference to Hitler's other victims), the frightening existence of survivors in concentration camps, and, following the war, the life-draining, hopeless prospects of the displaced persons camps. A great wave of sympathy and guilt tortured the consciences of many in the victorious nations. These sentiments were easily exploitable for compensating actions for the surviving Jews. Orchestrated conventional opinion held they would not want to return to their former homes but were uniformly eager to find insurance against any repetition of the tragedy in a nation of their own. To have quibbled about a few square miles of territory would have appeared unseemly and ungrateful, so the Zionist managers believed. They masked their disappointment over the territorial specifications of partition with restrained expressions of satisfaction with the promise of Zionist sovereignty over whatever territory they would acquire. With the same tactical suppleness that had led Chaim Weizmann to accept the Balfour Declaration, even though it promised less than the 1919 blueprint of Zionist claims, the 1947 leadership accepted partition with public grace while privately harboring profound reservations.[12] In 1948, after the decision had been made, David Ben-Gurion cryptically described the partition-prescribed Jewish state as having been established in only "a portion of the land of Israel." And he reminisced, "[I]f Moshe Dayan had been chief of staff during the war of 1948 against the Arabs in Palestine, Israeli territory might have been greater."[13]

Another authoritative source put it differently. In the official Zionist publication, *Zionist Review*, of January 30, 1948, Walter Eytan, who would become director-general of the Ministry of Foreign Affairs, contributed an article called "The Search for a Name" of the "Jewish State." He stated that *"Eretz Yisrael"* (Land of Israel) was discarded as "inappropriate for the state which was in only a part of Palestine." *"Medinat Yisrael"* (State of Israel) was finally adopted.[14] The distinction remains in much Zionist-Israeli terminology.

chapter 4

PARTITION—LESS THAN
HALF THE LOAF

General Assembly Partition Resolution No. 181 (*UN Res.*, pp. 4–14) noted that England had informed the United Nations it would "complete its evacuation of Palestine by 1 August 1948." Part I of the resolution declared, "The Mandate for Palestine shall terminate as soon as possible but in any case not later than 1 August 1948." For a variety of reasons, the British actually declared termination of their mandatory responsibilities on May 15, 1948.[1]

Zionist reservations about the territorial allocations were made *en famille*, in assemblies of the inner circle of policy makers or confined to Zionist publications with limited readership or, regrettably, no readership at all among the movers and shakers of diplomacy. There were massive rallies of cheering Zionists in New York and in Palestine. But far from the near-hysterical joyous crowds, more sober Zionist planners considered how to improve the disappointing boundaries that had been proposed largely based on demographics of concentrated Arab and Jewish populations. There was little regard for either the 1919 Zionist dream or for rational boundaries demarcating the proposed Arab and Jewish states. Also, contrary to Zionist aspirations, Jerusalem was to be a *corpus separatum*, a separate city, "under a special international regime and administered by the United Nations."

In Palestine, the Zionists acquired the means to translate private reservations into geopolitical facts. As early as 1946, terrorists led by Menachem Begin and the Irgun had begun offensive military action against the British. On July 22, with the agreement of the Haganah, the Jewish Agency's regular defense forces, the Irgun blew up the King David Hotel.[2] At the time, this was the most celebrated of the terrorist exploits, but Hirst inventories a long list of additional acts of violence.

> They also blew up bridges, mined roads, derailed trains and sank patrol boats. . . . They raided armouries and robbed pay vans. They blew up twenty warplanes on closely guarded airfields in a single night. They staged what the British press called the "greatest jail-break in history." Irgun and Stern [another, smaller terrorist group] . . . blew up the British embassy in Rome. They despatched letter-bombs to British ministers. . . . They sent an assassination squad into Britain, with the mission—which was not accomplished—of executing the former commanding officer in Palestine, General Evelyn Barker; its members included Weizmann's own nephew, Ezer Weizmann, one of the architects of the Israeli air force. . . . In Palestine they killed soldiers in their sleep. They captured and flogged officers; then they hanged two sergeants from a tree and booby-trapped their dangling corpses.[3]

The hanging of the British sergeants on July 30, 1947, and the booby-trapping of their bodies stirred the greatest anger in England and out-raged people in many parts of the world. Begin selected the earliest targets of terrorism—primarily the British. The political objective was to make administration of the mandate impossible. The Palestine problem would then be debated by the United Nations, leaving the Palestinians to the mercies of the Zionists.

The Jewish Agency consistently and publicly declared its disapproval of and separation from the terrorism and its perpetrators. The most eloquent—and widely accepted—disavower was Chaim Weizmann. In his autobiography, *Trial and Error*, Weizmann recalls the substance of his testimony in 1947 before the United Nations Special Committee on Palestine:[4] "I said before the U.N.S.C.O.P. in Jerusalem: The [British] White Paper [of 1939] released certain phenomena in Jewish life which are un-Jewish, which are contrary to Jewish ethics, Jewish tradition. 'Thou shalt not kill' has been ingrained in us since Mount Sinai. The dissident groups which sprang up in Palestine, and which terrorized the Government and to some extent the Jews, and kept up an unbearable tension in the country, represented to my notion a grave danger for the whole future of the Jewish State in Palestine."[5]

Earlier, before the Anglo-American Committee of Inquiry (1945), Ben-Gurion was asked by a British committee member "whether he agreed with Dr. Weizmann's condemnation of violence." Ben-Gurion is reported to have replied that "he associated himself with it." He then added that the Jewish Agency had discontinued "collaboration" with the British "in suppressing the terrorists . . . because it was futile."[6] But in 1948, *after* the terror had driven the first mass of Palestinian refugees from the territory assigned by partition to the Jewish state, Weizmann, no longer despondent over the "un-Jewish" character of the terror, called the results of the violence "a miraculous simplification of Israel's tasks"![7]

There was good—even if closely guarded—reason for the Jewish Agency's equivocation about Begin's extremist exploits in terror prior to the UN decision. The Zionists anticipated a close call in the General Assembly for the decisive vote. The U.S. government's position would be decisive. But it was in the United States, more than in Europe, that Zionism was generally perceived as a humanitarian refugee movement. In fact, the agency had never been more than halfhearted in its efforts to identify the terrorists and put a stop to their activities. There had been on-again-off-again negotiations since 1946 between Begin and his Irgunists, on the one hand, and the agency's military arm, the Haganah, on the other hand.[8]

In July of that year British Command Paper No. 6873, "Palestine Statement Relating to Acts of Violence," noted that during the preceding eight or nine months the "Haganah and its associated force, Palmach, working under the political control of prominent members of the Jewish Agency, had been engaged in the carefully planned use of violence and sabotage under the name of the Jewish Resistance Movement."[9] The British document also said the Stern Gang (more radical and violent than the Irgun and in which Yitzhak Shamir was a leader) had been cooperating with the Haganah, and the Irgun's "illegal radio transmitter calling itself the 'Voice of Israel' was working under the general direction of the Jewish Agency."[10]

The Irgun's 1946 campaigns realized its immediate *political* goals when a war-weary Britain determined to leave Palestine and put the problem before the United Nations. It is clear that by raising nonaccountability to an art form, the official Zionist establishment, with the

Jewish Agency internationally recognized as its representative, was a now-you-see-it, now-you-don't partner with the terrorists.

The General Assembly's partition decision dictated the next logical target. The date of May 15, 1948, which the British had determined for their withdrawal from Palestine, became crucial in the early months of 1948 and set the agenda for the political and territorial issues to be addressed in the armistice agreements. The Zionists lost no time preparing to take by force many of the territories of their 1919 plan that the partition threatened to deny them.

The Arab States, the Palestinians, and the British

The Arabs of Palestine reacted almost immediately against the recommended partition, but they were no match, either militarily or organizationally, for the Zionist forces. The disparities were attributable largely to British policy during the mandate. There had been times when the British had displayed some concern for the Balfour Declaration's pledge that "nothing shall be done to prejudice the civil and religious rights" of the Arabs. But in practice, the British administration, politically harassed by a determined Zionist machine, closed its eyes to Zionist policies that persistently stretched the Balfour agreement's promise to the Zionists to its limits and often beyond them. British respect for Arab rights usually consisted of damage control, reaction to Zionist faits accomplis. The Jewish Agency had consistently evaded halfhearted British attempts to prohibit the importation of military equipment and the influx of illegal Jewish immigrants.[11] The Palestinian Arabs lacked both the central organization and the means to mobilize, train, and equip a comparable fighting force.

Arab resistance to the UN decision was directed both against the partition—on principle—and against the Zionists. Zionist objections were directed against the territorial allocations of partition, while the principle was accepted. In its conceptualization, therefore, the civil war was uneven. On the Zionist side was the weight of general, worldwide support, even if only partially informed. Weighing against the Palestinian Arabs was rejection by international consensus and a decisive imbalance in the means to fight a war.

The early engagements between the adversaries were numerous but rather small scale. The Zionist attacks were generally planned to secure geographically strategic points whether within the proposed Jewish state or not. Arab attacks were on a kind of hit-or-miss basis, lacking any overall strategic design or central control.

The partition recommendation (Section B) specified "Steps Preparatory to Independence." The paper plan was designed to provide an orderly transition from mandatory Palestine to the partition of the country into the so-called Jewish and Arab states. The General Assembly was to elect a commission of representatives from five member states. Paragraph 2 (Section B) introduces the commission and invites the cooperation of Great Britain to coordinate implementation of its declared intention to withdraw with the optimistically blueprinted expansion of the commission's authority.

> 2. The mandatory Power shall to the fullest possible extent coordinate its plans for withdrawal with the plans of the Commission to take over and administer areas which have been evacuated.
>
> The Commission shall have authority to issue necessary regulations and take other measures as required.
>
> The mandatory Power shall not take any action to prevent, obstruct or delay the implementation by the Commission of the measures recommended by the General Assembly.[12]

The British, however, declared they would not cooperate. They refused to allow the commission to enter Palestine before their scheduled withdrawal on May 15. The Arab Higher Committee, which was the closest the Palestinian Arabs came to any representative central authority, refused to recognize the commission because the Arabs, on principle, rejected partition. Consequently, "the Commission members never left New York."[13] British noncooperation with the plan for partition went beyond refusing to assist the commission. As early as April 1947, War Minister Emanuel Shinwell, a staunch Zionist, directed the armed forces "not to become involved in the Arab-Jewish conflict." The commanding general's responsibility was restricted "to ensure an orderly withdrawal."[14] The inevitable result was a vacuum of authority and a collapse of law and order. "Between December 1, 1947 and February 1, 1948, according to a UN report, there were 2778 casualties, including 1462 Arabs, 1106 Jews and 181 Britishers."[15]

The power vacuum was more advantageous to the Zionists than to the Arabs. By April, Begin's Irgun was prepared for disciplined attacks on Arab population centers that could provide strategic bases for Zionist territorial expansions toward the maximum goals of their 1919 map.

Jerusalem became a prime target for the Zionist irregulars to frustrate the partition recommendation to separate the Holy City from both states and to be governed by an international regime. The Irgun carefully planned its assault on the city's approaches and environs.

The notorious massacre at Deir Yassin was an integral part of this strategy. In addition to the Zionist objective of moving on Jerusalem, the savagery and brutality of the attack on the villagers played the important role of turning the original flight of the noncombatant Palestinian Arabs into a stampede from their homes. The cry of "Deir Yassin" became a warning of horror, spurring several hundred thousand refugees to flee in the weeks before the scheduled termination of the mandate and providing a great leap forward toward the Zionist goal of reducing the Arab population and the realization of ultimate demographic domination by Jews. As Menachem Begin boasted in *The Revolt* (pp. 164–65), "Panic overwhelmed the Arabs of Eretz Israel. . . . the Arabs began to flee in terror even before they clashed with Jewish forces," such as in Haifa, where the Palestinians fled "in panic, shouting Deir Yassin!"

The details of that grim and tragic episode at Deir Yassin have been well reported elsewhere. Critically relevant for this account is the scattered but unmistakable evidence that again, while the Jewish Agency was playing diplomat at Lake Success and bidding for favorable public opinion in capital cities around the world—particularly in Washington—its acknowledged militias, Haganah and Palmach, were providing support to the terrorist attack on Deir Yassin. "The rifles and hand-grenades had been furnished by the Haganah." Once the Zionist terrorists had wreaked their havoc on both homes and humans, "The Haganah moved into Deir Yassin to take over the village. The first party to reach the area was led by Eliyahu Arieli, a scholarly veteran of six years' British army service who commanded the Gadna, the [Zionist] youth organization. The spectacle he found was, in his eyes, 'absolutely barbaric.'"[16]

Using Zionist sources, Hirst's account of Jewish Agency collaboration is more detailed.

For this operation, as for the blowing up of the King David [Hotel], the Irgun was acting in collaboration with the Haganah and the official Jewish leadership. "I wish to point out that the capture of Deir Yassin and holding it is one stage in our general plan." So ran the letter, quickly made public by the Irgun, in which the Jerusalem commander of the Haganah had outlined his interest in the affair. . . . The raiders called it "Operation Unity," for not only had Irgun and Stern joined forces, Haganah had made its contribution too. It had furnished weapons, and a unit of the Palmach, the Haganah's elite commando forces, was to play some part in the actual fighting—supplying covering fire according to its own account, demolishing the Mukhtar's house with a two-inch mortar according to the Irgun.[17]

Robert John and Sami Hadawi add to the Deir Yassin record: "The Jewish Agency could not afford to jeopardize their political struggle at the United Nations. They condemned the massacre strenuously . . . but on the same day the Zionist General Council ratified an agreement . . . for cooperation between the Hagana and I.Z.L. [Irgun]."[18]

From that point on, collaboration between the Jewish Agency forces and the Irgun (and Sternists) gradually increased, accompanied by frequent resort to the art of nonaccountability or plausible deniability. The agency's public denials were considered essential to retain credibility with the United Nations. But by 1954, Ben-Gurion considered it safe to confess at least some of the truth. He dated the beginning of "our War of Independence" in April 1948. "As April began, our War of Independence swung decisively from defence to attack. Operation 'Nachshon' . . . was launched with the capture of Arab Khulda near where we stand today and of Deir Muheisin, and culminated in the storming of Qastal, the great hill-fortress near Jerusalem."[19] On another occasion when candor might be exercised at low cost, the prime minister added:

> The primary task of the Hagana was to safeguard our settlements and lines of communication, but here the best defence is attack. . . .
> In operation "Nachshon" the road to Jerusalem was cleared at the beginning of April, almost all of New Jerusalem occupied, and the guerillas were expelled from Haifa, Jaffa, Tiberias, Safad while still the Mandatory was present. . . . Arabs started fleeing from the cities almost as soon as disturbances began in the early days of December [1947]. . . . The exodus was joined by Bedouin and fellahin, but not the remotest Jewish homestead was abandoned and nothing a tottering Administration [i.e., the British Mandatory] could unkindly do stopped us from reaching our goal on May 14,

1948 *in a State made larger and Jewish by the Hagana.* (emphasis supplied)[20]

The following is an inventory of Zionist attacks before withdrawal of the major British forces and the May 15 intervention of the Arab states' armies. Some of these offensives resulted in occupation of the territories. Most uprooted the local Arab inhabitants, producing new facts on the ground, to use Moshe Dayan's euphemism. These attacks took place *before a single soldier from any Arab state entered Palestine* and *two months before* the UN date for establishing a Jewish state:

(a) In the territory reserved for the "Arab state" the village of Qazaza was attacked and occupied as early as December 1947; Salameh in March; Saris, Qastal, Biyar Adas and the town of Jaffa, in April; and the town of Acre in May 1948.

(b) In the territory assigned to the "Jewish state" the towns of Tiberias and Haifa in April; Safad and Beisan in May 1948, besides hundreds of Arab villages.

(c) Within the area reserved for "Jerusalem International Zone," the village of Deir Yasin was attacked where the massacre of 250 men, women and children took place on April 9, 1948; and the Arab quarter of Katamon in Jerusalem City on April 29.

During this six-month period over 300,000 Arabs were driven out of their homes and became refugees—contrary to the expressed intentions of the United Nations.[21]

Map 4 indicates that the Israelis came to the armistice negotiations with long-held conceptions of the dimensions they envisaged for their state. This geographic plan gave them a distinct advantage in the negotiations. They were on the offensive for more territory than partition had allocated to them. The Arabs, on the other hand, had rejected partition, and both the Palestinians and later the contiguous Arab states were on the defensive. As Zionist military achievements mounted, the Arabs negotiated, hoping only to salvage as much territory as possible in Palestine and beyond the international borders, where fighting had taken place and Israelis already occupied territory where sovereignty of Arab states had been internationally recognized.

The map shows Zionist military campaigns before May 15, 1948, indicating Zionist incursions into territory assigned by partition to the

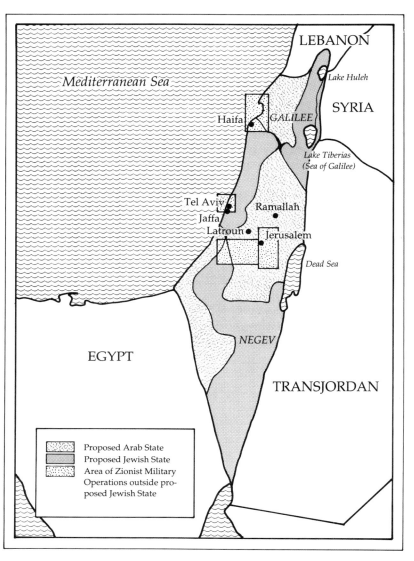

Map 4. Zionist military operations beyond proposed UN partition borders, April 1–May 15, 1948.

Arab state. The Arab states' reasoning for their own intervention is summarized as follows:

> Had the British Government fulfilled its obligations "to maintain law and order" up to the date of the termination of its Mandate; and had the United Nations from then on undertaken its responsibilities of ensuring peace and security for the Arab inhabitants, Arab States intervention would have been unnecessary.
>
> The Arab States armies were at no time inside the area set aside for the "Jewish state" under the Partition Resolution.[22]

This account is probably *technically* correct. There is no hard evidence that any *regular* forces from any Arab state entered even those parts of Palestine assigned to the Arab state before May 15. A U.S. source reported, however, in an undated State Department memorandum, "prepared, presumably, between January 24 and January 26, 1948," that irregulars were infiltrated, largely from Damascus.

> *Summary:* Reports from the U.S. Mission at Damascus indicate that Syria is the center of recruitment and training of the so-called irregulars, which are intended for infiltration over the Palestine border and subsequent guerilla work in Palestine. There is evidence that such forces have already proceeded across the border to a considerable extent. . . .
>
> (1) *Recruitment.* Active recruiting of "irregulars" under Fawzi Qawuqji has been carried on in Syria.
>
> (2) *Training.* Syria appears to be the training center for recruits from Palestine, Egypt and Iraq. (*FRUS* 5, part 2 [1948], p. 556)

A secret, urgent telegram from the U.S. consul at Jerusalem, on May 3, to the secretary of state says, inter alia, the British commander had informed the U.S. consul "categorically that Arab armies have not entered Palestine." It continued, "Arab irregulars and volunteers are still dribbling in" and estimated the "present strength" of the "liberation army" at 7,000. "[The] fact that they are trained and equipped by government neighboring states is well known but they do not form component regular armies" (*FRUS* 5, part 2 [1948], p. 889).

On May 16, the secretary-general of the United Nations formally notified Warren Austin, the U.S. representative, that Egypt had informed the Security Council on the fifteenth that "it has engaged in 'armed intervention' " in Palestine. The secretary-general added, "I received a cablegram from the Arab League making similar statements on behalf of the Arab states."

And from Israeli journalist Simha Flapan comes the following explanation of Arab miscalculation: "If there was one matter on which the Arab states were unanimous, it was the view of Zionism as an alien invader, an expansionist cancer. By the spring of 1948, the destruction of Arab villages, the massacres and the mass Palestinian flight made continued inaction by the Arab states untenable. . . . In addition, the Arab states greatly feared that Israel and Transjordan would carry out their agreement to divide Palestine between themselves, eventually perhaps leading to a Hashemite kingdom extending over Syria and Lebanon."[23] The problem was already under discussion by the Security Council (*FRUS* 5, part 2 [1948], p. 1000).

This extended review of history and legal documentation, beginning with the 1919 Zionist territorial proposals, is essential to any appreciation of the place of the armistice negotiations in the protracted problem of Palestine and the Palestinians. It demonstrates that Zionist/Israeli negotiating strategy and tactics reveal a planned, determined pursuit of territorial and even demographic objectives and largely explain the continuing frustration to this day of attempts to secure a lasting peace.

chapter 5

WARRING THEIR WAY TO "PEACE"

The Zionists had reluctantly supported partition because at the time they despaired of obtaining all of Palestine. They were far from content with the proposed allocation of territory despite the fact that partition had awarded them approximately 55 percent of mandate-controlled Palestine,[1] of which Zionists actually owned about 7 percent. Much of the territory allocated to them by partition was inhabited by Arabs whose families had lived for generations in these villages and towns. The recommended partition boundaries would have resulted in leaving a majority of Arabs (509,780) in the proposed Jewish state where there were 499,020 Jews.[2]

To the Arab inhabitants of the towns and villages allocated to the Jewish state, Israeli sovereignty would mean foreign rule, their status to be reduced from that of a majority to a minority in their own country. The whole character of their social, economic, and communal life would be threatened by an alien culture and alien values reinforced by the authority of a state preordained to be Jewish. The personal and communal property rights of these Moslem and Christian Arabs would be subrogated to the interests of Israeli settlers. And to the governors of the proposed Zionist state, so large a population of remaining, resentful Palestinians meant perpetuating trouble. Palestinians had no option but to resist Israeli domination.

Bernadotte's September 1948 proposed revision of the partition boundaries was an attempt to produce a better match of population concentrations to geography. But Zionist military actions had, by that time, overtaken demographic rationality. Tens of thousands of Arabs had become refugees, and Israeli military superiority was a factor that could not be dismissed unless the Israelis voluntarily withdrew from the strategic points they had occupied beyond the partition borders. The armistice negotiations would reveal early on that these concessions were not a consideration of Israeli negotiating strategies. Although it would not become a slogan until after the 1967 war, it was in the context of these first armistice negotiations that the formula in which Israel might trade territory for peace first presented itself. The Zionist state was as adamant in rejection then as it has been in later years.[3]

This impasse confronted Ralph Bunche when he was appointed acting mediator on September 18, and the situation continued to deteriorate. As able as Bunche had proven to be as an administrator, at the time he lacked the commanding international stature Bernadotte had enjoyed. Despite their military superiority, the Israelis felt threatened by the growing worldwide support for the Bernadotte proposals. In the United States some indications began to appear of a possible reversal of earlier acquiescence to Zionist-Israeli demands. On September 21, 1948, Acting Secretary of State Robert Lovett, attending the General Assembly in Paris, released a statement urging the parties and the General Assembly "to accept [Bernadotte's proposals] in their entirety as the best possible basis for bringing peace to a distracted land. . . . It is our sincere hope that the parties concerned will realize that their best interests and the interests of the world community will be served by accepting in a spirit of fair compromise the judgment of Count Bernadotte" (*FRUS* 5, part 2 [1948], pp. 1415–16).

But the Israelis were not buying. Their advances had been largely dictated with an eye to future geopolitical strategy, camouflaged as "security" or "necessary for defense." Israel had violated the truce early in September. It had two strategic objectives in mind. One was occupation of Jerusalem. The Israelis were concerned that they would suffer world condemnation if they violated the truce designed to isolate Jerusalem from battle damage that would follow certain resistance by Jordan's Arab Legion. The other objective was designed to frustrate Bernadotte's proposal to award the Negev to the Arabs. The plan involved renewed fighting with the Egyptians on the southern front. In a series of coordinated moves their forces advanced on approaches to Faluja and

Beersheba. A further Israeli battle plan in the south was to establish bases for a later attack on Jerusalem from the rear.

Bunche charged Israel with "a serious breach of the truce" and ordered it "to halt [its] forces and to withdraw them behind the October 14 lines, the date when, with 15,000 troops, Israel had launched its major offensive, known as 'Operation Ten Plagues.'"[4] The October 14 date and the freezing of the belligerents' positions had been called for in Security Council Resolution No. 61 (November 4, 1948, operative paragraph (1) and was reaffirmed on November 16 in the preamble of Resolution No. 62 (*UN Res.*, pp. 129–30).[5] Three thousand Arab civilians and a large unit of Egyptian and Sudanese soldiers had been trapped at Faluja by the Israeli advance. The disposition of these forces and civilians would play an important role in the armistice negotiations with Egypt.

Two more developments in 1948 were of major significance for the armistice agreements. First, on October 28 Israel launched a major offensive with the objective of seizing all of western Galilee (which partition had allocated to the Arab state). Second, Truman's red light on further U.S. support for Bernadotte's proposals was turned on by an intensive Zionist public relations campaign that started during the last week of September after the General Assembly had publicly released the murdered mediator's proposals. Truman's advisors, Clark Clifford and David Niles, were in positions to play decisive roles. Truman confessed later that the pressures exerted on him were unlike anything he had ever before experienced.[6] The earlier American endorsement of Bernadotte's proposals was substantially diluted. The U.S. switch from consort with the majority UN opinion to acquiescence to Israeli defiance of the international body began a long record of American abandonment of cooperation with world opinion in the search for peace in Palestine. The U.S. pro-Israeli bias would become increasingly apparent throughout the armistice negotiations.

chapter **6**

FIRST TRY FOR PEACE—
WITH EGYPT

Reluctant Negotiators

The historical, military, political, and demographic facts provided incendiary materials inherited by Ralph Bunche as the UN's chief representative when, on January 12, 1949, Egypt and Israel reluctantly agreed to discuss replacing the precarious truce with a more durable, negotiated armistice. Egyptian reluctance to engage was attributable to its adverse military position at the time and because of a conviction that "Arab allies had deserted in the hour of need." Israel was reluctant to bring its successful military campaigns to an end. But pressures from both the United Nations and the United States finally persuaded it to agree to negotiations.[1] On January 7 a formal cease-fire went into effect on the Egyptian front. Egyptian-Israeli talks began on the island of Rhodes on January 12, with Bunche acting as mediator. The Israelis came with great confidence.

Zionist leaders had been disappointed with the Balfour Declaration. Lord Balfour's promise compared badly with their earlier dream state. It denied *all* of Palestine as the locus for the national home. One safeguard clause protected the "civil and religious rights" of the Palestinian Arabs. The phrase carefully avoided reference to any national rights of the indigenous Arabs. Nevertheless it strongly implied some national home obligations with respect to the status of inhabitants of Palestine who were not Jews. The second safeguard or limiting clause stipulated, with greater specificity, that the Zionists were to do nothing to "prejudice the rights and political status of Jews" in any country other than Palestine. This limitation reflected the position of Jews who rejected recognition in international law or agreements of all Jews—the Jewish people—as a political-national entity. These anti-Zionist Jews wanted neither to acquire nor to exercise collectively national-political rights in any sovereignty other than the one in which they possessed citizenship.[2]

Despite Zionist misgivings about the internal contradictions of the Balfour Declaration, for the three decades between the issuance of the declaration and the armistice talks the Zionists, with more successes than failures, had manipulated British policy to their general satisfaction. With British help, they continued their success under the League of Nations' stewardship of the mandate.[3] By 1947–48 these forces had imposed on the Palestinians the skeletal structure for an exclusive Jewish state. By May 15, the Palestinian refugee problem had been created. The armies of the Arab states had been fought to at least a kind of standoff. And the combined military successes of the Zionist forces, regular and terrorist, had expanded the occupied territory beyond the partition borders. After the 1948 American presidential elections the Zionists had reason to believe that the political pressure tactics, which had worked in England, would continue to assure them the support of the emergent leader of the free world. And in those years they also had the political support of the Soviet Union.

The Arabs, on the other hand, approached the armistice negotiations divided, unsure of themselves, little equipped militarily or politically to cope with the formidable coalition of forces supporting Zionism and its new state. Finally, but no less significant, Arab efforts at public relations were pitiful compared with the Zionists' talents in this increasingly important political effort. Zionist appreciation and skillful utilization of this weapon tilted the odds even more sharply against the Arabs. Zionist propaganda exploitation of the Holocaust was a most effective weapon. The well-organized efforts of American Zionists, whose leaders knew what worked in American politics, contributed their share, as did more general U.S. empathy with the "people of the book." And finally, the disparity of numbers between the Zionists in Palestine and populations of the Arab states made David vs. Goliath an emotional script of almost exquisite efficacy.

Talking with the Egyptians

The confident Israeli attitude is reflected in the editor's Introduction to the *Companion Volume* of the Israeli documents. "The start of armistice negotiations with Egypt was postponed for many weeks, mainly because of Israel's refusal to accede to Egypt's demand, based on the 4 November resolution, to allow the evacuation of the besieged Egyptian garrison from Faluja prior to opening the talks." The same entry continues: "Both countries responded to the Security Council appeal to cease hostilities on 7 January; the Egyptians simultaneously announcing their agreement to immediate armistice talks. These opened officially in Rhodes on 13 January 1949."

The editor summarizes the Israeli approach: "The Israeli representatives came bolstered by the advantage of military control of the area claimed by Israel and victory in the war. . . . [I]t became clear that this *advantage, important as it was, did not suffice to guarantee realization of all Israeli expectations* . . ." (emphasis supplied).[4]

Israel occupied territory that partition had allocated to the Arab state. But its initial demands were "total Egyptian withdrawal from the confines of Palestine, viz., the Gaza strip and the Bethlehem area." Although the (Israeli) Provisional Council of State argued that this demand should serve only as a "bargaining point and not an irrevocable condition," the negotiating delegation was instructed to be "inflexible . . . not to agree to withdrawal from any outpost which is held by the Israeli army" (*C.V.*, p. 15).

The summary in the Introduction to the *Companion Volume* continues: "Consequently the Israeli delegates rejected Egypt's demands for the withdrawal of Israeli forces from Beersheba, Asluj and Auja. [All were outside the partition "boundaries."] On the tactical level, the delegation was directed not to deviate from the above-mentioned basic framework nor to make any concessions. However, they were not to break up the negotiations without first consulting with the political and defence authorities in Israel."

Without apology, forty years after the event, the Israeli interpretation admits that "the Egyptians were capable of capitalizing both on their very willingness to negotiate, and on the authority of Security Council resolutions" (*C.V.*, pp. xiii-xv). Judging by the available records, however, they did neither.

If Security Council resolutions have the weight of inscribed international law and if law is some prescription for protection of rights and property and an instrument for achieving justice, then Egypt's position was closer to these landmarks of whatever international morality exists than the Israeli reliance on superior military power and territory occupied by conquest. The point is relevant to the propaganda campaigns that accompanied Israel's consistent aggression and helped it win the political support of Western democratic governments. There is no law regulating propaganda. And in this burgeoning factor of international relations, the newborn Jewish state enjoyed a clear advantage.

The Israelis were aware of their transgressions of generally recognized law, on the one hand, and the superior legal position of the Egyptians, on the other. The Israelis put their dilemma this way: "Some factors to be reckoned with were the former Palestinian-Egyptian border, the November 1947 partition borders, the fighting line and the lines established in Bunche's 13 November memorandum. The Egyptians based their stand mainly on Bunche's memorandum, while Israel based its demands principally on the actual military situation. The partition plan, though not mentioned explicitly, frustrated the realization of the Israeli demands on the Gaza strip and the Auja area."[5]

Egypt's opening position was to reclaim everything the Israelis had occupied beyond the boundaries recommended by the partition proposal. Consistent with the UN Charter and a Security Council resolution of August 19 (No. 59 [1948]), Egypt rejected Israeli claims to "military or political gains" resulting from violations of the original truce. Their specific demands were "(a) continued Egyptian presence in the Gaza strip; (b) removal of Israeli forces from the northern Negev south of the 14 October line, except for defensive forces in the Jewish settlements; (c) demilitarization of Beersheba and the appointment there of an Egyptian civil administrator; (d) Egyptian control of the Asluj-Rafah road and the appointment of an Egyptian civilian governor in the village of Asluj; (e) withdrawal of Israeli forces from the entire strip of desert on the Palestinian-Egyptian border, including Auja—junction of the roads to Beersheba and the heart of the Sinai; (f) demilitarization of the southern Negev area" (*C. V.*, p. xiv). Many of the early exchanges involved bickering over military technicalities: definitions of various kinds of arms (such as heavy equipment and personal arms), vehicles, the size of military units (such as battalions and companies), and numerous similar details.

Early on, the impasse over the Faluja "pocket" was resolved, partially separated from the broader questions of the armistice. A formula was developed permitting the "immediate unconditional evacuation to Egypt, under UN supervision, of sick [and] wounded" (*M.V.*, p. 24). The rest of the military personnel and equipment would be phased out, according to a detailed schedule, over a period of time. The final stage was to be delayed until final negotiations for the armistice were completed and signed (*M.V.*, p. 698).[6]

With the vexing Faluja problem temporarily disposed of, negotiations for a full armistice could proceed. The crucial questions concerned where the final armistice demarcation should be drawn "without prejudice to the claims of either party" in any final settlement. The Israeli forces occupied many strategic points beyond both the partition boundaries and the provisional demarcation lines delineated by Bunche. Despite appeals by Bunche and some concessions by Egypt, the Israelis were adamant about three key areas: Bir Auja (on the approaches to Jerusalem), Beit Asluj (south of Beersheba), and Beersheba itself (*C.V.*, p. xviii). None of these was within the partition borders for the Jewish state. Reluctantly, the Israelis gave up hope of an Egyptian withdrawal from the Gaza Strip. The Israelis were prepared for trading on some positions. But rigidity on Auja, Asluj, and Beersheba was essential to their long-range targets: the Negev, which Bernadotte had recommended be given to the Arab state in exchange for western Galilee, and Jerusalem, which the United Nations continued to insist should have some form of international control.

When negotiations began on the hard, substantive matters of territory, the determination of permanent lines, allowable troop strengths, types of military hardware, and establishment of neutral zones (which Bunche had recommended to separate the military forces and minimize a renewal of fighting), the Israelis found themselves at a disadvantage by the terms of reference governing the Rhodes negotiations. Their military superiority and illegal occupation of territory should not have outweighed the clear, legal weight of Bunche's and the Egyptians' reliance on the UN Charter, the Security Council resolutions, and the general Egyptian strategy to return to the status quo ante and the partition recommendations, modified to conform to the Bernadotte proposals.

With the legalities against them, the Israelis decided that if they were to attain their objectives, they would have to mount a public propaganda campaign that might enlist a wide, politically active audience. They had two specific political objectives in mind. One was their petition for admission to membership in the United Nations. The other was to deepen and expand the still somewhat uncertain commitment of the United States as a reliable backup partner in the negotiations. Realization of this second objective would have a powerful influence on the first. But the political goal was in constant potential jeopardy from the professional diplomats and Middle East experts in the State Department.[7]

To outflank this resistance and reach the president, who possessed the final authority to determine foreign policy, it was necessary to influence the president's in-house personal political advisors, Clark Clifford and David Niles. These two pro-Israeli stalwarts needed plausible reasons for the president to ignore the advice of his Middle East experts. It was necessary for the president to have simplistic rationalizations to take to committees of Congress and to professional politicians of his party so as to be prepared for the time when it would be required to provide public explanations. The pro-Zionist-Israeli advocates had the experienced Zionist public relations machinery in the United States to serve as both ally and mentor.

The Egyptians, on their side, had only the professionals in the State Department, together with a few Christian missionaries and anti-Zionist Jews.[8] There were also the less than publicly eloquent lobbyists for the American petroleum industry. The handful of American missionaries who had served in the Arab world, the few academics who had been associated with the American academic institutions in Beirut and Cairo, and the small group of anti-Zionist Jews, who were more opposed to Zionism's Jewish nationalism than they were advocates of Arab claims and rights, were no political match for the Zionist team. The oil people registered their reservations about U.S. support for Zionist aspirations in subdued voices, consistent with the usual less than courageous corporate attitudes when controversial political issues were involved.

The Israelis negotiating at Rhodes had more respect than the Israeli cabinet for this complexity of forces with the potential of influencing the outcome. The cabinet, sitting in Tel Aviv, was concentrated on the long-range, still unfulfilled military-territorial and demographic objectives. One objective contemplated for the near future was "the General Staff's plan for an advance to Elath" (*C. V.*, p. xx).

Wearing Down the Egyptians

The Egyptians were not unaware of the historic Zionist pattern of advancing two feet, falling back one foot when necessary, in order to advance another two feet. They were eager to conclude the negotiations and to have the results become operative immediately upon the signing. The Israeli negotiators at Rhodes confronted a tactical problem. On the one hand, they wanted to avoid the appearance of obstructing an agreement, so they had to provide plausible counteroffers to this Egyptian plan for concluding an armistice. At the same time, however, the government in Tel Aviv was in no hurry to reach any binding agreements because it had not yet reached all the strategic positions it considered essential for the campaigns it still had in mind to attain maximalist territorial gains. This difference in timing prompted Walter Eytan[9] to send Sharett a long letter as early as January 16. The following excerpts are revealing.

Eytan began by saying that the letter was devoted, "in fact . . . to general considerations on which Reuven [Shiloah][10] and I are agreed." He continued, inter alia:

> The fact of signing this armistice with Egypt is in itself of far-reaching importance irrespective of the terms of the agreement. . . . Lebanon, Syria and Transjordan, all these countries are willing to sign an armistice if the negotiations with Egypt succeed—succeed, that is, in the sense of ending in agreement, signed, sealed and delivered. Stav[ropoulos][11] also spoke to the Iraqi Minister in Damascus, who spoke to him along the same lines as far as Iraq was concerned. A series of such armistice agreements would transform the political situation in the Middle East. They are possible only if the talks with Egypt lead to results. If we here fail, it sets back indefinitely the chances of armistice with all these countries. We consider, therefore, that the signing of an armistice agreement with Egypt in itself transcends in importance this detail or that. . . . It is perfectly clear that [the Egyptians] have orders to reach agreement and reach it quickly. They want the agreement to come into force immediately on signature, or at the latest within a matter of hours (not days) afterwards.
>
> All this being so, I hope that the *traditional military considerations* will not be allowed to carry too much weight. . . . (*M. V.*, pp. 26–28; emphasis supplied)

But a week later, on January 22, Eytan was apparently giving more weight himself to military considerations. He informed Sharett that

> We made it absolutely clear that politically we could under no circumstances accept any settlement which provided for an

advance of Egyptian forces even in token strength or the appointment of even the most unreal and symbolical Egyptian civil
administrator on the Palestine side of the frontier. This was a
political principle from which we could not under any circumstances recede, and in the specific case of Auja it was reinforced
by equally unalterable military considerations. Unless this basic
principle were conceded without reservation, there could be no
agreement.

If our hopes prove justified—and as a matter of fact we all still
feel reasonably optimistic—the talks may have to go on for another
four or five days. *It is simply a matter of wearing the Egyptians
down.* The process is rather callous and extremely tiring, but we
think it worthwhile making the extra effort over the next few days
in view of the great political possibilities which success would
open up for us. (*M. V.,* p. 55; emphasis supplied)

Two elements in Eytan's letter deserve emphasis. First, his use of the
phrase *Palestine side of the frontier* is unusual at this point because the
Israelis were insistent on using the name *Israel* now that the state existed.
As a professional diplomat accustomed to precise language, Eytan's use
of "Palestine" must be interpreted to mean the Israelis were not reconciled to the partition borders even in the southern sector bordering the
Gaza Strip. Al-Auja had been allocated to the Arab state. The Israelis
had in mind to maintain several bases contiguous to the strip once they
were reconciled that Gaza would be under some form of Egyptian control. All these bases were in territory allocated to the Arab state.

The second point worth emphasizing in Eytan's January 22 communication is the candid admission that Israeli strategy to wear the Egyptians down was callous. He admitted the extra effort to prolong the
negotiations was extremely tiring but was justified by "the great *political* possibilities." One possibility was the demonstrated ability of American Zionists, coordinating with the Israeli diplomatic corps and particularly through Aubrey (now Abba) Eban, to manipulate U.S. political
support for the Israeli political objectives. Prolonging the Rhodes negotiation to wear down the Egyptians was related to the ability of the
American Zionist–Israeli government combine to hold and increase
U.S. support for Israeli territorial and military objectives at Rhodes.[12]

The smooth sailing of Clark Clifford's and David Niles's influence on
the White House was fading.[13] The situation emerging in the Middle

East had been predicted by the State Department's specialists, and the department's credibility commanded greater respect at the White House. Not the least important, the 1948 election and the threat of the Jewish vote were now history. The Arab states continued to protest partition, but by late January–early February 1948 a subtle change of tone was apparent in their attitudes. Egypt, for example, was "anxious to get the Palestine question settled so that they could get along with the development of the Egyptian economical and social system." The Egyptian ambassador, Mahmoud Fawzi, "had the authority to enter into discrete informal conversations with the American and British Governments regarding the boundary lines which should be established in southern Palestine" (*FRUS* 5, part 2 [1948], pp. 624–25).

This was de facto acceptance of the Jewish state, although questions of boundaries remained. In a comprehensive memorandum of January 27, 1949, Samuel H. C. Kopper, special assistant to the director of the Office of Near Eastern and African Affairs at the State Department and advisor to the U.S. delegation at the United Nations, reported:

> Most of the Arab leaders seem to realize that their cause against the establishment of a Jewish state in Palestine is now hopeless. They are not, however, as yet able to take a position in public recognizing the state of Israel. . . . In spite of their aversion to the policy of the U.S. the great majority of the Arab leaders recognize the realities of the position of the U.S. in the world today and many of them hope that the situation in Palestine can be ended so that they can resume more normal relations toward the U.S. . . .
>
> The tone and feeling of the Arab Delegations in the General Assembly of 1948 as compared with the previous session was much more friendly towards the U.S. in spite of all that transpired between November 1947 and September 1948. . . . In spite of insinuations a year ago that the Arab states might leave the United Nations, they have not done so although they are undoubtedly quite cynical about the role of the UN . . .
>
> When the General Assembly was considering the establishment of the Palestine Conciliation Commission during the latter part of November and early December of 1948 there was considerable speculation as to how the Arab states would vote. . . . However, since the particular objective seemed to be conciliation by peaceful means and there did not appear to be any strong reaffirmation of

the November 29, 1947 resolution the Arab leaders were able to indicate to their Asiatic friends their willingness to have them abstain or vote in favor of the December 11, 1948 [General Assembly #194] resolution. (*FRUS* 5, part 2 [1948], pp. 704–5)

These reports by professional diplomats suggest that the Arabs did not much like what had happened but were ready to negotiate a settlement. Although they were resigned to U.S. support for Israel, they still hoped for a fair measure of justice in territorial questions along the lines of Bernadotte's proposal, incorporated in the December 11, 1948, General Assembly resolution. Of prime importance to the Arabs was operative paragraph 11, calling for the refugees to be offered a free choice between repatriation and compensation for those who elected not to return.

Washington: Star-Spangled Eminence?

A three-way exchange from January 23 to January 29 among Eytan in Rhodes, Sharett in Tel Aviv, and Eliahu Epstein (later Elath),[14] the provisional government's special representative in Washington, sheds light on the Israeli perception of the new U.S. approach. Epstein cabled Sharett on the twenty-third that it would be advisable to accept a "reasonable compromise" with the Arabs (*M.V.*, p. 63; *C.V.*, p. 18). The alternative would enhance the authority of the Conciliation Commission, composed of "unfriendly Turkey, unreliable France and vacillating U.S.A." But on the twenty-ninth, from Rhodes, Eytan urged Sharett to send Epstein "further guidelines," for continuing contacts with the U.S. government. Sharett apparently complied, and on the twenty-ninth Epstein met with a team from the State Department.

The department's "Memorandum of Conversation" records that the U.S. assistant secretary of state for the Near East and Africa told Epstein the Egyptians considered Israeli evacuation of Faluja the key to further progress. Epstein replied, "We will let them [the Egyptians] out of Faluja if they will agree to our staying at El Auja." He added that Israel "would never agree" to a "token Egyptian force" remaining in El Auja—a U.S. proposal. Epstein commented on "the long-range aspects of the Arab refugee problem," saying "he was sure the Israeli Government would welcome back the *Christian* Arabs" (emphasis supplied); "such a welcome would not be accorded the Moslem Arabs." But he added that "the

Mohammedans [*sic*] would not wish to return in any event as they did not feel comfortable as a racial or religious minority group." Rather gratuitously, the Israeli continued, "certain of the Arab states, such as Transjordan and Iraq, were in need of extra population and might be able to take a considerable portion of the refugees" (*FRUS* 6 [1949], pp. 708, 709).[15]

The negotiations were now stalled on dead center. On February 3, Tel Aviv informed Eytan that Ben-Gurion "objects to the handing over of Auja or any other place in the Negev to UN rule." This was a rejection of a Bunche proposal that Eytan had explored with both the Egyptian and Israeli delegations to break the impasse on El Auja, Beit Asluj, and, most importantly, Beersheba. On the fourth, Eytan informed Tel Aviv that once again the Egyptians were taking their stand on the UN resolutions and on Bunche, who was attempting mediation by invoking full respect for the same resolutions. "Bunche favors them," he added, "because they have accepted the draft proposal" (submitted on January 22) (*C.V.*, p. 23; *M.V.*, pp. 56–57). Israel continued to rely on "tiring the Egyptians."

While publicly posturing as an impartial referee, supporting the United Nations and Bunche's efforts to hold the negotiations as close as possible to his UN mandate, the United States continued to tilt toward Israel. On January 27, Secretary of State Dean Acheson sent Truman a memorandum recommending de jure recognition of Israel and Transjordan. James G. McDonald, a pro-Zionist activist before the Israeli state was formed, was to be nominated as ambassador to Tel Aviv. The president approved. Both actions were formally announced by the White House on January 31 (*FRUS* 6 [1949], pp. 702, 713). A footnote (p. 719) reports, "In a note of February 4, Egyptian Ambassador Rahim expressed to the Secretary of State the very deep regret of his Government that 'certain powers' had recognized the 'so-called State of Israel,' despite the failure to find a solution for the problems of Palestine. . . . [W]hile such recognition was not to be interpreted 'as a definite stand in favor of Zionists, yet the Zionists had exploited it in this sense'."

The Israelis reciprocated elevation of Israeli status by announcing on February 1 that on August 2, 1948, the Israeli cabinet had decided to terminate the military governorship of Jerusalem and "to institute in that city governmental arrangements obtaining *in other parts of the State of Israel*" (emphasis supplied). Shertok (the Israeli foreign minister, who later changed his name to Sharett) advised McDonald that "to avoid international misunderstanding" the Israeli action was merely an "administrative" move "and not annexation of Jerusalem."[16] Contradicting Shertok's disclaimer, the exact language of the cabinet's statement, reported by the U.S. consul in Jerusalem, was "that all laws of the State of Israel apply to the area of Jerusalem under Israeli occupation." William Burdett, the U.S. consul, added, "Initial local public reaction is that [the] announcement [is] tantamount to annexation [of the] Jewish sections [of the] city [of] Jerusalem to [the] State of Israel" (*FRUS* 6 [1949], p. 717. A copy of Burdett's telegram was sent to Amman, notifying the Transjordanians.

On February 8, 1949, Burdett forwarded to Washington a lengthy report by Mark Ethridge of a conversation with Shertok in Jerusalem on January 7, 1949.[17] Ethridge confronted Shertok with a report that the Provisional Government of Israel (PGI) planned a constituent assembly in Jerusalem where it would offer a resolution calling for annexation of the city. The provisional government also "intends [to] hold municipal elections" there. Ethridge reminded Shertok that such actions "appeared to be contrary to the spirit, if not the letter of GA [General Assembly] resolution December 11 [#194]" (*FRUS* 6 [1949], pp. 736-37). Shertok responded that on Jerusalem, the Israelis "had acquiesced in the international status in 1947 . . . but situation had subsequently changed because of failure of international community or any other authority to protect it except Jews themselves. PGI could not now entrust security of Jews in Jerusalem to any outside agency nor could their economic security be safeguarded except by integration in Israel. . . . Holding of constituent assembly would not result in *fait accompli*. On other hand, *Israeli* Jerusalem to all practical intent and purpose is now part of Israel" (emphasis supplied) (*FRUS* 6 [1949], p. 736).

In the cable Ethridge went on to report Shertok's response to a question raised about the refugees by the French representative on the Conciliation Commission, Claude de Boisanger:

> [The] refugee problem can only be settled as part of peace settlement. There can be no significant return of refugees before *and possibly after that event*. . . . Since they fled voluntarily and at British instigation PGI policy has been based on status quo. Exodus was primarily caused by aggression of Arab states. Return now would undermine security of Israel and would impose impossible economic burden on Israel to integrate refugees in Israeli economy.

Arab refugees are essentially unassimilable *in Jewish Israel*. Efforts can now be made [for] radical sound solution, namely integration in neighboring Arab states, especially Iraq, Syria and Transjordan which Shertok claims are underpopulated and require more people. (emphasis supplied)

The telegram also contains Shertok's statement of the Israeli provisional government's position on two other items: territory and the modality for conducting negotiations. On separate negotiations with each Arab belligerent, "Shertok stated regarding general peace settlement that Israel desires to negotiate separate peace treaties and did not wish general conference. Shertok reasoned Israeli-Lebanese problems, for example, were of no concern to Egypt" (*FRUS* 6 [1949], pp. 736–37).

On January 28, Bunche had informed Israel that Jordan, Lebanon, "and perhaps Syria as well are willing to join the Rhodes talks." Bunche "wishes to know Israel's position." From Rhodes, Eytan informed Sharett the Israeli delegation was holding out for separate negotiations with each of the Arab states: "Additional parties might stiffen Egypt's stand, the delegation is seeking a way to endorse the proposal yet postpone its implementation until an agreement with Egypt is signed or at least until the final stage of the negotiations." Using a "divide and rule" strategy, Sharett cabled Eytan the official Israeli opposition "to broadening the range of the Rhodes talks" (*C.V.*, p. 16).

Conspiracy for Betrayal

What Shertok did not tell the commission—and what apparently Bunche did not know—was that from early December 1948, Israel and Transjordan had been engaged in secret negotiations. The Israelis were attempting to persuade King Abdallah to sign "a general armistice" and begin "peace talks" (*C.V.*, p. 46). The Transjordanian negotiating position presented by Abdallah's emissary, Colonel A. Al-Tall, was based on the Jericho Conference of early December 1948. Attending had been "delegations from towns and villages of the Jordan-controlled part of Palestine," some military authorities (unidentified in the Israeli record), "officers of the Arab Legion and military governors, representatives of the Supreme Moslem Council and [also unidentified] guest delegations from Jordan, Syria and Lebanon." The conference resolved "no confidence in the Arab Higher Committee and the 'Gaza Government' and established the Union of Jordan and Palestine as the Arab Hashemite Kingdom. Abdallah was proclaimed king." Syria, Lebanon, Saudi Arabia, and King Farouk of Egypt, the secretary-general of the Arab League, rejected these resolutions (*C.V.*, p. 156). Secret Israeli-Abdallah negotiations continued. But on Rhodes, Israel insisted on negotiations with Egypt alone.

Burdett's February 8 telegram to Washington reported a second item summarizing in detail Shertok's address on territory before the Conciliation Commission: "Shertok explained . . . that Israel had accepted 1947 partition [provided] Arab Palestine would become independent state. If it now became part of Transjordan situation was radically altered and Israel's previous acceptance no longer valid. . . . Israel claimed, for example, widening of 12-mile coastal strip between Haifa and Tel Aviv for security reasons. PGI had decided it would not agree to foreign bases in Palestine section of an enlarged Transjordan on basis of present British treaty with Transjordan. . . . Shertok voluntarily disavowed intention of seizing non-Israeli Palestine unless provoked" (*FRUS* 6 [1949], p. 737).

And on Jerusalem: "Shertok stated that discussions 'between Israeli and Arab Military Commission should be encouraged to continue,'" but the talks "were limited to demarcation of military areas and that he doubted whether Commission would be of assistance to them. . . . Shertok stated demilitarization of Jerusalem was only possible if there was outside force or no need for protection. As neither condition existed demilitarization was not possible" (*FRUS* 6 [1949], p. 738).

In a footnote, Burdett's telegram added that Ethridge had described "Shertok's presentation" of the Israeli "views regarding Jerusalem . . . unyielding." Israel "does not accept world opinion regarding internationalization" and "intends to take steps looking toward eventual incorporation of Israeli Jerusalem in Israel." Ethridge's comment continued: "It may be true PGI does not intend to transfer its capital from Tel Aviv to Jerusalem. . . . [But] facts that constituent assembly is opening here, that certain central administrative offices are operating here, that Israeli civil law applies here and that municipal elections under Israeli auspices will be held here seem to bear out my analysis. . . . It seems logical, however, present policies will continue and may only be counteracted by firmness on part of command [*sic*] governments there represented" (*FRUS* 6 [1949], p. 738).

Ethridge added that Shertok's stated position on the refugees "offended

[the] Commission." "It also astonished me in view imperative necessity for friendly relations between Israel and Arab States and importance of early establishment of economic connections with Arab hinterland. . . . It might be wise in long run to resettle greater portion Arab refugees in neighboring Arab States; nevertheless, it appears contrary to Israel's best interests at outset to take inhuman position" (*FRUS* 6 [1949], pp. 737–38).

Nearly 750 pages in the *Main Volume* of the Israeli records are devoted to the armistice negotiations with Egypt, Jordan (Transjordan), Lebanon, and Syria. The weight attached to the talks with Egypt is evident by the fact that this diplomacy occupies just slightly less than half of the pages. Both sides agreed that significant precedents might influence the negotiations to follow with other Arab states. The fundamental negotiating positions of the two sides were therefore important, as were Bunche's reactions. Bunche's opening statement on January 13, 1949, clarified that he saw his role to be "implementing the Security Council resolutions of 4 and 16 November 1948" (*M.V.*, p. 13). He—and the Egyptians—regarded those resolutions as the governing law for the discussions.

Operative paragraph 1 of the November 4 resolution called on "the interested Governments to withdraw those of their forces which have advanced beyond the position held on October 14." The acting mediator was authorized to establish provisional lines beyond which there was to be no movement of troops.

On October 15, the Israelis had "smashed the Egyptian lines in the northern Negev. Israeli forces occupied Beersheba and the coastal strip from Isdud south to Yad Mordechai, as well as a strip across from Beit Jibrin to Majdal. [They] also expanded the territory under their control in the Hebron area and in the Jerusalem corridor. An entire Egyptian brigade was trapped in the 'Faluja pocket' " (*C.V.*, p. xii).

These advances violated the Security Council resolution. Disregarding their own violations, the Israeli basic position was that the Egyptians must withdraw from "the confines of Palestine." The delegation was instructed "to be inflexible on this last matter, and consequently the Israeli delegates rejected Egypt's demands for the withdrawal of Israeli forces from Beersheba, Asluj and Auja. . . . The delegation was directed not to deviate from the above-mentioned basic framework nor to make any concessions. However, they were not to break up the negotiations without first consulting with the political and defence authorities in Israel" (*C.V.*, p. xv).

The period between approximately January 25 and February 15 was crucial to the Egyptian-Israeli talks and established the pattern for later talks with the other Arabs. Bunche had cabled UN Secretary-General Trygve Lie that "prospects for an armistice agreement are virtually nil" (*FRUS* 6 [1949], p. 707). The impasse involved the 3,000 Egyptians trapped in the Faluja pocket. Israel refused to withdraw and release them until an armistice was arranged. A second stumbling block was Beersheba and a third El Auja. Bunche had appealed to the president of the Security Council to convene a meeting "to arbitrate the disputed points." The president declined, advising Bunche he could not call a meeting unless Bunche sent "a full report," identifying "specific issues to be debated" (*C.V.*, p. 27). The Israelis feared that if Bunche went to the Security Council, the council would support Bunche's position based on the Security Council resolutions of November 4 and 16 (*M.V.*, p. 93). Then Bunche would use the Security Council's support to impose "his solution on both parties" (*C.V.*, p. 27).

Tactically, matters were going well for the Israelis. They had defeated multilateral negotiations in a single conference with all Arab belligerents. They had also prevailed that the armistice demarcation lines should be based on existing fighting lines rather than the positions of October 14 and should be the starting point for negotiations, contrary to Security Council Resolution No. 61 (1948). But strategically they found causes for apprehension. First, there was Bunche himself and his dedication to the UN resolutions. Sharett described the acting mediator as "liable to prove extremely dangerous" (*C.V.*, pp. 12–13).

And despite past U.S. support for Israeli positions, the Israelis were apprehensive about the staying power of the American commitment. The United States had much broader and more complicated national interests than Israel. It was a member of the Conciliation Commission. Eliahu Elath, Israel's ambassador to Washington, had described the three members as "unfriendly Turkey," "unreliable France," and "vacillating U.S.A." (*M.V.*, p. 63). Also a fairly energetic effort was under way to coordinate American and British policy on Palestine. England had a treaty with Transjordan and, on the whole, was inclined to be more supportive of the Arab than of the Israeli position. The U.S. tilt toward Zionism and Israel had created misunderstandings between the two traditional allies (*FRUS* 6 [1949], p. 691).

A high priority Israeli objective, beyond a satisfactory conclusion to the armistice negotiations, was the pending application for membership in the United Nations. Israel had submitted its first application on November 29, 1948. The Security Council rejected it on December 17 because of "noncompliance with the United Nations resolutions."[18] U.S. lobbying had been essential for adoption of the partition plan. In his frustration over negotiating the armistice with Egypt, Bunche had threatened several times to turn the matter back to the Security Council. The Israelis did not want to risk a second rejection. The mediator's threats, therefore had several times wrung concessions from the Israelis.

This mix of facts and attitudes was not lost on the Israeli policy makers. For the moment they were more than satisfied with their military accomplishments. But they were confronted now with the more difficult task of attempting to legitimate their war gains and, indeed, to legitimate the state itself.

In an effort to reconcile these somewhat divergent interests, Elath and his first secretary, Uriel Heyd, obtained an appointment on January 28 with the middle-level State Department officers directly involved with the Rhodes negotiations. That same day Elath reported to Sharett:

> Found them most conciliatory and open our arguments. No more mention made by them of Security Council resolutions nor did they challenge us or try argue Egyptian case. They carefully inquired whether Auja main stumbling block Rhodes and whether we will implement Faluja agreement when general agreement reached. We replied affirmative. McClintock agreed Egyptian fear that Auja our hands threatening their communications unfounded, if we maintain there mere outpost, taking main force back, . . . supervised UN.
>
> Satterthwaite urged we should not break off negotiations Rhodes and they meanwhile try influence Cairo *as requested.* (*M.V.*, p. 83; emphasis supplied)

Ralph Bunche—Frustrated Mediator

The nub of the impasse, which had led Bunche to conclude "that prospects for an armistice agreement are virtually nil," was the rigid Israeli refusal to withdraw from el-Auja and Faluja and "unconditionally to release [the] Faluja garrison." To the Egyptians the Faluja matter was a "token evidence of good faith." The Israelis insisted on holding the Egyptians—troops and civilians—as hostages until Egypt agreed to the armistice. El-Auja (and Bir Asluj) were strategically important points on the drawing board of Israeli campaigns to take the Negev—contrary to the Bernadotte proposal and to Security Council Resolution No. 61. The U.S. response to Elath's January 28 presentation was to request the British to make a "particular effort [with] Cairo [to] attempt to persuade the Egyptians [to] reach compromise with Israelis at Rhodes" (*FRUS* 6 [1949], pp. 706–7).

The United States was shaving its commitment to the United Nations and, despite its Conciliation Commission membership, was gradually reinforcing Israeli strategy. The reasons for the shift of American policy to a more consistent tilt toward Israel are complicated. But two considerations appear to be dominant. First, the pro-Israel propaganda campaign continued and was intensified, producing greater political pressures on the White House than previously. Probably of even greater weight was the extension of Truman's cold war ideology to the Middle East, following Washington's realization that British power and influence were on the wane. Middle East historian J. C. Hurewitz wrote, "United States rivalry with the Soviet Union went to absurd lengths."[19] The Soviets and the Eastern bloc had begun to support Arab positions at the United Nations. The American reaction was to increase political support for Israel gradually while attempting to avoid serious damage to U.S.-Arab relations.

In an attempt to break the stalemate, on January 31 Bunche submitted a draft "Egyptian-Israeli General Armistice Agreement" to the Israeli delegation. In a letter of transmittal to Eytan, Bunche admitted that because "these armistice negotiations are very narrow in scope," no political implications were discussed "even when these are clearly visible just below the surface." He therefore found "it necessary to employ guarded phraseology and symbolic or token devices which leave much to be desired" in order "to keep some doors open in anticipation of ultimate peace negotiations" (*M.V.*, pp. 96ff.).

The draft referred explicitly to Security Council resolutions of November 4 and 16. It called for the withdrawal of the Egyptian forces from "the al-Faluja area," to begin on the day "immediately following the signing this agreement." They were to withdraw "beyond the Egypt-Palestine frontier." There would be no "restoration of previous fighting lines" and "no advance of military forces of either side beyond positions held at the time this Armistice Agreement is signed" (*M.V.*, p. 99).

Paragraph 3 of Article IV of the draft referred to several points that had been strenuously disputed during the several previous weeks of talks. It embodies a principle that most of the UN resolutions stated and that came to be, more or less, standard language in subsequent armistice agreements and warrants reproduction here inter alia:

> [T]erritorial custodial or other claims or interests which may be asserted by either Party in the areas in which their forces have been engaged shall not be prejudiced or otherwise affected by the signing of this Agreement. . . . [I]nterests which may be asserted by Egypt in southern Palestine, including such interests as may be claimed to relate to the Beersheba and Bir Asluj areas deriving from the 4 November 1948 resolution of the Security Council and the 13 November 1948 Memorandum for its implementation, as well as claims on other grounds which either Party may assert, shall be entitled to consideration in the discussions with the United Nations Conciliation Commission and in the final settlement between the two Parties on the same basis as though that Resolution and Memorandum had been fully implemented. (*M.V.*, p. 99)

Paragraph 2 of Article V restricted the armistice agreement to military considerations, leaving determination of future "political or territorial boundaries" to an "ultimate settlement of the Palestine question." Article VIII deferred resolution of the el-Asluj problem by establishing "a Special Neutral Zone from which both Egyptian and Israeli armed forces shall be totally excluded." The neutral zone "shall be under the full supervision and effective control of the United Nations, whose flag shall fly there and shall be held in custody by the United Nations pending final settlement of territorial dispositions in southern Palestine." Violations, "when confirmed by the United Nations, shall constitute a flagrant violation of this Agreement and an act of force directed against the United Nations." A Mixed Armistice Commission of seven members was to be responsible for execution of the agreement. Three members were to be designated by each side. The chairman was to be chief of staff of the UN Truce Supervisory Organization (UNTSO) or a senior UNTSO officer designated by him (*M.V.*, pp. 98–102).

A major issue throughout the talks had been southern Palestine. El-Auja, Beersheba, and Bir Asluj were all strategic prizes. The Egyptians, apparently, had been satisfied with the arrangement for UN control of the el-Auja area and agreed that Egyptian troops might return to the area "in defensive strength only" and "under supervision of the United Nations." But they insisted on retaining military occupation of the Gaza area and on civilian administrators in Beersheba and Bir Asluj, "following the withdrawal of Israeli forces" (*M.V.*, p. 105).

Bunche rejected these demands about Beersheba and Bir Asluj if they were predicated on the armistice agreement. But in a compromise dated January 30, he allowed an Egyptian assertion "of interests" in "southern Palestine," based on the November 4 Security Council resolution. He also allowed an Israeli "assertion" of claims in these areas (*M.V.*, p. 108).

Concessions were made to Israel's rejection of the October 14 fighting lines, but "the advance of Egyptian forces anywhere in Palestine cannot be considered." At their disputed points, both Israel and Egypt would be permitted forces "in defensive strength only" during the period of the armistice. It was explicitly stated that all of these compromises and their supporting claims by either party "shall be entitled to consideration in the discussion with the United Nations Conciliation Commission and in the final settlement between the two parties on the same basis as though that resolution and [his November 13] Memorandum had been fully implemented" (*M.V.*, p. 106).

With such language and circumlocutions around the impasse of Israeli demands for the armistice lines to be based on the existing fighting lines, on the one hand, and the Egyptian insistence on the relevant UN resolutions, on the other, Bunche tried to move the negotiations from dead center while still upholding the authority of the United Nations.

In this connection, a telegram from Eytan to Shertok, dated February 1, is significant because it illuminates again the Israeli intention to emasculate UN authority, if possible. The following summary of the telegram is from the *Companion Volume:* "In view of the Security Council's present composition Eytan proposes working for repeal of the 4 November resolution, which determined cease-fire lines that are out of accord with the present military situation. He also suggests the possibility of cancelling all obsolete Security Council resolutions on Palestine" (p. 21).

Colonel Yigael Yadin of the Israeli army, who served the Israeli delegation in Rhodes as its military expert, expressed the same idea in somewhat different terms. In a meeting with the Israelis on January 31, the Bunche draft-armistice agreement was subjected to the most minute linguistic criticism. At one point Yadin offered a new formulation of paragraph 3, Article IV of Bunche's original draft: "I understood that in signing this armistice whatever claims the Parties will have in the future will not be based on [November resolutions] 4/11 or 16/11. Insofar as these are concerned, they will be finished here" (*M.V.*, p. 114).

Bunche agreed but only if these resolutions were "signed away" in a final agreement. "But there would be no automatic signing away to this effect." Later, on the same subject, to the Israelis, he added, "You cannot gainsay any Security Council resolution that has not been repealed. The point is that the resolutions will be repealed if the armistice works. If it does not, they will be kept in force. If there is no danger to the peace, the Security Council will wipe the slate clean" (*M.V.*, pp. 114–15).

Bunche's draft agreement raised the question of what was meant by southern Palestine, a phrase he had used several times. Transjordan's Arab Legion had been Israel's military adversaries in the eastern Negev. During the negotiations, the Egyptians had made several claims to territory where they either had no troops or their troops had not been a significant factor. In the southern Negev there had been some coordination of Egyptian forces and those of the Arab Legion.

The Egyptians knew little, if anything, about the secret negotiations involving King Abdallah and the Israelis, and the Israelis never entertained the idea of abandoning their plan to acquire the southern Negev, which would provide a southern outlet to the sea. The Egyptians had guessed at this objective because of the Israelis' insistence on including, as part of their territory, Beersheba, which was outside the partition-recommended borders for the Jewish state. The Egyptians counterclaimed the right to occupy southern Palestine on the grounds of custodial responsibility for territory Bernadotte had recommended to be part of the Arab state.

The Israelis hoped to remove as many military obstacles as possible on the road to Elath by negotiating with Abdallah. They argued, therefore, that the Egyptians had no legitimate basis for negotiating anything in the eastern Negev. That was to be left to armistice negotiations with Abdallah (*M.V.*, p. 117).

Some of the most illuminating disclosures of the attitudes of Bunche, the Israelis, and the Egyptians are recorded in detailed reports of conversations between Bunche and the Israeli delegation on January 31 and February 1. The subject was one that had plagued the talks from their inception: whether fighting lines or the Security Council resolutions should be the basis for establishing the armistice lines, for the withdrawal of troops, for determining who should have authority for troop movements, for categories of weaponry, and for UN instruments to monitor the armistice. There were also questions involving territory where both parties were to share control. The Egyptians insisted that the Security Council's pronouncements should govern. Israelis, in violation of the Security Council resolutions that called for a truce, had occupied many places beyond the borders of the partition resolution. They were equally determined about the reality of the fighting lines to establish the armistice. One important agenda item was where to establish headquarters for the Mixed Armistice Commission. The Israelis—with an eye to future claims for sovereignty and particularly concerned about acquiring the Negev—wanted as little UN authority as possible in territory they had already occupied. The Egyptians, Bunche reported, "do not wish to sign away any territory which might be Arab" (*M. V.,* p. 132).

The November 4 Security Council resolution (No. 61) had ordered all forces to withdraw to the positions held on October 14. It provided support for the Egyptian negotiating strategy. The Israelis argued for the fighting lines held by their forces after that date, contending that territory acquired by fighting after October 14 should be Jewish state territory. El-Auja, Bir Asluj, and Beersheba were in this category and all were essential to the Israeli planned military campaign to acquire the Negev. At one point Eytan admitted to Bunche, "We are allergic to the [November] 4/11 resolution. . . . [A]ny expression of its terms in the armistice agreement is setting up what is today an utterly artificial structure, which carries in it the seeds of its own destruction" (*M. V.,* p. 132).

Beersheba was the most important strategic point. El-Auja was a control point on an important road across the Negev. Once it had been agreed that Egypt was to be allowed to retain forces in Gaza, it became important for the Israelis to thwart any possible Egyptian attack from Gaza into the Negev. Bir Asluj was to defend Beersheba against an attack from the south as well as supply a base to launch the Israeli campaign to occupy the southern Negev. The location for the Mixed Armistice Commission headquarters therefore became a pawn in this larger game. Both parties were attempting to position themselves advantageously for what they speculated might be future developments. In these January 31–February 1 talks with Bunche, from the legal standpoint of the UN Charter's prohibition against "acquisition of territory by war," the Israelis were more guilty by several degrees than the Egyptians.

With the responsibility of enforcing the UN resolutions, Bunche told the Israelis at one point:

We are here trying to draw a line between positions taken by the two delegations, and we have had to speak with both delegations. On the one hand we are told that the whole thing must be on a completely reciprocal basis: what is done in your territory must be done in Egyptian territory. I would agree with you fully if I had some basis from you or your Government of saying to the Egyptians: "Look here, this territory, Auja or Beersheba, is sovereign territory of the State of Israel in the same sense that el-Arish is sovereign territory of Egypt, and they must be treated on a reciprocal basis." If there is such a basis for explaining this to the Egyptians, then the picture becomes much clearer. We tried to steer a middle course in these negotiations and tried to cut through the fog. I'm not sure we may not have added more to it. (*M.V.*, p. 133)

Eytan's response was typical of Israeli tactics: "It is true that Israel has not asserted formal political sovereignty over Beersheba or Auja. That does not matter very much in the terms of an armistice. But what in fact matters is that militarily the Government does exercise sovereignty, and this is so with regard to both Beersheba and Auja" (*M.V.*, pp. 132–33).

But Israel was satisfied to defy the November 4 resolution and to assert de facto control over both contested areas. This was consistent with its strategy to denigrate UN authority, on the one hand, and to minimize Egyptian claims, on the other. The disputed areas were essential to communications and transport for the Negev. The Israelis, therefore, were satisfied for the moment to stabilize the status quo, beyond the partition-recommended boundaries. To accomplish this it was necessary to neutralize the United Nations without antagonizing so many of the member-states that Israel's membership application might be jeopardized. It was also necessary to defeat Egyptian aspirations to authority over Palestinian territory that had been allocated to the Arab state.

An exasperated Bunche finally rebuked the Israelis, saying "I do not know what the nature of your thinking was when you accepted this invitation [to the armistice negotiations]." Eytan responded by claiming the November 4 resolution (No. 61) obsolete and the Egyptian position no longer compatible with the fact of the Israeli military advances. He put it this way:

You asked just now on what basis we thought we were coming here for discussions which involved 4/11 and 16/11 [November 4 and

16, 1947]. We regarded the resolution of 16/11 as a very great advance on 4/11. The whole context of the 4/11 resolution is a truce. 16/11 is an armistice. And it got us a great deal nearer realities and peace than any previous resolution of the Security Council. It never occurred to us that 4/11, which represented an outdated state of affairs, would work as a brake on the 16/11. . . . That, properly speaking, is what we had in mind. . . . The Egyptian position of holding up 4/11 as if it had a special sanctity of its own, which has to be considered separately even when one is talking in entirely different terms, was a thing which had scarcely occurred to us. . . . I have said they were being excessively legalistic, etc. They were trying to put a brake on, by appealing to something which to all intents and purposes has lost its applicability. It gives them certain advantages, but only in terms of a situation which no longer exists. That is the answer which seems to us to be a common-sense point of view. (*M. V.*, pp. 133–34)

Eytan's argument is an early example of Zionist-Israeli diplomacy by fait accompli: establish military facts and then bend and twist law and diplomacy to legitimate acquisitions by force. It is a practice that continues in the creeping annexation of the West Bank, the declared annexation of Jerusalem and the Golan Heights, and the unilaterally established "security zone" in southern Lebanon. These acts of aggression, except for largely rhetorical objections by the major world powers, are often acquiesced in by the United States, which rarely finds Israel in violation of the UN Charter and thus subject to consequent penalties.

The Eytan argument cannot stand against the text of the November 16 Security Council Resolution No. 62. The first paragraph of the preamble reaffirms "previous resolutions concerning the establishment and implementation of the truce in Palestine"; the last makes specific reference to Resolution No. 61 of November 4 and to "the actions of the Acting Mediator" (*UN Res.*, p. 130). The Israeli tactics were circular. By refusing to withdraw to the October 14 lines, they had violated the November 4 resolution. Then they insisted on basing the armistice lines on the territory they had occupied in violation of the Security Council order.

On February 1, Eytan informed Sharett that the Egyptians had to go to Cairo for consultations, dashing Bunche's hopes for a quick windup of the talks. Eytan saw the delay as an opportunity to reinforce the Israeli demands by recruiting Washington's help. His message to the minister for foreign affairs described the Egyptian negotiators as "cronies" of his colleague Reuven Shiloah, meaning they were "patsies" for the Israelis. Israel's position on Beersheba, Auja, and Asluj would prevail, he said. "If our case on Beersheba, Bir Asluj and Auja is strongly supported from Washington, there may be some chance of getting away with it" (*M. V.*, p. 144).

The Negev

Both the Israeli and American documents record an exchange of views among Washington, Cairo, and Tel Aviv that was the most heated of the long weeks of talks. One of the principal remaining issues had a direct bearing on the future of the Negev. The Israelis insisted on the right to maintain "mobile forces outside . . . scattered Jewish points (settlements) in the north." The Israelis considerably expanded the role played in the armistice negotiations by their mission to the United Nations. Abba Eban, head of their delegation, was paying particular attention to the U.S. delegation. On February 3 Eban called Sharett, informing him that John Ross, deputy to the U.S. ambassador, had told him that the question of where Israeli forces might remain in the Negev after the armistice was considered crucial. Ross had apparently told Eban the United States "could not understand why it was necessary" to maintain military forces "outside settlements." Eban's explanation discloses Israel's ultimate political goals. He told Sharett: "I explained difference is between Negev in obvious effective Israel control and Negev of undetermined authority except scattered Jewish points in north. This difference might be decisive politically. I emphasized urgency American pressure Cairo since we had gone to great lengths conciliation and our attitude Faluja, Gaza, Auja village, cease-fire, offered ample material [for the] Egyptians emerge honorably. . . . Our impression American pressure is on us, not Cairo" (*M. V.*, pp. 147–48).

The Israeli concessions had all been beyond the recommendations of the partition in territory to which Israel had no claims except the right of conquest (*M. V.*, map facing p. 138). They were demonstrations of the fait accompli diplomacy used by Zionists to expand the Balfour Declaration's "national home for the Jewish people . . . in Palestine" into a full-blown national Jewish state.

The Egyptians were as aware as the Israelis that title to the Negev was at stake in this vigorous dispute over seemingly minor territorial differences. And both parties were becoming increasingly aware that, although not a direct party to the armistice negotiations, the United States—behind the scenes and in the United Nations—was exercising increasing leverage in the critical discussions. Consequently, representatives of both Egypt and Israel converged on the U.S. State Department on February 5. Both were received personally by Secretary of State Dean Acheson. The Egyptian ambassador came first. As reported in "Memorandum of Conversation by the Secretary of State" (*FRUS* 6 [1949], pp. 725–27), he reviewed negotiations at Rhodes, emphasizing that Egypt "had accepted and was willing to carry out Security Council resolutions of November 4th, 16th and December 29th," as well as the "last compromise suggested by Mr. Bunche, which involved a recession on their part from the November 4 resolution." But "unfortunately 'the other side' had consistently refused to accept any compromise and adhered to its original position." His government therefore had instructed him to ask the United States to "intervene" to prevent the breakdown of negotiations.

Acheson replied the United States "could not 'intervene,' but it would continue to use its good offices." He added that the United States agreed "to the desirability of our getting back on closer and friendlier relations." The memorandum of the conversation concludes with Acheson's admission that "we were aware of the cooperative attitude displayed by the Egyptians at Rhodes and were most appreciative of it." Acheson's conversation with the Israeli ambassador is recorded in a top secret memorandum that was sent to President Truman. It may be significant that the initiative for the meeting had come from Acheson.

The American secretary chided the Israeli with the information that Bunche and the U.S. delegation to the United Nations had sent reports to Washington "which caused us considerable concern." The Egyptians had accepted "the Mediator's proposals . . . practically in full, although with reluctance." But Eban, the Israeli "representative in New York had told our representative that the Israeli Government could not accept these proposals." Bunche had "expressed grave fears that the negotiations would break down and that the matter would have to be reported to the Security Council by him." Acheson warned Elath, "It appeared that in such a situation the collapse of the negotiations would rest on the Israeli Government" (*FRUS* 6 [1949], pp. 727–29).

Acheson then emphasized the seriousness with which he hoped the

Israelis would receive this information. He was, he said, "speaking . . . with the knowledge and approval of the President" who had been "caused . . . deep concern" by the situation (*FRUS* 6 [1949], p. 727). The president believed the time was ripe for an armistice agreement. The rest of the memorandum warrants extensive verbatim excerpts because it reflects the waffling that characterized much of the U.S. "good offices" during the negotiations. It illustrates also the Israeli tactic of cultivating the U.S. perception of Israel as an authentic democracy that, for security, needed the territories it had acquired by war beyond the partition boundaries.

Acheson noted that Truman believed an armistice could be crafted "without injury to the vital interests of any of the parties, if the Israeli Government would approach these discussions in a spirit of broad statesmanship and make concessions which were wholly in accord with the moral position of Israel." He continued: "I hoped therefore that his [Israel's] Government would not reject the proposals but would accept them as a basis for further discussion and work out an armistice along the lines proposed. I did not believe that the attitude of the Egyptian Government was brittle but did believe that there was sufficient flexibility so that with a conciliatory attitude on both sides, a solution could be reached. I said that if this were not done, if the negotiations failed, and if the matter was so reported to the Security Council, the position of Israel, both morally and otherwise, would be prejudiced" (*FRUS* 6 [1949], p. 728).

Acheson's memorandum recounted the Israeli ambassador's response. "He stated that his Government knew that it had no more sympathetic friend than President Truman and that his views would be pondered with the greatest respect. He said that I could assure the President that . . . his Government was not making a flat rejection of the Mediator's proposal but was finding difficulty on security reasons to eliminating its forces from certain places." Acheson then began to give ground: "We both agreed that we would not go into the details of the matter and he understood that what I had said did not mean that we believed that the proposal as made in all its details ought to be the one finally accepted" (*FRUS* 6 [1949], p. 728).

At this point, the Israeli ambassador changed the subject to the history of the Jews, stressing the Holocaust theme. "The Ambassador then spoke of some of the problems which his Government had as the government of a democratic country in carrying its own people with it. He then spoke at some length about the spiritual and moral forces which had enabled the Jews to survive their hardships and which lie at the basis of the state of Israel" (*FRUS* 6 [1949], p. 728).

Acheson acquiesced in the switch of substance. He had called in the Israeli to discuss the military strong points that Israel insisted on retaining beyond the partition boundaries. But now the secretary of state offered a kind of half benediction to the Israelis' pitch about moral forces. "I hoped they [the Israelis] would approach the proposals for an armistice from the point of view of these considerations and that what he had said assured me that they believed that reliance upon these forces were more effective than military strong points here and there, and that as I saw it the thing that his Government would wish to avoid more than anything else would be impairing in any way its moral position. He agreed that this was so and that considerations of *noblesse oblige* bore strongly upon the Jewish attitude" (*FRUS* 6 [1949], pp. 728–29).

On February 9 the Israeli cabinet reviewed the negotiations to that date. Compromises were accepted on Auja. It might serve as the seat of the Armistice Commission; the Egyptians were to demilitarize a zone on their side combined with a reduction in the size of the demilitarized zone. But the area "must not be placed under United Nations control." The way to the southern tip of the Negev was still clear. The Israeli record was consistent: They did not want the United Nations in the neighborhood. "The Cabinet realized that failure to achieve agreement with the Egyptians might be politically dangerous should the matter be brought before the Security Council, while, it was hoped, some further concessions would make agreement on all military matters possible, thus facilitating the implementation of the General staff's plan for an advance to Elath (Operation Uvda)" (*C. V.*, p. xx).

Before proceeding here with the negotiations with the Egyptians it is useful to examine the success of the Israelis' strategy in these earliest rounds. On the whole, it had benefited them handsomely. Consequently, they pursued—or tried to pursue—the same pattern for upcoming discussions with Lebanon, Transjordan, and Syria. It is important to understand this strategy as part of a well-thought-out long-range plan that might otherwise appear to be only a series of good-faith but expedient accommodations to attain peace at any reasonable price. Not only did the Israelis attempt to denigrate the stated, general objectives of the relevant Security Council resolutions, but they invested the *specifications* of the partition recommendation with as little sanctity as they "could get away with," to use Eban's words. At the same time they invested the *concept* of partition with the most inviolate authority for the legitimacy of their state.

All of the territorial points contested with the Egyptians had been assigned by the partition to the proposed Arab state. The Bernadotte proposals had revised the partition boundary recommendations and assigned the Negev to the Arab state. Following the declaration of Israel's establishment, there had been no Egyptian invasion of territory designated for the so-called Jewish state. It was Bernadotte who had proposed that the Negev be included in the Arab state. By February 5, 1949, Israel had determined, as a matter of policy, to use force to reverse this Bernadotte proposal.

During the 1948–49 fighting, Israel had occupied key strategic points that would be indispensable to the success of the military campaign—already planned—to take the Negev. Egypt, on the other hand, considered itself a partner in the Arab stewardship to protect the part of Palestine that partition or Bernadotte had assigned to the Arab state. But throughout the negotiations the Israelis constantly denied that the Egyptians had any rights to occupy any part of Palestine. With equal consistency, the Israelis vigorously defended their right of conquest to remain in parts of Palestine that had been designated Arab. At the third joint informal meeting of the two delegations, with his staff present, Bunche commented on the phrase *right of conquest* that Eytan had invoked to support Israeli claims to Auja and Beersheba. Bunche's challenge is instructive: "I would like to raise two points in regard to Auja, as a matter for the record. I wonder if you really, in view of the wide implications this could have in terms of the overall Palestine situation, meant to base your presence in Auja not only on practical necessity or security reasons as you pointed out, but also on the concept of something strange in the framework of the truce; namely, the right of conquest. Right of conquest is one thing, but there is a different framework in terms of the truce, and you might for the sake of the record wish to qualify it in some way" (*M. V.*, p. 188).

Realizing that Bunche saw through the Israeli pretext of security to justify its aggressions, Eytan backtracked, dropped the demand for recognition of its "right," and substituted a more credible explanation of its conduct. He responded to Bunche:

> I am well aware that "right of conquest" is a technical term in international law. I was not using it in its technical sense. I think

the meaning which I was trying to convey might be equally well expressed by the term "fact of occupation." What I was trying to point out is that in el-Auja we have a situation where the whole area up to the Egyptian border is held, occupied, and controlled by Israeli forces. . . . I was trying to point out that this military situation which exists is not one which can be completely disregarded. We are in occupation of that area, and when we voluntarily recede from a position there, we are receding from a position which we actually hold. I was trying to point out the contrast between this, and the alleged concessions of the Egyptians of land which they do not hold. (*M.V.*, p. 188)

In other words, Israel had the right of conquest and Egypt had no rights because it did not conquer.

In a February 7 letter to Eytan, Bunche cut through the Israeli linguistic fog, instructing the Israelis that the Security Council truce permitted *no* advances by either side while the truce obtained. Then, with impeccable logic, he added, "If your forces are often asked to withdraw, it can only be that they have often advanced under the truce. If the Egyptians are not called upon to withdraw, it is only because, for whatever reason, they have nowhere advanced. Indeed, in one instance, al-Faluja, they have been ordered to withdraw and have been prevented for months from doing so for reasons well known to you" (*M.V.*, p. 210). The Israelis had occupied Auja in violation of the truce. If no negotiated agreement were reached, the Auja problem would automatically revert to the Security Council for action. The Israelis were anxious to avoid the public debate that would follow.

In the same February 7 letter Bunche strongly intimated he saw through Israeli rigidity on the three strategic Negev areas (Auja, Bir Asluj, and Beersheba) to their design for acquiring the entire Negev. He put the charge with a modest amount of diplomatic indirection:

It has never been my understanding that you are insisting that in the armistice agreement the Egyptians must recognise your right to any territory, whether in the Negev or elsewhere. For if that were the case, there would be obvious difficulties, since it is not yet known officially whether you are claiming all or part of the Negev, and whether or not you are claiming places outside the 29 November 1947 lines such as Beersheba and el-Auja. It is inconceivable, also, that if you were claiming all of the Negev, you would be willing to sign an agreement permitting Egyptian forces to remain there during the period of the armistice.

I point all this out to emphasize that not only because of Security Council resolutions, but also because your own position is unknown, there is a distinction that can be drawn between what is clearly defined as Egyptian territory and what is not yet clearly defined as yours, and that, in any case, it is not the responsibility of an armistice agreement to settle territorial disputes. The Egyptians could scarcely be called upon to recognize claims not even advanced. . . .

On the other hand, nothing in the agreement envisaged should prejudice any rights, claims or interests you may wish to advance when the settlement stage is reached, and in its present draft I am positive that nothing does.

For these reasons I am appealing to both parties to . . . return to . . . the basic premise of the intended armistice, viz. the liquidation of the military phase of the conflict.

. . . I am in full accord with you that your security interests must be fully safeguarded and I think that the Egyptians also will be amenable in that regard. (*M.V.*, pp. 211–12)

So, in these first Israeli-Arab conversations, in what many hoped would be the beginnings of the first peace process, the Israelis established another strategy that they pursue to the present: they demand security and recognition but refrain from declaring either their optimum negotiating positions or permanent borders.

This letter and another, more formal in style to Sharett and also dated February 7, indicated that Bunche was losing patience with Israeli delays. On the same date, Eytan confirmed this in a cautionary letter to Sharett. In the following excerpt, Eytan confessed to his own foreign minister that the Security Council, if called on to act, might make evident it was "fed up with our failure to comply with orders":

The threat of Security Council action has of course lurked behind Bunche's conversations with us ever since we came here, but it has never come out so clearly before. The basic question which the Government has to ask itself is whether it is prepared to face the Security Council on these issues. I take it from your cable to Bunche that the answer is in the affirmative, though I do not for the life of me know what the Government would do if the Security Council, egged on by Bunche and fed up with our failure to comply with orders, took a really strong line to force us to withdraw from Auja, return to November 13th lines, etc.—or be branded as violators of the truce and mockers of UN, with all that this would mean in respect of our chances of becoming members of that organisation in the near future. For all the strength of our military case—and it is this of course that we have been pressing all along—we should have a very sticky time attempting to justify ourselves in terms of the international order as represented by Security Council decisions. I presume that this aspect of the present armistice negotiations is being borne in mind by the Government, and that the Government has decided that it doesn't give a damn. (*M.V.*, pp. 216–17)

On February 8, Eban informed Sharett that he had briefed David Niles and Clark Clifford on the Rhodes talks and left "a short paper—urging stronger pressure on Egypt [to] sign without further demands."[20] The same day, Uriel Heyd, first secretary of the Israeli Embassy, informed Sharett that Clifford had told Abe Feinberg that day that "Bunche [a] few days ago suggested U.S.A. should press us for further concessions Rhodes, but White House instructed Acheson against one-sided pressure on Israel" (*M.V.*, p. 220).[21]

On February 18, Warren Austin, the U.S. representative to the United Nations, informed Secretary of State Acheson that Bunche had asked the U.S. "for any possible assistance" with the Egyptians, who had agreed to Israeli forces in "the surrounding area" but were adamant about withdrawal from the town itself. They argued that Beersheba "is an Arab town" and "is intended in territory allotted to Arab state by November 29 resolution" (*FRUS* 6 [1949], pp. 755–56).

The Israelis, however, "are adamant in refusal . . . to withdraw from town" but "are in fact building camps outside the town." This might be interpreted to mean "that Israelis plan informally to withdraw their forces." The reasons they offered were that Bunche was not on the Egyptian front, and until an armistice was negotiated with Transjordan they needed a military base in the event of a renewal of fighting by Abdallah's forces. Bunche therefore observed "that Beersheba is more of an issue between the Security Council and Israel than between Egypt and Israel, if it is an issue at all" (*FRUS* 6 [1949], pp. 755–56).[22]

On February 21, James McDonald, the U.S. special representative in Israel, informed Acheson that Sharett had told him that Bunche had narrowed the difference about Beersheba by designating the "eastern front 'irrelevant' until armistice negotiations open with Transjordan." "Beersheba," the telegram continued, is "well east [of] dividing lines. Hence its noninclusion in Israel evacuation zone." McDonald concluded his message by adding an appeal from Sharett for a "word from Washington to Egypt urging unqualified acceptance latest Bunche draft might result signature armistice Wednesday or Thursday this week. He pleads urgent action by Department" (*FRUS* 6 [1949], p. 760).

This recommended exclusion of the Transjordan front from the Israel-Egyptian discussions had been incorporated in a new draft of Article VIII of Bunche's draft agreement of February 12, after consultations with the military experts of both parties. The revised draft declared the Israeli and Egyptian negotiators recognized that "the proximity of the forces of a third party [Transjordan] . . . in certain sectors . . . makes impractical full application of the provisions of the agreement to such sectors." In addition to the eastern front, the territory "south of Bir Asluj down to the southernmost tip of Palestine" was excluded from the Israeli/Egyptian agreement, "pending conclusion of an Armistice agreement, to replace the existing truce" with the "third party [Transjordan]". At that time "the matter shall be subject to review by the Parties." A note to the draft agreement adds "acceptance by the Parties" of this paragraph (identified as paragraph 5) "shall be on the agreed understanding, *not to be incorporated in the agreement*, that "(a) The line described in paragraph 4 shall follow the road through the town of Beersheba itself; (b) Israeli forces now in the town of Beersheba shall be gradually withdrawn, but in any case not later than one month after the Agreement is signed, and garrisoned in nearby camps and settlements; and (c) A United Nations Observer team shall be stationed in the town of Beersheba" (*M.V.*, pp. 239–40; emphasis supplied).

This concession to the Israelis was not to be published when the armistice agreement might be made public. It also eliminated some obstacles to Israel's determination to occupy the entire Negev. And the Transjordanians were to be kept in the dark about when formal negotiations would be started for an armistice with them.

On February 14, Eytan updated Sharett on the negotiations and recommended that Shabtai Rosenne, legal advisor to the Israeli delegation, "be ready to come" to Rhodes "to help in the final drafting." He reported the Israelis were prepared to agree to a demilitarized Auja area provided it was smaller than Bunche had proposed; also it should "not be a UN zone nor in any way under UN rule or control." The Armistice Commission might be based there but "nowhere else." Egyptian defensive positions were to be restricted, and the road "from Taba via Quseima" would be denied to "any military force whatsoever . . . for the purpose of entering Palestine" (*M.V.*, p. 245). Eytan reported he had accepted the larger demilitarized Auja area finally proposed by Bunche. Measured by the terms of the November 29 partition proposal, Eytan noted this final determination was another victory for Israel. His vague reference to the elimination of a "danger for the future" is significant in the context of the Israeli plans to invade and claim the entire Negev: "This has the one great advantage over the area previously suggested by Bunche for the UN zone that it bears no relation at any point to the 29 November line. . . . [T]he earlier area had the apex of its triangle on the 29 November line, which Bunche maintained was purely fortuitous, but which to us spelled danger for the future. In the new area this is removed. I have no doubt that we shall reach agreement with the Egyptians on this basis, and that we shall never have to make the maximum concession of accepting Bunche's full plan for a UN zone" (*M.V.*, p. 247).

On the question of Beersheba, Eytan informed Tel Aviv that he had told Bunche that he "objected strongly to the attached 'Note,' which states that 'acceptance of this Article is to be on the agreed understanding, not to be incorporated in the Agreement. . . .' I thought the principle of the thing was unsound. If a matter could not be incorporated into a written agreement, but had to be dealt with by the subterfuge of an 'understanding,' it was a bad thing and we had had an unfortunate experience before" (*M.V.*, p. 247). The "note," Eytan observed, is "the only trouble" with the draft agreement, but he expressed the belief the problem would be settled and "the agreement will be all but signed" after four more days of work (*M.V.*, pp. 246–48).[23]

The time prediction was optimistic. On February 21, the day Acheson received McDonald's telegram conveying Sharett's request for the United States to persuade Egypt to accept the "latest Bunche draft," Acheson did, in fact, comply with the Israeli request. His instructions to the U.S. Embassy in Cairo were something less than accurate. He reported the Israelis had "accepted without reservations" Bunche's final draft of the "complete text armistice agreement and appendices." He added that the U.S. government had been "further informed that Egyptian delegation at Rhodes has made reservations to status proposed by Bunche for Beer-sheba." Acheson's only source of information about the Egyptian position had been McDonald's report of what Sharett had told him. Accordingly, Acheson noted, the U.S. government "understands that provision in Bunche draft agreement looks toward safeguarding of any political rights or claims. Status Beersheba will be determined at time of final peace settlement and USG believes question should not be permitted obstruct signing of armistice agreement" (*FRUS* 6 [1949], p. 760).

Then, ignoring Israeli claims to Auja and Asluj that conflicted with the recommended partition borders, Acheson offered self-congratulations for U.S. "good offices" that had "worked to persuade Israeli authorities modify their former adamant position, which was holding up negotiations. Tel Aviv subsequently made several accommodations in order to meet Bunche proposals such as status El Auja and Bir Asluj" (*FRUS* 6 [1949], p. 761).

Acheson then instructed the Cairo embassy to twist Egyptian arms by informing the Egyptians that the "USG would deplore any action likely create further obstacles at time when armistice agreement seems near. . . . In spirit of friendship for Egypt and in its desire see peace return to NE [Near East], USG urges Egyptian Govt accept Bunche draft without insistence [on] reservations" (*FRUS* 6 (1949), p. 760).

Events in the Middle East and on Rhodes were outpacing developments at Lake Success and Washington. On February 20, Eytan sent Sharett "one copy of the 'Draft Egyptian Israeli General Armistice agreement'" with the information it had been completed "at 10 o'clock this morning." Eytan added that at 4:00 P.M. a "formal meeting" with the Egyptians was scheduled, "at which time we shall indicate our assent to the draft, and they likewise." The question of Beersheba remained "the main outstanding point," but "it is the clear impression of all of us, including Bunche, that the Egyptians will not allow Beersheba to stand in the way of final agreement." Eytan also reported that "two or three" of the Egyptians were flying to Cairo for final authorization to sign the agreement (*M.V.*, pp. 258–59).

On February 22, Jefferson Patterson, the American chargé d'affaires in Cairo, informed Acheson that he had seen Egyptian Prime Minister Abdul Hadi Pasha and conveyed Acheson's message to him: the United States believed that "Beersheba should not prove [an] obstacle to signature armistice agreement because Bunche's draft had safeguards for political rights or claims to that town which should be determined during final peace settlement" (*FRUS* 6 [1949], p. 764).

The prime minister was reported to have replied that the "Egyptian attitude toward Beersheba was not arbitrary, but was based on importance of town as symbol of UN November 4 resolution; as strategic point important for Egypt's defense (although such importance now diminished by Zionist fortified villages in vicinity); and as communications center on an important highway. For these reasons Egypt had been anxious to maintain a civil administration at Beersheba without troops or fortifications." Patterson concluded that his "final impression" was that the prime minister "would use his influence to remove Egyptian reservations respecting Beersheba" (*FRUS* 6 [1949], p. 764).

The Cairo telegram to Acheson then introduced, for almost the first time in the armistice negotiations, a reference to Egyptian concern about the Palestinian refugees. The only other important reference to the war refugees was in the February 8 message to Acheson from the American consul in Jerusalem, reporting Sharett's statement to the Palestine Conciliation Commission (*FRUS* 6 [1949], p. 737).

The American consul's telegram of February 22 reported that having virtually agreed to the U.S.-Israeli position on Beersheba, "possibly with [a] view of making a Palestine settlement more palatable to Egyptian public," "Hadi Pasha urged at considerable length importance of US support for return of Palestine refugees to their homes since temporary relief would not suffice and also US aid to Egypt" (*FRUS* 6 [1949], p. 765).

In response to the Egyptian request for American economic aid, Patterson suggested to Acheson that "if a Marshall Plan for the Middle East were not practicable, at least the US Government should insist that Marshall Plan dollars supplied European countries should, when such countries required Egyptian cotton, be used to pay for at least a portion of such cotton in dollars" (*FRUS* 6 [1949], pp. 764–65). There is no record of a U.S. response on the refugee problem or to the question of economic assistance during the concluding negotiations for the armistice.[24]

Eytan's recommendation at the beginning of the negotiations to wear down the Egyptians had succeeded, aided by some duplicity and the eventual blessings of the United States. The armistice was signed at Rhodes on February 24. On the same day, President Truman, in a public statement, declared, "I am immensely gratified." He also expressed the hope that "this pattern for peace will be followed rapidly in the conclusion of similar agreements between Israel and the other Arab states [and] lead to permanent peace" (*FRUS* 6 [1949], p. 765).

FRUS 6 (1949) records in an editorial note that "hostile" public reaction "in Egypt has been practically nil." Perhaps not surprising, since, "while criticism has been barred from the press by government directive no indirect criticism, even by the opposition press, has yet appeared. The press has, in fact, devoted itself to statements up-holding the valor and honor of the Egyptian Army and calling attention to Egypt's respect and support for international organizations working for peace. The view is taken that the military experience gained in the Palestinian affair has more than compensated for sacrifices involved" (p. 766).

On February 24, Patterson telegraphed Washington that the Egyptian government's official communiqué "states 'agreement has no political character. It deals exclusively with military questions and does not affect in any way the political destiny of Palestine.' . . . Press reproduction of agreement forbidden by censor although radio heard in Egypt carries full text. Security officials warned Embassy officer violent reaction possible when agreement is published" (*FRUS* 6 [1949], pp. 768–69).[25]

The Israelis' handling of the press was more sophisticated. Eytan's February 21 letter advised Sharett that the final text of the agreement was to be considered a "top secret document" until its simultaneous release in Tel Aviv, Cairo, and Lake Success. He also recommended to Sharett that "we should not trumpet this agreement abroad as a great achievement or victory, except in the political sense" (*M.V.*, p. 261). In other words, it would not be prudent to emphasize the territories Israel had acquired beyond the recommended 1947 lines.

The Profits of Defiance

But privately, to Sharett, Eytan could hardly contain his exuberance. He provided a detailed inventory of what Israel had achieved over and above what it would have had to settle for had it abided by the original UN/Bunche conditions. First, the mediator's November 13 memorandum called for a return to the October 14 lines:

> This would have meant the total withdrawal of all Jewish forces from the Negev, except for those actually maintained in the settlements themselves for the purpose of [static] settlements defence. The effect of this would have been the full implementation of the Bernadotte plan in military terms. Taken together with the ap-

pointment of an Egyptian civil administrator for Beersheba, the
return of Egyptian military forces to el-Auja and elsewhere, etc.,
this would have meant the loss of our effective military control of
the Negev, which was achieved by the campaign which started on
14th October as well as by subsequent fighting, and with it the
probable loss of our political and territorial prospects in the whole
of Palestine south of Majdal and Faluja. For all these reasons—and
they are obvious reasons—we uncompromisingly opposed the
Egyptians' original demands, *though this meant*, between you and
me and Moish, *opposing a Security Council resolution which we
had in principle accepted as long ago as November 18th*. This
need not be stressed to the foreign press, but I presume that everyone realises that the Egyptians' insistent and *legitimate* reliance
on the 4th November resolution made our position very difficult
and forced us practically to argue our heads off in the presence of
Bunche, who, as a loyal official of the United Nations, could not
too openly take our side in this matter. (*M. V.*, p. 262; all emphases
supplied)

The following paragraph features another assist for Israel's contemplated expansion in the Negev. Eytan points out that "the essential
feature of the armistice agreement is the reduction of forces on both
sides to *defensive strength* only" (emphasis supplied). "[But] the point
to stress here is that both we and the Egyptians are reducing our forces
in such a way that there will be complete equality on both sides. The
Egyptians will not maintain offensive forces any nearer to us than el-
Arish. The coastal strip between Gaza and Rafah is included in the area
in which the Egyptians must reduce their forces. (*Our two main bases
for offensive* forces are in any case Julis and Beersheba, both of which
bases are outside the scope of the agreement with Egypt. *This of course,
is not for publication*)" (*M. V.*, p. 262; all emphases supplied).
    Second, in the Gaza-Rafah area, Eytan noted that "we have given the
Egyptians the satisfaction of taking the 13th November line as the basic
Armistice demarcation line." But, he added, "in point of fact we shall be
remaining on the 'wrong' side of the line in at least one place (Deir
Suneid) *but I strongly advise against mentioning this specifically to
journalists*" (*M. V.*, p. 262).
    Third, on February 15, Sharett had informed Eytan in Rhodes that
"the only way to 'frustrate' [Abdallah's] plot" to take over the southern

Negev was to establish "tangible Israeli control" in the territory.[26] "[H]e alludes to a military operation *which is being planned* with a view to occupying that area." The campaign was named Operation Uvda.

> The best timing for such a campaign is the period between signing of the agreement with Egypt and the commencement of official negotiations with Jordan. Sharett therefore recommends that the agreement with Egypt be concluded as soon as possible, to be followed immediately by negotiations with Lebanon and Syria, while negotiations with Jordan should be postponed to a later stage. He proposes "dragging out" the direct negotiations which the Israeli and Jordanian representatives have been conducting lately and instructs the Israeli representatives in Rhodes to induce Bunche to give priority to the negotiations with Lebanon and postpone the beginning of talks with Jordan. (*C.V.*, pp. 59–60)

The best time for the Negev campaign was now at hand, and Eytan's February 21 letter explained how, in the negotiations with Egypt, the Israelis had maneuvered around Bunche and the UN resolutions to facilitate the Israeli military aggression.

> The Memorandum of 13th November forbids the maintenance of any Jewish forces whatsoever in the Negev except actually *in* the settlements themselves. The words, "based on the settlements" represent a compromise. They mean that, while the forces shall be based on the settlements, there is nothing to prevent them [from] moving freely about the area. There is nothing, for instance, to prevent a patrol from staying away from its "base" for ten days, nor anything that forbids the maintenance of defensive forces in outposts ("Mishlatim") anywhere we choose, as long as the troops who man these outposts are nominally based on a settlement. (*M.V.*, p. 263)

Eytan recommended that this Israeli stratagem would best be concealed from the world, except for Israel: "I think this point is worth explaining to the Hebrew press, *but should not be overdone with foreign journalists*" (*M.V.*, p. 263; emphasis supplied).

Finally, one of the major points that Eytan's February 21 letter stressed is that "after much argument" the Egyptians "reluctantly conceded in principle" that "anything that happened in the eastern part of the Negev was no concern of the Egyptians and must therefore be outside the scope of an armistice agreement with them, but refused to draw a line dividing the eastern from the western part." "We got around this," Eytan continued,

> by agreeing that the line be drawn by the UN Chief of Staff. The line drawn by the UN Chief of Staff is, in fact, in every detail the line that we wanted. The formal position, therefore, is now that we have complete freedom of action in the eastern sector (i.e., east of a line from Beersheba to Bir Asluj and from there to the southern-most tip of Palestine on the Gulf of Aqaba), except insofar as this freedom of action is restricted by the existing truce, while in the western sector we are not tied down to static settlement defence, but can move freely except for certain spots (e.g., Auja) as provided specifically in the agreement. (*M.V.*, pp. 263–64)

Denial of any Egyptian concern for the eastern Negev was, legally, not as absolute as Eytan makes it appear. The original partition recommendation had assigned the Negev to Israel. But Beersheba, Auja, and Asluj were *not* included. The Bernadotte proposal had recommended that the Negev be assigned to an Arab state. But in the absence of any effective, recognized Palestinian authority and in view of the expressed purpose of the Arab states that they had joined the war to defend the rights of the Palestinian Arabs, neither Transjordan nor Egypt could be arbitrarily ruled to have no concerns for the proposed Arab state. However, as Eytan put it in this February 21 letter, with the Egyptian-Israeli armistice agreement neutralizing Auja and Asluj and allowing Israel to remain in Beersheba and with the restrictions put on housing and movements of the United Nations and the Conciliation Commission, a vacuum was created at strategic points in the Negev. The Israeli's planned Operation Uvda, already on the drawing board, ensured that the vacuum would not long remain.

On February 24—the day the armistice agreement with Egypt was signed—Eban requested the Security Council "to give renewed consideration to his country's membership in the United Nations" (*FRUS 6* [1949], p. 766). And on March 4 the Security Council found Israel to be "a peace-loving state . . . able and willing to carry out the obligations contained in the Charter" (*UN Res.*, p. 131). On May 11, 1949, the General Assembly, in Resolution No. 273 (III), noting that Israel "unreservedly accepts the obligations of the United Nations Charter and undertakes to honour them from the day when it becomes a Member of the

United Nations and *Recalling* its resolutions of November 29, 1947 and December 11, 1948 and taking note of the declarations and explanations made by the representative of the Government of Israel before the *Ad Hoc* Political Committee in respect of the implementation of said resolutions . . . decides to admit Israel to membership in the United Nations" (*UN Res.*, p. 18).

The *Companion Volume* was not published until 1983—more than thirty years after the armistice with Egypt was signed. In the Foreword, the editor summarizes the Israeli viewpoint of the results of the armistice negotiations with all the belligerent Arab states. Her assessment of the agreement with Egypt reflects the near-complete satisfaction Eytan expressed in his February 21 letter to Sharett.

> Neither side achieved all its demands: Israel had to accept Egyptian military presence in the Gaza strip and to withdraw its troops from the Beit Hanun area [but it was] permitted to maintain seven outposts along the Gaza strip; the besieged Egyptian brigade at Faluja was released; Israel was forced to agree to the establishment of a demilitarized zone in the Auja area, which did, however, extend over both sides of the border; Auja was to be the seat of the Mixed Armistice Commission, but *Israel succeeded in preventing the placing of the area under United Nations control*; the Egyptian demand that Beersheba be included within the area of defensive forces was rejected, but Bir Asluj was included within this area; Israel managed to guarantee the mobility of its forces in the northern Negev, and attained the temporary exclusion of the entire eastern sector of the southern Negev, bordering on Jordan, from the territory covered by the agreement with Egypt; it did not succeed in preventing the frequent reference to the Security Council resolution of 4 November and to Bunche's 13 November memorandum in some clauses of the agreement which reserved the right of the parties to raise their political demands in the course of future negotiations.
>
> Notwithstanding all the concessions, the agreement gave Israel considerable advantages; militarily, it guaranteed Israel's control of the northern Negev, and in fact left it free to occupy the southern Negev without violating its agreement with Egypt. Politically, it strengthened Israel's international standing and its chances for admission to the United Nations Organization. The signing of an agree-

ment with the largest Arab state opened up possibilities for agreements with other Arab states and inspired hopes—soon dashed—that the armistice would lead to a final peace. (*C. V.*, p. xxvi; emphasis supplied)

One other *Main Volume* document pertaining to the Egyptian negotiations is of more than ordinary significance, particularly to Americans. On March 3, Abba Eban wrote a confidential letter to Eytan, its purpose to inform Eytan—and presumably any other Israelis who might be involved in future armistice negotiations with the other Arab states—of "intimate connections between events at Rhodes and influences from Lake Success and Washington" (*M. V.*, p. 275).

Eban's first point was that Bunche "possesses a great power" because he "is able to determine the target" for adverse public opinion when a party to the negotiations "is considered culpable in preventing an agreement." Pointedly, Eban noted that Bunche "is both an American and an officer of the United Nations." "The United States Government, and, to a more limited extent, the Secretary-General, have an important influence on his conduct, and therefore on the atmosphere of the negotiations" (*M. V.*, p. 276).

Second, Eban pointed out that Bunche sent "the Secretary-General a detailed survey of the negotiations with summaries of all relevant documents." He then emphasized a pivotal role—but clearly (at least to Eban) a somewhat irregular and privileged one—played by the United States. He added, "There is obviously an agreement whereby these [detailed reports] reach the United States Government immediately. If a crisis or complication occurs," John C. Ross, U.S. deputy representative at the Security Council, "refers the matter to Washington, where the State Department exercises the requisite pressures on the negotiating parties" (*M. V.*, p. 276).

Third, Eban stated as an unqualified—and undocumented—fact that "until the final phase, Bunche used his powers of reporting . . . to secure American pressure upon ourselves." "Our duty," he continued, "was to withstand this pressure and to divert it in the Egyptian direction [also] . . . to keep contact with all Security Council members in an effort to create an impression of Israeli moderation and Egyptian intransigence" (*M. V.*, pp. 275–78).[27]

This tactic was used by Eban in New York and by Elath in Washington to accomplish these manipulations. According to Eban and to Elath's representation to the State Department, there were communications "including the Secretary of State himself, defending our position and advocating pressure upon the Egyptians; and similar conversations between myself and members of the United States delegation at Lake Success." The Israelis did not limit these communications to regular channels. Eban noted "contacts between our embassy and White House friends [anonymous, of course] to ensure that the President received a fair impression of our viewpoint and interests." He (Eban) maintained "close contacts with the Secretary-General to ensure a supply of information [he does not say who gave what to whom] and the use of his influence with Bunche" (*M.V.*, p. 277).

Fourth, Eban admitted that "great pressure was exercised on the Egyptians, both at Washington and at Lake Success" and, in a not-too-modest bid for kudos, added, "It is possible that the activities detailed above may have played some part in that result." He specified that following a talk between Acheson and Elath "and the submission to the President of our Rhodes memorandum, the United States showed less inclination to bludgeon us, and a greater activity in their Egyptian contacts. . . . The whole weight of international pressure," Eban boasted, was brought to bear "to make one of the parties yield on Beersheba. The whole weight of international pressure was brought to bear upon the Egyptians." But the secretary-general did not apply his pressure "convincingly," Eban complained, meaning that Trygve Lie's implementation of this world pressure was halfhearted. Lie explained to Eban that "he had been asked to suggest our withdrawal from the town of Beersheba; but that if he were we, he would not do such a thing, since he had looked at the maps and seen that the town was obviously vital for Israel and of no account to Egypt."[28]

Fifth, having chronicled this "modest" record of accomplishment, Eban criticized the communications between Tel Aviv and Rhodes and Elath and himself. Often the Americans, he wrote, produced cables or displayed "knowledge of intimate detail which had not been communicated to Eliahu [Elath] or myself." This may suggest that Israeli employment of "White House friends"—with an inside track to the White House and the president—worked better and faster than the bureaucratic channels leading from Tel Aviv to the recognized Israeli representatives in New York or Washington. The friends may also have been able to short-circuit Washington's own bureaucratic maze. Eban expressed the hope that "in the next stages, which are likely to be even more influenced outside Rhodes, we shall be better equipped" (*M.V.*, p. 277).

Sixth, Eban reported he found "the Soviets and the French deeply resentful" of the back door pipeline between the UN Secretariat and the White House "while they were kept in the dark." Or so Washington may have pleasurably thought. The emergent "only ally of the United States in the Middle East"—and the most "trustworthy"—was not inhibited from playing both ends against the middle. Early in the game, it became clear that Israeli and U.S. interests were not wedded "in sickness and health." The Israelis were serving up to the French and Soviets such tidbits of secret information as served Israeli purposes. Eban offered the admission without apology. "They were therefore visibly grateful to us for redressing this balance and keeping them well informed, not only about the negotiations themselves, but *also about United States efforts to influence them*" (*M.V.*, p. 278; emphasis supplied).

Seventh, Eban apparently had not been informed of Sharett's directive to Eytan to stall negotiations with Transjordan until after Operation Uvda. He may also not have been "cut in" on the secret dealing between Abdallah and the Israelis. His letter to Eytan indicated that he believed the talks with Transjordan would follow completion of the negotiations with Egypt. He cautioned that the Transjordan talks will be complicated (for Israel) because "Great Britain will be standing in tangible support" of Abdallah. He recommended beginning frank conversations immediately with both the State Department and the American delegation, "pointing out that equilibrium will be achieved only if the Americans make it their main effort to support our legitimate interests and counterbalance British pressure. *It will no longer be appropriate for them to bring pressure for concessions upon both sides*; still less . . . to concentrate it mainly upon us" (*M.V.*, p. 278; emphasis supplied).

Eighth, and finally, Eban reflected the historic Zionist—and now Israeli—awareness of the importance of public opinion and the necessary attention to it as a responsibility for all engaged in Israeli diplomacy. Because of British support, "Transjordan will no doubt have a better press than did the Egyptians. Our delegation at Rhodes would accordingly be well advised to watch Bilby, Sam Brewer, and company more vigilantly than was necessary before."[29]

In view of the Israeli insistence that, as a starting point, the negotiations with Egypt should accept Israeli claims to territory beyond the partition-recommended borders, Eban's advice to Eytan said a good deal about the Israelis' proclivity for operating on a double standard and managing the news: "It is urgently necessary to implant the view that Transjordan has no automatic right to any of the territories it now occupies west of the Jordan; and that anything conceded to them there is in reality a substantial concession even if they occupy it already. The impression is too strong that their occupation forms the starting-point of negotiations and that the margin for bargaining concerns only the territory occupied by Israel in excess of the November 29th Resolution" (*M.V.*, pp. 275–78).

Eban's activities had been concentrated in New York, with occasional trips to support Elath in Washington. The two journalists he specifically mentions worked for the leading morning newspapers in New York, "newspapers of record." It is obvious that Eban's offered advice on the subject of public opinion had the American public primarily in mind. Attentive to public opinion as the Israelis were in 1949—particularly to American public opinion—just as oblivious were the Arabs to the importance of merchandising their diplomacy.

Arab derelictions with respect to publicity and their own explanation of their case has improved little four decades later. The American communication media are biased, but not all the bias is attributable to built-in mendacity. The ineptness, the inadequacy, the grudging, miniscule funding of any public relations programs, and the lack of competent personnel are devastating flaws in Arab diplomatic efforts.

Eban's March 3 letter to Eytan is the last document in the Israeli archival collection pertaining to the Egyptian negotiations. Some generalizations about Israeli negotiating strategies may therefore be in order. Those strategies were frequently predicated on U.S. support at critical points and therefore some notice must be taken of American conduct. Before engaging in this exercise the caveat made early must be kept in mind: There is no available English record of intragovernmental Egyptian memoranda and conversations. Consequently, there is no authoritative or official evidence of their negotiating strategy except as reported by the Israelis and the *FRUS* records of the United States. That deficiency should be remedied. Whenever and however this happens, future historians should be able to draw a more complete picture than is now possible of Egypt's motivations. As matters now stand, what must be characterized as only hearsay evidence (even if of a high quality) in the

Israeli and American records is available. With these cautions, the following conclusions seem supportable by evidence in Israeli and *FRUS* 1948 and 1949 volumes.

(1) From the first sessions with Bunche, Israel resisted any multi-lateral, coordinated Arab negotiations. This strategy was consistent with the old Zionist maxim that "Arab disunity is one of Zionism's most reliable allies."

(2) Throughout its pre-state history, Zionism had successfully practiced what has come to be called "fait accompli diplomacy."[30] After the state was established, Moshe Dayan used a less self-incriminating phrase, "establishing facts on the ground." By whatever name, the process meant to take by financial or military force any property that would be of strategic importance in the long-term planning for attainment of the ultimate goal. Israel deployed its military forces beyond the partition-recommended borders during the 1948–49 fighting, confronting the Egyptians—and Ralph Bunche—with territorial faits accomplis. These forward positions served either as jumping-off bases for further, already planned expansions or as defensive points for territory the Israelis had already acquired, to which they had no legal claims but thought the Egyptians might attempt to regain by force or diplomacy. Auja was an example of this kind of diplomacy. Beersheba was a base essential for Operation Uvda to take the entire Negev.

(3) Before the negotiations, Israel had a clear picture of the Palestine it eventually wanted to govern as the Jewish state. The Egyptians, on the other hand, had no clear vision of the proposed Arab state and no military plan to defend the territory from an Israel on the offensive. The original motivation of Egypt—and the Arab League states that joined in the fighting—was to assist the Palestinian Arabs to defend themselves against Zionism. But there was no effective organization to mount and sustain a credible defense by the indigenous population. As the fighting progressed, disadvantaged by longer lines of supply and communications, the Egyptian strategy became essentially incapable of protecting the rights and properties of the Palestinians.

(4) And, finally, it bears repeating that the sophisticated Zionist-Israeli use of public information and the unrelenting application of political pressures, particularly in the United States, combined with Arab derelictions and virtual ignoring of public opinion, made the political struggle in both U.S. and UN decision making grossly unequal.

These ingredients of the Palestine problem are still operative in Israel's international conduct. Both the Israelis and later chroniclers agreed the Egyptian armistice negotiations were an almost unqualified success for Israel. With this first armistice concluded, the Israelis confidently turned to the next stage. Although secret negotiations with Abdallah had been in progress for some time, the next formal negotiations, following Sharett's directive to Eytan, were with Lebanon.

chapter 7

LEBANON

First Try for the Litani

Compared to the complicated and protracted negotiations with Egypt, Israeli negotiations with the Lebanese were fairly simple. They began with a preliminary agreement, signed on January 14, 1949, in which Israel agreed to evacuate its troops from five Lebanese villages if the Lebanese agreed to enter negotiations for an armistice (*M.V.*, p. 282; *C.V.*, p. 36). The agreement is described "as a good will gesture and a prelude to further discussions" of the Security Council resolution of November 16, 1948.

On January 30, Bunche invited Israel to begin the negotiations and to name its delegation. He also recommended that the talks be held at Ras en-Nakura (Rosh Haniqra), a village close to the international border, in a kind of no-man's-land between the armed forces. Shabtai Rosenne, legal advisor of the Israeli delegation, was pleased with the border site. He emphasized that the talks were to be direct, with minimal participation of the "UN representative," in contrast "to the almost total lack of direct contact between the parties which characterized the talks with Egypt." Bunche assigned Henri Vigier, a member of his staff, to serve as chairman. Rosenne complained that "Vigier is biased in favour of the Lebanese, [but] his predilection has no fundamental influence on the course of the discussions" (*C.V.*, pp. 39–40).[1] Bunche had prepared a "Draft Israel-Lebanese General Armistic Agreement" that he presented to both parties to serve as a starting point for the negotiations (*M.V.*, p. 285ff.).

The preliminaries out of the way, on March 3 the two delegations turned to the substance of the negotiations. The Israelis raised two difficulties, not specifically addressed in the draft agreement: (1) "The presence in Lebanese territory of certain military units [Syrians] . . . under Lebanese command which . . . do not belong to the national Lebanese army" and, related to the first, (2) the signing of an armistice between Lebanon and Israel which would call for "a complete withdrawal of Israeli forces" from Lebanese territory. The Israelis wanted to "link" the withdrawal from Lebanon to "the conclusion of an armistice between Syria and Israel" (*M. V.*, p. 295).

Vigier suggested that the second point be put aside until the armistice with Lebanon was drafted, when the two governments would decide "if and when it will be signed and when it will be applied." The proposal was accepted on the condition that the final agreement contain a sentence, proposed by the Lebanese, "guaranteeing the Lebanese territory would not be used for any hostile purpose by a third party" (*M. V.*, pp. 295–96).

Implementation of this reservation proved to be more complicated than stating it. It raised the question of whether a "third party" [Syria] should be included in the agreement." This point was raised by General Riley, an American who was serving as chief-of-staff of the United Nations Truce Supervisory Organization. Vigier also opposed the reference to a third party and accused Israel of "going back on its promise" to proceed with a draft agreement, "through postponing the signing until an agreement is reached with Syria." He threatened to adjourn the conference. Riley saved the situation by organizing a meeting between the parties at which the Lebanese legal advisor "agreed to convey the Israeli position to his government." In return, the Israeli delegation was "to inform its government Lebanon would not sign an armistice that permitted Israeli soldiers to remain on Lebanese soil" (*C. V.*, p. 40).

Bunche considered the impasse serious enough to telegraph UN headquarters on March 17. The text of the telegram was forwarded to the U.S. Department of State on the same day: "Mr. Bunche stated that an Israeli-Lebanese armistice agreement was 'held up solely by Israeli intransigence'; that he had informed Mr. Shiloah 'in most emphatic terms that Israeli position in this regard is utterly unreasonable and that if it is not changed before end of this week, I must report to SC [Security Council] that Israelis are deliberately blocking Lebanese agreement in apparent attempt to bring pressure on Syria'; and that 'Israeli good faith was involved' " (*FRUS* 6 [1949], p. 846, n. 1).

Fraser Wilkins, the State Department officer in charge of Palestine-Israel-Jordan affairs, was in Rhodes monitoring the armistice negotiations. He also cabled Washington:

> Bunche considers Israeli article introduces new element . . . which was not raised at time Lebanese and Israelis agreed to negotiate under UN chairmanship in accordance with SC resolution November 16. Lebanese delegation and Israeli delegation agreed on March 15 to refer issue to their governments and meet again on March 23. Bunche subsequently informed Israelis at Rhodes he considers their continued insistence on Lebanese signing agreement sanctioning presence Israeli troops on Lebanese soil for indefinite period so unreasonable that he feels compelled to report matter to SC and seriously to consider withdrawing from all negotiations.
>
> In order avert threatened stalemate in Lebanese negotiations it is recommended Israeli government be informed by Department that proposed Lebanese clause seems to have same effect as proposed Israeli article and that early acceptance would facilitate Bunches task and commission's work. (*FRUS* 6 [1949], p. 846)

A footnote to Wilkins's message adds that, in his March 17 telegram to the United Nations, Bunche stated that "if the Israeli position did not change in the next few days, he would 'seriously consider' withdrawing from both the Lebanese and Transjordanian negotiations and return to New York" (*FRUS* 6 [1949], p. 847, n. 2). The American volume contains no record of any U.S. action on Wilkins's recommendation. But on March 19, Wilkins advised the department, "Israelis have informed Bunche they are prepared to sign Lebanese agreement immediately with provision concerning Israeli troops on Lebanese soil" (*FRUS* 6 [1949], p. 847, n. 3).

Syria: The Negotiator Who Was Not There

That information however, was premature. It had apparently been obtained from Bunche who, in turn, had been informed on March 18 by Shiloah on Rhodes of Israel's "willingness to sign an agreement with Lebanon." Bunche, in return, informed Shiloah that an "affirmative reply" was expected from the Syrians "to begin talks with Israel." Bunche also "hinted he would support Israel's demand for evacuation of the Syrian army from its territory" (*C.V.*, p. 42).

Shiloah had not been informed, however, of a meeting in Tel Aviv, where Ben-Gurion had presided, in which it was determined that Israel would "sign the agreement only if it included a paragraph concerning the withdrawal of Syrian forces from Lebanese territory." The Syrian withdrawal "if possible" should "be completed concurrently with that of the Israeli forces" from the occupied Lebanese villages. The Israeli delegation was instructed to ensure "Israeli civilian traffic" on a road between Metulla and Misgav Am (*C.V.*, pp. 41–42). Both of these villages were barely on the Israeli side of the internationally recognized border but well within the territory occupied during the fighting.

The point of the Israeli condition was that if Israel withdrew from *all* the territory occupied during the fighting, Lebanese troops could be deployed cheek by jowl with the road connecting these two villages and could, theoretically, harass traffic on the connecting road. It was a reasonable request, assuming an armistice terminating all fighting could be agreed upon, particularly in view of the Israeli concern that an armistice with Syria might not be arranged. Also, the Israelis were planning to build a new road farther east, connecting Metulla in the north with another village, Rosh Pina, which was well within the territory the partition assigned to Israel. These new Israeli proposals also demanded the withdrawal of the Lebanese army from all Israeli territory, specifically mentioning Rosh Haniqra (*M.V.*, p. 314).

The new conditions threatened the promising atmosphere in which the negotiations had been progressing, and Shiloah protested to Tel Aviv that he regretted not having been informed of them "before he informed Bunche of Israel's willingness to sign the agreement." Vigier "declared that these new conditions frustrated all his efforts to bring about an agreement" (*C.V.*, p. 42).

Sharett was still in New York at the United Nations, and on February 19 Eban informed Walter Eytan in Tel Aviv that the secretary-general of the United Nations "formally conveyed [his] concern" that the Lebanese negotiations were breaking down. He had also informed Eban of Bunche's "threat [to] report [to] the Security Council, blaming us" and threatening to withdraw from both the Lebanese and Transjordan negotiations (*M.V.*, p. 318).

Eban discussed the situation with Sharett and reported to Eytan that Sharett

agrees (1) B[en]-G[urion], Reuven [Shiloah], yourself, should sign. (2) Insistence our remaining Lebanon is difficult task argue Council. We virtually committed include evacuation in armistice agreement. Lebanon enjoys greater sympathy U.S.A. than any Arab State. France, which supports us most issues, is here definitely engaged Lebanon side. . . . (3) We suggest our delegation signs agreement, endeavouring secure safeguarding clause binding Lebanon not intervene if hostilities break out between Israel and third party. Bunche indicates they [Lebanese] may be willing pledge their territory unusable for warlike acts against Israel. Simultaneously we express to Secretary-General our surprise at ultimatum tactics and tone Bunche's communications. (*M.V.*, p. 319)

Eban's reference to American sympathy and French interest and the observation that it would be difficult for Israel to offer a good defense in any Security Council debate all suggest Israel's own awareness of its dependence on favorable international public opinion. None of these easily observable factors appears to have played a major role in the determination of Washington's posture when the conventional obeisance to the intimidating visage of the Zionist lobby and domestic politics held center stage. On the points at issue the Israelis had the better substantive case. Washington's timid approach in this first round of Israeli-Arab diplomacy was not warranted by *apparent*[2] facts or by any threat to use Israeli political power to frustrate a reasonable U.S. position. Since that date, the knee-jerk formula of weighting U.S. policy with greater importance given to domestic political perceptions than to objective assessments of national interests or moral values has become legendary, with dismal consequences for any hopes for peace.

In Paris, Eliahu Sasson, director of the Middle East Division of the Ministry for Foreign Affairs, was holding informal talks with the Lebanese minister to France. Sasson relayed rather complete reports of these conversations to Tel Aviv. On March 18, he forwarded the following information in a letter addressed to Walter Eytan.

He had attempted to persuade the Lebanese diplomat that "from every point of view" it would be "to the interest of Lebanon" to conclude "not simply any armistice agreement but a full peace alliance." He also urged

Eytan to urge Ben-Gurion to agree to sign the armistice agreement, "even if Syria persists in its refusal to participate in the negotiations." Sasson argued that Israel's rigid stand was "pushing the Lebanon into the waiting arms of Syria and giving the Lebanese an argument for refusing" any future Israeli proposals without first obtaining Syrian agreement. Sasson predicted the Syrians "would be forced, sooner or later, to enter into negotiations . . . and the evacuation [by Israel] of Lebanese villages will give us the right to demand the evacuation of our territory by the Syrians" (*M.V.*, pp. 315–16).

Concurrently, at Rosh Haniqra, General Riley was strenuously working to arrange compromises with the Lebanese to satisfy the new Israeli demands. In a confidential exchange with Riley, Lebanon agreed to allow Israeli use of the Metullah–Misgav Am road for thirty days, following the signing of the agreement. Riley "agreed to try to prolong the arrangement until the planned, alternate road was completed." The Lebanese continued to object to including the demand for Syrian withdrawal. Riley persuaded the Lebanese to insist on Syrian withdrawal to a line stretching from Tripoli to Aleppo. Finally, Rosenne's messages of March 21 informed Sharett (in New York), Sasson (in Paris), and Shiloah (in Rhodes) that Ben-Gurion had instructed the delegation at Rosh Haniqra "to conclude the agreement that same day, at all costs" and the delegation "therefore decided to agree to the proffered arrangement" (*C.V.*, p. 43). Rosenne's comments: "(1) This agreement will bolster our position in Elath; (2) it will strengthen our position in the discussions with Transjordan; (3) it will facilitate the military action in the Triangle if we have to undertake it. It will strengthen our demands vis-à-vis the Syrians. Also, it is advisable for us to link one Arab country with another" (*C.V.*, p. 153).

The stage was set for the signing on March 23. Unlike the Egyptian talks, the Lebanese-Israel agreement changed few facts on the ground. The internationally recognized boundary was accepted as the armistice line without requiring Israeli withdrawal from western and central Galilee. Israeli control over these territories, which had been allocated to the Arab state, was consolidated. The northern border of the Zionist state, for all practical purposes, was established, expanding its territory beyond both the partition recommendations and Bernadotte's proposals. The presence of a large Arab population in the Galilee would be a vexing problem for a Jewish state later. And, as the armistice with Egypt had done, the Lebanese negotiations left a quota of loose ends, agreements to be arranged outside the framework of the formal negotiations. These loose ends were never knitted into the whole. They continue as sources of hostility and—in 1982—were undoubtedly one casus belli for the Israeli invasion of Lebanon.

All parties, including the United States, expressed satisfaction—perhaps relief would be a more accurate description—at the conclusion of the negotiations. But the continuing tragedy of a "nonpeace" is attributable, in a major part, to a general acquiescent ignoring of what law had been legislated in the UN resolutions. Long gone in the dustbin of history is Ralph Bunche's original declaration that UN resolutions would govern the military armistice conversations. The spirit dominating the talks had been "Let's get on with it."

chapter 8

TRANSJORDAN

Playing Both Sides against the Middle:
Israel and Abdallah vs. the Palestinians

The disposition of the Syrian forces that were in northern Palestine, in territory that the partition had assigned the Jewish state, had not been resolved in the negotiations with Lebanon. Logic, therefore, might have dictated that talks with the Syrians might be the next order of business. Anticipating such a development, Rosenne informed Ben-Gurion and Sharett on March 24 that the acting secretary-general of the Lebanese Ministry of Foreign Affairs had informed "the Syrians that the Israeli delegation to the talks with Lebanon was composed of serious and moderate people, and advised them to send a similar delegation to the talks with Israel" (*C. V.*, p. 44).

But logic does not always drive politics. A number of factors thwarted the logical progression from the Lebanese negotiations. On the same date, Rosenne registered his "doubts the Mediator will support Israel's demand for Syrian withdrawal to the international border." The Israelis had invited such a reaction by their refusal to withdraw from Arab state territories in their negotiations with Egypt. Rosenne continued, "The [Israeli] UN representatives emphasized that the early stages of talks with Syria would be difficult and slow, and speedy results should not be expected. Vigier said he would rather not chair this conference and would try and persuade Bunche to take on that function" (*C. V.*, p. 44).

The presence of Iraqi troops in the Samaria district of the eastern

front presented a further complication. Iraq resisted any armistice negotiations that, in the spirit of the UN resolutions, might lead to a final
peace. Israel maintained that no satisfactory negotiations with Transjordan were possible while Iraqi forces remained in a dominant position
at the very heart of Israel. No Transjordanian action

> could remove the threat to Israeli security so long as Iraqi troops
> remain on Israeli territory a few miles distant from the coast and
> from the most densely populated centres of Jewish population.
> There are contradictory reports of Iraq's intention to abide by any
> agreement signed by Transjordan. The Transjordan delegation has
> now informed Dr. Bunche that they are now empowered to repre-
> sent Iraq. It is obviously necessary, however, to have this undertak-
> ing from the Iraqi Government itself. (*FRUS* 6 [1949], pp. 809–10;
> memorandum from Warren Austin, U.S. ambassador to UN, to
> Secretary of State Acheson, March 9, 1949)

A third complication was that, in fact, two separate negotiations—
with quite different objectives—were in process between Israelis and
Transjordanians. The Israeli records (*C.V.*, p. 45) report that Eliahu Sasson had met Lieutenant Colonel Al-Tall (also Tel) of the Arab Legion in
Jerusalem. (Individual contributors to the *C.V.* cited the same man as
Abdullah Tall and Abdullah Al-Tall. The spellings of the original documents have been retained.) The meeting was apparently in response to
an "untraced" message from the Israelis (apparently to Abdallah) at an
unspecified date before December 11, 1948. Moshe Dayan was also present. Al-Tall reported the king was prepared "to start open peace talks"
after ten days. Abdallah hoped to enlist "other Arab leaders." "If not, he
would begin talks on his own" (*C.V.*, p. 45).

King Abdallah wished to discuss "Jaffa, Ramle, Lydda, Beisan and
Jerusalem, the Negev and southern Palestine." Tall added that he was
"not acquainted with the King's claims on each and every subject." The
king also asked Israel to "refrain from attacking the Iraqis during the
next ten days," adding, according to Al-Tall, that the Iraqis "knew about
and approved his [the king's] contacts with Israel" (*C.V.*, p. 45).

Al-Tall told Sasson the king intended to implement the resolutions of
a conference in Jericho in December that had "proclaimed Abdallah
King of all Palestine." On December 2, upon Abdallah's insistence, the
resolutions of this conference

included an expression of no-confidence in the Arab Higher Committee and the "Gaza Government," and established the union of Jordan and Palestine as the Arab Hashemite Kingdom. Abdallah was proclaimed king and it was decided that Palestinian representatives be admitted to the Jordanian Parliament. King Abdallah was authorized to solve the problem of Palestine as he saw fit. The resolutions . . . were approved by the Jordanian Cabinet on 7 December and ratified by Parliament on 13 December. The resolutions were criticized by the heads of the Gaza Government, King Faruk and the Secretary-General of the Arab League, as well as by Syria, Lebanon and Saudi Arabia. (*C.V.*, p. 156)

Sasson countered he could not respond to such "serious" ideas without knowing "all the details and understanding what means the King intended to use in implementing these resolutions." Al-Tall promised to deliver the king's reaction to the proposals for both an armistice and peace negotiations on December 13 (*C.V.*, p. 45).

On that date Al-Tall reported Abdallah agreed to "a general armistice and peace talks, although he was not yet able to fix a date." He had to delay a final answer for a week to discuss these matters with the Iraqi regent and with the Jordanian prime minister. If the latter refused to "undertake the task" of negotiating these matters, "the King would demand his resignation . . . to make way for a more courageous man" (*C.V.*, p. 46).

Sasson responded that if the king "was determined to put the resolutions [of the Jericho conference] into effect, he should do so as soon as possible in order to present his rivals with a *fait accompli*." He should not discuss "the Israeli aspect with the Palestinian Arabs" but should "present his moves as an act of deliverance which would guarantee their peace and tranquility." Sasson also asked the king not to take "a final stand" on Jerusalem but "to discuss its fate with Israel." Al-Tall wanted to know if Israel would agree "to divide the city between Israel and Jordan." Sasson refused further discussion of the subject "pending the start of negotiations." Sasson urged Abdallah to declare "a general armistice before undertaking the implementation of the Jericho resolutions." This would make it possible to withdraw the Arab Legion from the Palestinian front, and, if necessary, "to use them against Egypt and Syria." He advised Al-Tall that "Jordan must be prepared" for attacks by both Egypt and Syria (*C.V.*, p. 47).

Sasson advised the king "to do his utmost" to remove the Iraqis from

Palestine. In return, the Israelis "presumably" would not invade "the Triangle pending conclusion of the peace talks." If the Iraqis refused to withdraw, "Israel might be obliged to remove them by force." Tall repeated the king's promise to discuss the matter with the Iraqis. Sasson, undoubtedly having in mind the difficulties certain to arise between Israel and Egypt in light of Israeli designs on Beersheba, Auja, and the southern Negev, asked what Jordan's position would be if hostilities with Egypt were "renewed." Tall replied that "Jordan would remain strictly neutral." Finally, Sasson "advised the king" not to trust "foreign mediation rather than direct negotiations with Israel" (*C. V.*, p. 47).

If the king would agree to these conditions, Sasson promised Israel would try to generate the "sympathy of the enlightened world" for Jordan's efforts "to implement the resolutions of the Jericho Conference." Tall replied Abdallah was "interested primarily in the sympathy of the United States," and he urged Sasson "not to go too far in his contacts with the other Arab states." Sasson responded that the king "could depend on Israel's friendship," and urged him "to speed up the implementation of the resolutions of the Jericho Conference in view of the possibility of a rift between him and the Arab League" (summarized from *C. V.*, pp. 45–47).

On December 25, Shiloah had a further meeting with Abdallah's representatives. He reported the results to Ben-Gurion and Sharett. This time, Abdallah's personal physician, Dr. Shaukat al-Saty, joined Al-Tall, and Dayan accompanied Shiloah, who had now been appointed head of a delegation for the anticipated overt negotiations with the Transjordanians. Al-Saty and Shiloah both reported they were authorized by their respective governments to begin armistice talks as a preliminary to discussions for a permanent peace. They also agreed that, in view of the king's "delicate position," the talks would be held in secrecy. Shiloah cautioned that "such secrecy could be only temporary." The Jordanians agreed and asked that plans for publication should be agreed to by both parties (*C. V.*, p. 48).

Al-Saty then inquired if "Israel would agree" to return Jaffa, Lydda, and Ramleh "to the Arabs and would allow a number of Arab refugees to return to these towns." Shiloah gave the standard Israeli reply: No "single problem" could be "isolated from all the others." All outstanding questions would have to be discussed in the course of the negotiations. He added that "despite Israel's desire to help King Abdallah in view of his delicate position, Israel did not consider itself obliged to make any sort of gesture towards the Arabs; it had not started the war nor was it the vanquished party. Shiloah said that Israel would agree to discuss all proposals in a serious manner, and promised to transmit the King's message to his government"(*C.V.*, p. 48).

Shiloah then wanted to know if the Jordanian prime minister knew about "the contacts with Israel," if there was disagreement between the king and the prime minister and whether the British knew of the talks and were being consulted. Al-Saty promised an early answer, and the two sides agreed on further discussions, to be alternated between "the Jewish area of Jerusalem and Shune, Jordan" (*C.V.*, pp. 47–48).

The next meeting, accordingly, took place in Jerusalem on December 30. Shiloah and Dayan represented Israel and Al-Tall, Jordan. Shiloah began by proposing an exchange of credentials by the two governments, indicating the desire to make these bilateral talks official. It was also agreed that instead of full minutes of the meeting there would be "a summary of the talks," signed by both sides. The meeting lasted "over two hours" and began to address issues of specific substance instead of the procedural questions of the previous talks.

Tall inquired, first, if Israel intended to negotiate on the basis of the partition resolution or of the Bernadotte plan. The king, he said, favored a combination of the two. Shiloah countered that Israel "was prepared to negotiate on the basis of the existing military situation." This approach would give Israel both the territorial and demographic advantages gained in the fighting and by the flight of the refugees that had been precipitated by the campaigns between regular military forces and the Zionist terrorist forces, the Irgun and the Sternists. Dayan asked if "Tall intended to extend the talks to areas in which Israeli and Jordanian forces did not confront each other. Tall replied the King intended to discuss the Palestine question *in toto*. A comprehensive agreement was necessary because the other Arab states would eventually evacuate the Arab parts of Palestine" (*C.V.*, pp. 49–52).

Who Speaks for Whom?

Shiloah announced that "at this stage Israel was prepared to discuss only problems outstanding between it and Jordan." To discuss "the general problem, Israel must know whether the King was authorized to represent the other Arab states." Al-Tall answered "the King thought he would have this authority by the time the Conciliation Committee reached Israel" (*C.V.*, p. 50).[1]

The published record of the December 30 meeting lists eleven items the Israelis wished to discuss. The Jordanian agenda contained four. It was finally agreed to separate the problems between Israel and Jordan from those between Israel and other Arab states.

Shiloah's list included the border between Israel and Jordan and between Elath and the Dead Sea. Israel proposed the Palestine-Transjordan border to be permanent.[2] At the Arab Triangle "the present military line was not acceptable to Israel as a permanent border" despite its earlier proposal favoring "the existing military situation." "Israel did not take for granted the annexation" by Jordan of the Arab-held part of Palestine. The General Assembly "had adopted no resolution to that effect." Again, the Israeli position was inconsistent with its earlier stipulation that the "existing military situation" be the "basis for negotiation." This position of "what we hold is ours and what you hold is up for negotiation" was the same strategy Israel had employed in the Egyptian negotiations (*C.V.*, p. 50). There were also questions of the potash works and properties at both the northern and southern ends of the Dead Sea.

For his part, Al-Tall raised the question of Jerusalem, suggesting the city be divided between the two states. Israel would be allowed *access* to the Hebrew University on Mount Scopus, but there was to be "no territorial continuity between the University and Jewish Jerusalem." "As a gesture to world opinion," the two parties "would agree that a specified area separating the two parts of the city be placed under international control." Also on the agenda, with no indication of the positions taken by either party, were Latrun, a hydroelectric power station at Nahryim, the railway to Jerusalem, prisoners and compensation, and future "political and economic relations." Al-Tall added that the king wanted Lydda and Ramleh under his control and "Jaffa to remain an Arab city within Israel, with an arrangement of free passage for the Arabs" (*C.V.*, p. 5).

Dayan raised the question of Arab refugees. Would Jordan be willing to rehabilitate them? Al-Tall replied, using essentially the formula put down in the December 11, 1948, General Assembly resolution, "The refugees had the right to determine for themselves where they wanted to live; those who did not wish to return to their homes were entitled to compensation for their property. Nevertheless the King was prepared to consider a plan for absorbing them where they were." The king was also prepared "to leave parts of the Negev in Israel's hands," provided Arabs could use "the Beersheba-Gaza road" and the Gaza Strip should become Jordanian territory (*C.V.*, p. 51).

The problem of the Iraqi troops still in the Samaria area remained unresolved. Al-Tall reported that the king had "initiated moves to evacuate the Iraqi army from the Triangle" and had "persuaded the Iraqi regent not to attack the Jews." When Dayan asked for credentials authorizing Abdallah to represent Iraq, Al-Tall "promised to consult the King" and asked "that no attack be launched against the Iraqis." The Israelis replied they were "not prepared to include [the Iraqis] in the special cease-fire agreement" with Jordan but added that "the General cease-fire applied to the Iraqis" (*C.V.*, pp. 50–52).

On January 5, 1949, Shiloah, Dayan, and Al-Tall met again. The Israelis presented credentials from Ben-Gurion and Sharett. Al-Tall had only a letter from the king, authorizing him "to negotiate . . . on the basis of a discussion of the general problem." The Israelis were not satisfied with this vague document. They requested "official credentials similar to the document" they had provided. Al-Tall promised to produce one at the next meeting (*C.V.*, p. 52).

The cat-and-mouse game Abdallah thought he could play with the Israelis is revealed in a January 6 report by Shiloah to Ben-Gurion and Sharett, reporting the substance of the previous day's meeting. Al-Tall had told the Israelis that the king "does not view the talks as armistice talks because he views the events of the past months not . . . as a war but merely a 'regrettable conflict' . . . [and] as a direct continuation of the contacts with the Israelis prior to the fighting and of others held recently in Paris" (*C.V.*, p. 52). But the Israelis were not to be put off any longer in maneuvering the Jordanians to substantive discussions. They wanted to know how the king planned to implement "a solution combining the partition resolution and the Bernadotte proposals."

Al-Tall did not miss the implication involving Abdallah's intentions with respect to the Negev, which Bernadotte's proposals had assigned to the Arabs. The Jordanian, therefore, responded that the king was prepared "to satisfy certain Israeli interests in the Negev." He was "willing to agree for example" to Israeli explorations for oil on the southwestern part of the Dead Sea. The Israelis replied their interests "did not necessarily relate to oil, but rather to an outlet to the Red Sea, access to the Dead Sea and land for settlement" (*C.V.*, p. 53).

Al-Tall countered that one of the king's strategic objectives in the

Negev was "the road to Egypt." A land bridge connecting Jordan and Egypt remained an obstacle to a territorial settlement for many years. (It remains an obstacle, if the proposal to establish a Palestinian state in the West Bank and Gaza is accepted as part of a final settlement.) The king was also concerned about the fate of the Negev Bedouin. (The Israelis began a "resolution" of the Bedouin problem after Operation Uvda by raids that forced the tribes across the border into Jordan.[3])

Most of the rest of the January 5 meeting was spent in an inconclusive discussion about how to divide Jerusalem between the two countries. Unable to reach a mutually agreeable formula, the Jordanians suggested a rough division of the city, with the dividing line to be one internationalized street, "including the King David Hotel and the YMCA." The Israelis called this plan "totally divorced from reality." "World opinion," they said, "was interested in the holy places and not in the King David Hotel or the YMCA." As an alternative they suggested "international control over the Old City." Al-Tall replied that Jordan would agree to hand over the Jewish Quarter of the Old City to Israel and "allow Israel access" to it (*C. V.*, pp. 52–53). None of these formulas complied with General Assembly Resolution No. 194 (III).

The King Comes on Stage

The last item in Shiloah's January 6 memorandum to Ben-Gurion and Sharett reports that Al-Tall informed the Israelis "the British knew about and approved of the talks with the Israelis, and that they desired a peaceful solution" (*C. V.*, p. 54). British knowledge of these secret conversations is confirmed in the U.S. record (*FRUS* 6 [1949], p. 631, n. 3). There is a gap of about two weeks in the Israeli record. The next entry is a message from Sharett to the Israeli ambassador in Washington dated January 18 (*M. V.*, p. 343).

Abdallah had now decided to participate personally in these secret discussions, and on January 16 he and Al-Tall met Dayan and Sasson in the "strictest secrecy" at Shuneh in Jordan. The king, still avoiding written credentials, verbally informed the Israelis that Al-Tall "had his confidence" and was authorized to conduct "further negotiations." He also "declared [he] has no use for Arab League, determined act alone, denies right any other Arab state have say fate Palestine, which matter only for 'Israel' and Transjordan." He urged the Israelis "not cede Gaza

Strip; he would prefer see that strip go to Israel or Satan rather than Egypt."

For their part, the Israelis promised to stabilize the positions of the two forces in the Araba Valley provided they were free to move "behind our line throughout area [the Negev] down to Eylat" (*M.V.*, p. 343). Abdallah rejected this offer and suggested instead that the Palestinian territory on the Gulf of Aqaba should be annexed by Transjordan, which would then trade free access to Israel in return for free Transjordanian access to Haifa.

At the Shuneh meeting, Abdallah also said he would "be ready" to "enter formal armistice talks as soon Rhodes conference ends successfully." But he added, apparently in an attempt to resolve the Israeli-Jordanian issues in a combination of the bilateral talks, that he did "not see why go Rhodes." He expressed his preference for Palestine as the site to continue the secret negotiations (*M.V.*, p. 343).

Sharett conveyed this information to Eliahu Elath, his ambassador in Washington. Elath was instructed to inform President Truman and Under Secretary of State Robert Lovett of these developments in "strictest confidence for personal edification" and also to brief Eban "enjoining utmost secrecy even [about the] fact [of the] meeting" (*M.V.*, pp. 343–44).[4]

On Rhodes, Bunche was preoccupied trying to conclude the Egyptian-Israeli negotiations. He was unaware of the back-alley diplomacy between Abdallah and the Israelis. The Transjordanians were eager to complete the secret deal, fearing that the passage of time increased the danger of leaks to the other Arabs.[5] Israel, on the other hand, was interested in prolonging the secret diplomacy. It held most of the cards by its occupation of so much of the territory that partition had assigned to the Arab state, and it was refining its plan for Operation Uvda to acquire the entire Negev. The following chronology reflected these disparate tactics and the different senses of opportune timing.

On February 9, Bunche informed Eytan that the Transjordanians were ready to hold armistice talks in Jerusalem. Bunche opposed the idea because he felt he could not chair the sessions without raising complications with the Conciliation and Truce Commissions (*C.V.*, p. 56). On the fifteenth Sharett instructed the Israeli delegation at Rhodes "to induce Bunche to give priority to the negotiations with Lebanon and postpone the beginning of talks with Jordan" (*C.V.*, p. 60).

On February 19 Sharett informed Eytan that the Jordanians now were eager to begin negotiations at Rhodes but wanted one more session with

Sasson and Dayan "to reach an agreement before the start of official negotiations." Abdallah, apparently, wanted to confront Bunche with a fait accompli in the form of an agreement along the lines of the secret discussions, for the thrust of those talks was clearly inconsistent with Bunche's commitment to honor the UN mandate. Sasson was in Rhodes, and if the proposed preliminary meeting Jordan wanted was to be held his return to Jerusalem or Shuneh would have required another delay before returning the talks to the Bunche-UN jurisdiction. The Jordanian proposal suited Sharett, and he suggested to Eytan "taking advantage of it to implement the plan for the conquest of the southern Negev." He ordered Sasson "to return to Israel immediately" (*C. V.,* p. 62).

Meanwhile, on February 15, Eytan had proposed that the Israelis draw up "a series of demands, even excessive ones" to present to the Transjordanians as "a reasonable starting point for negotiations." These "excessive/reasonable demands" included incorporation of the "Triangle in the State of Israel," "free passage to Mount Scopus," Beersheba to be "included in the State of Israel," Jordan to declare it "will not invoke the Anglo-Jordanian Treaty of Alliance against Israel" and the treaty "does not grant the British any rights west of the Jordan," "free access to the Wailing Wall for Jewish worshipers and visitors," and the armistice agreement to "state explicitly that it does not grant the Jordanian government any sovereign rights over territories west of the Jordan" (*C. V.,* pp. 61–62).

These demands were wholly in conflict with the proposals Abdallah had tabled in the secret negotiations. They were also probably designed to prolong the negotiations, providing the Israelis with additional time that Sharett had indicated was needed to complete preparations for the conquest of the Negev.

Securing the Negev

Finally, on March 4, after much haggling over procedural details, the first formal meeting of the Israel-Transjordan armistice negotiating committees was convened on Rhodes. Bunche informed the session that "communications in process" were clarifying the authority of Transjordan "to negotiate on behalf of Iraq" (*M. V.,* p. 367).

On March 5, Israel began Operations Uvda and Yitzuv, a two-pronged military campaign to secure all of the Negev (*C. V.,* p. 165). One column of troops and armor was launched from Beersheba, the other from Bir

Asluj, two strategic points beyond the partition borders that the Israelis had refused to cede to Egypt.

As they had done with Egypt, the Israelis were again rejecting any restraints that compliance with the partition recommendation might impose on their territorial aspirations. They were also determined to eliminate Bernadotte's territorial recommendations that the Negev be part of the Arab state. The Israeli government's February 28 instructions to its negotiating delegation candidly declared Israel would not "found its claims on the 29 November partition resolution even where such an argument would enhance its claims" (*C.V.*, p. 63). That directive was intended to cover more than the border towns and villages Israel wanted for security. A more important reason for the nullification declaration was Jerusalem, for which the partition had recommended an international status. An Israeli acknowledgment of obligation to the General Assembly partition plan would jeopardize any future Israeli claim to the Holy City.

The February 28 instructions listed specific Israeli objectives in the Negev:

> Wadi Araba and Elath: The delegation will demand that the armistice line be established along the Palestine-Transjordan border [*not* the fighting lines or the partition-recommended borders], from the southern tip of the Dead Sea to the northern tip of the Gulf of Aqaba. Some minor border modifications are possible, but the delegation must insist on the evacuation of Ein el-Weiba and other outposts at present held by the Arab Legion west of the border. Under no circumstances will the delegation waive Israel's claim to freedom of access to Elath, and it will threaten to take the matter to the Security Council if the Jordanians insist on an armistice line which cuts across the southern part of the Negev. (*C.V.*, p. 63)

Occupation of the Negev had long been planned at the highest levels of the Israeli government. The exact timing for the advance of Israeli troops was determined by reports of a reinforcement of British troops at Aqaba. The Israelis feared that Abdallah had requested this reported increase of British forces to support his ambition to control at least part of the Negev, providing the kingdom with an outlet to the Mediterranean coast at Gaza.

Operation Uvda drove down the center of the Negev from Beersheba to Um Rashrash, as it was known in Arabic, or Elath, as the Israelis had come to call the southernmost tip. Operation Yitzuv moved eastward from Bir Asluj to the internationally recognized border and then south to link up with Uvda at Elath (*C. V.*, p. 165).[6] The two-pronged attack continued until March 10.

Both U.S. and Israeli documents are strangely silent about this period. Nor was any action taken at the United Nations. The next entry in the Israeli sources is dated March 10. It is a message from Bunche to Shiloah, on Rhodes. Bunche had been discussing with the Israelis a Jordanian charge that the Yitzuv operation had engaged in fighting with some Arab Legion troops in the south. The Israelis countered that the Jordanian forces were "west of the [international] border." The Israelis were again playing "now you see it, now you don't" with the partition recommendation. They insisted on "existing military positions" as the basis for determining armistice lines where they had advanced beyond the recommended borders. But they were equally insistent that whatever Arab party they were engaged with at the moment must respect the international boundary that, in the Negev, coincided with the partition proposal.

Bunche's March 10 message to Shiloah did not straightforwardly address this double standard. Bunche's firsthand knowledge about affairs in the Negev was inadequate. He had to ask Shiloah if, indeed, there had been a military encounter between Israeli and Jordanian forces. He apparently knew generally of the Israeli campaign. But he did not invoke Security Council Resolution No. 61 of November 4, which prohibited "military or political advantage through violation of the truce." Nor did he invoke Chapter VII of the UN Charter that the same resolution authorized if either party or both violated the truce. Resolution No. 61 primarily addressed the situation between Israel and Egypt. But the preamble recalls specifically Security Council Resolutions Nos. 50, 53, and 54, all of which addressed all parties. All of these resolutions had been supported by the United States. Bunche's March 10 message to Shiloah should be read with these legal declarations in mind.

Rhodes, 10 March 1949

In pursuance of our conversation of last evening another note on the same subject has been handed to me this morning by Colonel Jundi.[7] The text of the note reads as follows.

Military operations against Arab Legion in Wadi Araba continue. Israeli forces attacking Arab Legion positions with tanks and armoured cars. . . . The continuation of this state of aggression renders the negotiations turbid and may lead to their interruption. I therefore strongly protest and request you to kindly take up decisive action for the stoppage of such operations by Israel and the withdrawal of their forces to their original positions. I shall be glad if you will inform me as soon as possible of the action taken so that I may inform my Government, who are impatiently [a]waiting the reply. . . .

Do you have any information as to any recent clashes between your forces and those of the Arab Legion in this sector?

In my view it will be useful for you and Colonel Jundi to discuss this situation today. He is willing.

I also feel that it now becomes important to have the cease-fire agreement signed without further delay and I hope you will be in position to do so today. Colonel Jundi is prepared to do so. (*M.V.,* pp. 379–80)

Bunche had submitted a draft cease-fire agreement on March 1. The Jordanians had approved it on the third, and Shiloah had informed Sharett of this action. But on the fourth Sharett instructed Shiloah not to sign a cease-fire agreement, pending clarification of "Jordan's authority to deal with the Iraqi front" and "pending developments with regard to actual control in Wadi Araba and Elath." "In view of the plans [of an advance to Elath] Israel is interested in delaying conclusion of a cease-fire agreement" (*C.V.,* p. 66). The Israelis also raised questions of the "composition and powers" of the Jordan delegation at Rhodes, undoubtedly part of their delaying tactics. When questioned, Abdallah replied that the "Rhodes negotiations were of a purely military nature," and he "saw no reason to send a political representative" (*C.V.,* p. 164). For Abdallah, the dream of ruling Greater Syria—and therefore the secret negotiations with Israel—was more attractive than the Rhodes negotiations, where diplomacy in a fishbowl had to be respectful of UN resolutions and possible appeal and review.[8]

Finally, on March 11, after the Israelis had reached Elath, a cease-fire agreement was signed at Rhodes. The Israeli signature did not inhibit Sharett inquiring of Shiloah, "If we change our dispositions at southern end [Negev] after signing, shall we be accused of violating the cease-fire agreement?" (*C.V.,* p. 168). Shiloah replied that "if Israel redeploys its forces in the southern Negev, the Jordanians will accuse it of breaking the agreement." But he added he could not be sure of what Bunche might do (*C. V.*, p. 71).

Conscious of Bunche's ability to take the matter to the Security Council and of Israel's violations of previous Security Council resolutions, Sharett yielded without further conditions. The Israeli military occupation of the Negev had been completed. The cease-fire agreement was signed on March 11. There were the usual prohibitions of further troop movements by either party and of any civilian crossing of the lines. The agreement stipulated that the restrictions applied to "the lines or positions now held by the foremost elements of [the] ground forces." Israel had staked out another sector by force, and its position was secured with whatever legality the armistice agreement provided. It contained the usual boiler-plate provision that the agreement was "without prejudice to the rights, claims, interests and positions of either Party which may relate to the armistice negotiations now in progress or to the ultimate peaceful settlement of all outstanding issues between the Parties" (*M. V.*, p. 383). This verbal grab bag appeared in all the armistice agreements. The armistice negotiations were to be limited strictly to military matters. They were not to address political questions such as sovereignty over territory. But one substantive item on the agenda of the secret talks between Abdallah and the Israelis was how Jordan and Israel would divide control of Jerusalem.

The Israelis were aware of the uncomfortable position in which their Negev campaign and violations of previous truce agreements had placed the acting mediator. A March 13 message from Dayan, on Rhodes, to Tel Aviv confesses their awareness. The relevant parts of the message warrant reproduction here because it is one of the clearer expositions of Bunche's actual powerlessness and of the abandon with which both the Israelis and Jordanians indulged in horse trading, ignoring whatever authority actions of the United Nations were considered to possess. Dayan

found Bunche sulking over UN queries about Operation Uvda. Bunche thinks that the British will seek political gain from the operation, and is concerned lest he gets personally involved and might be obliged to give up the conduct of the Rhodes talks. He fears that if the matter is raised in the Security Council, the Arabs will claim that he assented to the Israeli advance in the Negev, despite the Rhodes talks and in violation of the truce. He will then have to demand Israeli withdrawal from the southern Negev. A refusal will lead to a deadlock which will force him to resign.

Dayan reassured Bunche that there had been no Israeli advance in the Negev, but rather a deployment of forces which replaced the control of the territory by reconnaissance; in Elath, too, there were no Jordanian forces, so that the advance had not been at the expense of the other side. Bunche replied that *any advance was prohibited under the truce,* even though he admitted that if no military clash had occurred and no lines had been breached, the truce violation was not so serious.

To Dayan's argument that the Jordanians had signed a cease-fire agreement with Israel on 10 March Bunche replied that despite the agreement the British were liable to protest in the UN and the Jordanians in Rhodes. . . . He said that the Jordanian delegation was already manifesting its displeasure. . . . Dayan replied that if the Jordanians wanted to get the territory held by the Iraqi forces, they must cooperate with Israel, not quarrel with it.

Dayan . . . inquires whether he should not make it clear . . . that if Jordan hinders Israel, Israel will not cooperate in the transfer of the Iraqi-held territory to it, or, alternatively, whether Bunche could be relied upon to settle the matter with the British. (*C.V.,* p. 74; emphasis supplied)

It is important, at this point, to recognize that although the Israelis on Rhodes were vaguely informed of the secret negotiations, neither of the other participants—the low-level Jordanian delegation and Bunche—was reliably informed about them. The most serious consequences were the acting mediator's honest efforts to preside over the official Rhodes negotiations with at least a respectable degree of compliance with UN legislation. His efforts to devise some formula for separating the military forces and to halt the fighting in Jerusalem were the most frustrating. His objective was to create a condition holding some promise for implementing international control of the Holy City. But Abdallah and the Israelis were discussing dividing the city. Numerous formulas were bandied back and forth. On March 15, Bunche presented both delegations with the suggestion that one delegate from each delegation be appointed "to collaborate" with him "in working out the details" (*M.V.,* pp. 419–23).

Both the Israelis and Jordanians rejected the proposal. Jordan "eventually agreed with the Israelis that no changes be made in the Dayan-Tall agreement at this point." Bunche had also been involved with the Jordanians in finding a formula for the withdrawal of Iraqi troops from the central front. This problem, too, was stonewalled at Rhodes, shifted to the secret talks, and then included in the armistice agreements as a fait accompli (*C.V.*, pp. 77, 86; see also *M.V.*, pp. 470–72).

A particularly revealing entry in the Israeli *Main Volume* is a letter, dated March 23–24, from Eytan in Tel Aviv to Sharett, who was then in New York at the special session of the General Assembly. The secret agreement was kept secret from even those members in the Israeli Foreign Ministry except "those . . . whose knowledge . . . was essential." Also, Abdullah Tall had asked for a British officer to be present at the secret meeting at Shuneh on March 24 at which time were discussed a final disposition of the Iraqi troop problem and the division, between Jordan and Israel, of the territory those troops had occupied. Tall explained as the reason for this request that the Jordanians at the meeting included some "ministers [who] had no more idea of map-reading than the King had and that it was essential for a military man to be present. . . . All the good Transjordanian officers were away at Rhodes." The Israelis reluctantly agreed to the request, realizing, "of course that the British know about the arrangement and presumably gave it their blessing" (*M.V.*, pp. 469, 471).[9]

"Too Good to Be True"

The concluding paragraphs of Eytan's March 23–24 messages express Israeli elation over outmaneuvering the Jordanians with an agreement that would outrage the other Arabs.

As it turns out, despite all the precautions for secrecy, Shiloah reported on March 23 that "Bunche knows about the talks with Tall and the Jordanians [probably only those of the second or third echelon at Rhodes] are at least surmising that something is afoot." Shiloah "cannot continue to ignore [Bunche's] queries." But the acting mediator, apparently, did not know the details of the signed agreement. Dayan disagreed with Tel Aviv and recommended that Bunche be shown the final agreement. The document provided for establishing a commission of "not less than two representatives of each Party" to "peg out the demarcation line agreed to; and there was also to be a chairman appointed by the United Nations Chief of Staff" (*M.V.*, p. 473). The recommended chairman was to be a UN person, so Dayan argued Bunche would learn the details anyhow. Logically, Dayan argued, "One cannot spring the agreement upon Bunche and then ask him to have his representative implement it." But Tel Aviv finally persuaded Shiloah and Dayan that Bunche was *not* to be informed "of the Agreement with the King at this point, however, he will have to be told at some point to ensure his cooperation in the implementation of the agreement" (*C.V.*, pp. 83, 85, 87).

During all this "good faith" bargaining, Bunche, on Rhodes, was conscientiously attempting to maintain respect for the UN resolutions. Two days after the secret agreement was signed at Shuneh and after Shiloah had informed Tel Aviv that Bunche knew of the secret talks, and a day before the Israelis agreed not to inform Bunche of the details, a "secret" *FRUS* entry (March 25) records a telephone conversation between Robert McClintock and Thomas Power, both of the State Department. McClintock was the deputy to Dean Rusk, director of the Office of United Nations' Affairs, and Power was deputy secretary-general of the U.S. Mission to the United Nations. Power had telephoned McClintock to advise him that Bunche had requested UN Secretary-General Trygve Lie to ask the British to reduce the number of their troops at Aqaba. The Israelis conditioned the reduction of their forces at Elath on a Jordanian agreement not only to reduce its own forces at Aqaba but to require Britain to reduce its forces there as well. Bunche, still lacking details of the Israel-Jordan deal but looking for a way to break the impasse, had suggested it would be helpful if the United States "put pressure on the British" (*FRUS* 6 [1949], p. 868).

Who Knew What—And When?

McClintock told Power "the British were as well aware as we [U.S.] of the secret negotiations . . ." and added, "The Israelis had very recently threatened King Abdallah that they might resume hostilities against the Iraqis in Samaria. Under these circumstances the British would certainly not feel disposed to reduce their garrison in Transjordan and I did not think the Department of State would be warranted in asking them to do so."

McClintock was reluctant to inform Bunche of the details of the secret negotiations, and he advised Power that he "did not think we [the U.S.] had any warrant . . . to tell our friend, the Mediator, of what was happening" (*FRUS* 6 [1949], p. 869).

In a superb example of the befuddlement inherent in this blindman's buff style of diplomacy, McClintock advised Power he did not think "we would possibly take the risk with Israel, *which had not informed the U.S. of what was going on*, using our action with Bunche as a pretext to denounce the agreement now reached secretly with Abdallah. I told Mr. Power that under no circumstances should USUN divulge to the Secretariat or to Bunche its knowledge of the secret negotiations between Abdallah and the government at Tel Aviv. Mr. Power seemed somewhat unconvinced. I later confirmed my position with Mr. Rusk and have informed Mr. Power" (*FRUS*, 6 [1949], p. 869; emphasis supplied).

It is possible to draw one of several conclusions from the contradictions in this McClintock message. First, it is possible McClintock knew little or nothing of the details of the secret deal. This would have been consistent with Sharett's January 18 instruction to Elath that only "the President and Robert Lovett," the under secretary of state, were to be informed in "strictest confidence" of Abdallah's deals with the British. A second possibility is that McClintock knew more than he was prepared to share with Power. But he inserted the idea that Israel had "not informed the U.S. of what was going on" to put Power off, at the same time relying on the possibility of exercising the bureaucratic prerogative of deniability (*FRUS* 6 [1949], p. 869). And finally, although there is no evidence that Israel was dissatisfied with the secret deal, McClintock's apparent incoherence suggests the United States might have been unhappy if the Israelis had denounced it, exposing U.S. complicity. The United States wanted Israel admitted to the United Nations, and public knowledge of the deal with Abdallah would have militated against its acceptance because virtually every detail of the off-the-record agreement flouted the UN resolutions. A more subtle U.S. reason for not wanting Israel to scuttle the agreement may have been that the United States preferred Jordan to take over the part of Palestine that Israel had not already occupied, because Abdallah, largely under British control, promised to be more "reliable" than the more independent and nationalist Egyptians and Syrians.

None of the available records contains a clear explanation for the internal inconsistencies in the McClintock conversation. But one conclusion emerges clearly. Insofar as the Bunche and UN decisions reflected international law, the U.S. commitment left much to be desired. Such hypocrisy in American–Middle East diplomacy has continued for most of the ensuing four decades and cannot escape a large measure of responsibility for the steady worsening of the Palestine problem.

Jerusalem! O! Jerusalem!

The U.S.-Israeli-Jordanian wheeling and dealing thwarting UN legislation offered scant hope that the complicated problem of Jerusalem would be discussed within the framework of the UN recommendations. General Assembly Resolution No. 194, December 11, 1948, paragraph 7, called for "a permanent international regime for the territory of Jerusalem." The Israelis and Abdallah together had conferred on plans to share a divided city. Bunche was still unaware of these secret agreements when, on March 12, he convened the fourth meeting of the two official delegations on Rhodes. In the opinion of the U.S. consul at Jerusalem, the military situation in the Jerusalem territory and the impotence of the United Nations and Bunche to enforce the withdrawal of all troops to their positions of March 1949 made Resolution No. 194 obsolete. In a March 19 telegram to Acheson, the consul (Burdett) reported the opinion of Mark Ethridge, the American representative on the Palestine Conciliation Committee:[10] "While we intend to continue efforts to achieve substantial degree internationalization Jerusalem we consider agreement on separate legal entity practically out of question unless USG willing apply strongest pressure. Mayor New City [on] sixteenth insisted to Jerusalem committee that Israel entitled to all Jerusalem" (*FRUS* 6 [1949], p. 848).

Dr. Henry Cattan, a displaced Palestinian now living in Paris and a recognized authority on the international law aspects of the Palestinian tragedy, noted that the principal achievement of the Conciliation Commission was to secure the agreement of the four contiguous Arab states (Egypt, Jordan, Syria, and Lebanon), on the one hand, and Israel, on the other, to the Lausanne Protocol that was signed on May 12, 1949. The protocol stated that the parties accepted the Conciliation Commission's proposal that the attached working document (map according to the partition resolution of November 29, 1947) would be taken as a basis for discussion with the commission. But despite its signature, in its discussions with the Conciliation Commission, Israel refused the UN partition resolution as a basis for discussion, insisted on the armistice lines, and even demanded more Arab territories, namely western Galilee and the Gaza Strip. The third progress report of the Conciliation

Commission states that, on the territorial question, Israel proposed its frontiers with Egypt and Lebanon should be the frontiers of Palestine that existed under the British mandate. As for its frontier with Jordan, Israel proposed a boundary corresponding to the armistice lines. In effect, Israel's territorial proposals at the Lausanne discussions in 1949 meant that the Palestine Arabs would be left with about 20 percent of the area of their own country. With these claims, Israel was asserting as a source of title to territory the right of conquest rather than the UN partition resolution.[11]

Burdett's telegram of March 19 continued with a compromise proposal. It recommended "an international regime" for "the Jerusalem area" and recognition of the de facto situation in which there were already two separate communities, one Jewish and one Arab. The Jewish zone, so called, was essentially in the New City, or western Jerusalem. The Arab zone was essentially in the Old City, or eastern Jerusalem. The "adjacent Arab state" (Jordan) and Israel would administer the territories, except that an "international authority" would "assure protection of free access to the holy places." It would also have the right to make "representations" to the local Arab and Israeli authorities, or to the foreign ministers of the two states, with respect to "human rights," "common public services," "maintenance of peace and order," and "demilitarization of the area." The Arab and Jewish states would also agree to submit to the World Court disputes that might be "seriously prejudicial to the welfare of the area" or to "the international interest," and they would agree that the "jurisdiction" of the court would be "compulsory ipso facto and without special agreement." The State Department informed Burdett it "prefer[red] you do not submit this draft" to either the Conciliation Commission or to "Arab representatives" (*FRUS* 6 [1949], p. 849).

At Rhodes, Bunche faced the fact that neither Israel nor Jordan was prepared to comply with the Security Council's call for both parties "to take steps looking toward the demilitarization of Jerusalem." The only practical alternative, they both agreed, was to establish a no-man's-land between two parts of a divided city. Bunche finally retreated to this position. The sequential questions became what part of the area would be included in the neutral zone and whether civilians—as well as military forces—would be excluded from it. Both delegations had maps, drawn to virtually street-by-street detail. Each party had its own pet projects, some of which were holy places that, based on the existing demography, were in the territory over which the other would claim control. Bunche finally asked both to try to formulate a plan in which the roads leading to places like Mt. Scopus, Hadassah Hospital, Latrun, the Wailing Wall, several Arab villages, and Hebrew University would be opened by "mutual withdrawal." Bunche described these roads as "the traffic arteries" and called them "the main difficulty in the definition of armistice lines in Jerusalem" (*M. V.*, pp. 401–3).

Bunche had another consideration in mind. During the fighting, there had been a mass movement of civilians from the proposed no-man's-land. While the delegations at Rhodes were sparring about a formula for the separation of forces, civilians still inhabiting this zone feared a renewal of fighting and continued to flee the area. Bunche wanted these civilians to be able to return to their homes as soon as possible.

One of the problems was that "a joint or two separate police forces" was considered to prevent incidents among the mixed population of Jews and Arabs who had lived in the proposed no-man's-land. They were eager to return to their homes, lands, and businesses. The Israelis were prepared to support "reciprocal withdrawal," "provided it does not lead to joint or international supervision, or to the *return of Arab* residents to the demilitarized zone" (*C. V.*, p. 72; emphasis supplied).

In a March 13 telegram to Tel Aviv, Dayan expanded the Israeli explanation for rejecting Bunche's proposal. He advised Tel Aviv that Bunche and General Riley, an American and chief of staff of the UN Truce Supervisory Organization who had been assigned as an aide to Bunche, were advocating the "demilitarization not as a solution but as a stage toward peace." That would not make any difference "to us," Dayan continued. To substitute police for the armies would, "in practice," mean "only change in the colour of the hats." The next few lines suggest what Dayan meant by *in practice.* They strengthen the suspicion that the Israelis were approaching the armistices without serious thoughts about the Security Council's explicit recommendation that the armistice negotiations were "to facilitate the transition from the November 16, 1948, truce to permanent peace in Palestine" (*UN Res.*, p. 130). With this in mind, the following from Dayan's telegram should be critically read: "In any case," Israel "cannot argue that the time has arrived for peace arrangements."

In the negotiations at Rhodes—and in the secret talks with Abdallah—the Israelis had demanded the "restoration of normal conditions on Mt. Scopus" and "use of the railway" from Tel Aviv to Jerusalem. We cannot argue for these arrangements, Dayan protested to Tel Aviv, "and at the same time oppose *a priori* replacement of the army by police. One must only be watchful of their plot with regard to a united Jewish and Arab Jerusalem, separate in its arrangments from the State of Israel" (*C.V.*, pp. 170–71).

The implications are clear—at least they become clear more than twenty years after the 1967 war. The Israeli focus in the armistice negotiations with both Egypt and Jordan was not limited to military considerations. The Israeli strategists' primary considerations were strategic points that would, at some future time, serve their plans to expand to the territory claimed in the 1919 Zionist proposals. Consequently, they objected to the return of any Arabs to the proposed no-man's-land; and they were determined to frustrate any blueprint for a united Jerusalem separated from the State of Israel. The prescribed law was eviscerated by crude horse trading. The Israelis possessed military superiority, and, for the time being, they held the winning bid. It was another example of force superseding the UN goal of establishing a rule of law.

The "Triangle"

When Bunche had been confronted with the Israeli fait accompli of Operation Uvda, knowing from experience that he could not rely on any of the "great powers"—including the United States—to support his loyalty to UN legislation, he found himself impotent to stem the erosion of UN authority. The negativism of this situation was intensified with the secret negotiations between Abdallah's emissaries and the Israelis, about which Bunche's knowledge was fragmentary, if he knew at all. The very fact that the two governments involved had agreed *not* to inform Bunche reflected their lack of respect for the acting mediator and the United Nations he represented. This barely concealed disregard for the surrogate of the expressed consensus of the international community manifested itself in the problem of disposing of the issue of Iraqi troops on the central front where the Israelis sought control but where Jordan wanted to take over from the Iraqis. The territory involved, where some 2,000–4,000 Iraqi troops were stationed, was just north and west of Jerusalem. The partition had assigned it to the Arab state. Jordan's claim as an Arab nation was therefore more valid than the Israeli insistence on being a party in determining control of the area in the armistice negotiations. However, since the armistices were to be limited to military considerations, the Israelis could establish a tenuous claim because, should the armistice give way to renewed fighting, the Iraqi troops would be in position to cut Israel in two. They stood directly opposite one of the narrowest places in the territory that had been assigned to the Jewish state. In this general area around Jaffa and Tel Aviv, Israeli territory was a mere ten miles wide. The Iraqis, therefore, could "threaten the most vital Israeli cities and lines of communication."[12] So, despite this debatable justification for participation in determining the Arab forces in the contested territory, the Israeli military experts had some geopolitical justification for apprehension over a continuing Iraqi military presence. The apprehension was not diminished by the fact that Iraq was not a party to the armistice negotiations, although Abdallah claimed he had Iraq's agreement to represent it.

This background makes understandable the Israelis' flat declaration to Abdallah that if his troops replaced the Iraqis, Israel "will view such an act as a manifest violation of the truce, and will not recognize it if it is implemented without Israel's agreement" (*C.V.*, p. 75). The Israelis' ultimatum, however, was tainted because they had been less than scrupulous in respecting the UN-ordered truces.

The Israelis were not deterred by such moral dilemmas. They were simply deliberating among themselves the possible political repercussions if they again violated a truce and initiated "an action against the Iraqi-held territory" (*C.V.*, p. 77).

Bunche might actually carry out his repeated reminder that he could always turn the problem of the armistices back to the Security Council. The Security Council's call for a truce carried with it the threat of sanctions under Chapter VII of the charter (see *UN Res.*, p. 129, Security Council Resolution No. 61, November 4, 1948, Preambular para. 3). Probably mindful of these considerations, Eytan sought Eban's advice at the United Nations, asking "the likely reaction of the Security Council and his advice on tactics best calculated to soften likely Security Council blow" if Israel should move against the Iraqi forces (*C.V.*, p. 173). The Tel Aviv exploration of the wisdom of violating the truce apparently had ended in an affirmative. From Eban, Tel Aviv wanted only his on-the-spot assessment as to how much damage Israel could "get away with" if it renewed active hostilities.

Later, in Israeli terminology, "the Iraqi front" came to be called "the Triangle" because the territory north of Jerusalem and stretching almost to the Mediterranean was bounded by an imaginary line joining three heavily populated Arab towns: Nablus, Tulkarm, and Jenin. This demographic fact undoubtedly dictated that the Triangle be assigned to the Arab state.

As mentioned, there was some strategic justification for Israel's coveting this territory. Without it, the width of the coastal territory allocated to the Jewish state at a central point was reduced to roughly ten miles. Conceding the Triangle to the Arabs put many Israeli coastal settlements within range of Jordanian artillery. The territory also provided a desirable military route to the Jordan River and to possible control of the West Bank. Menachem Begin had consistently berated the Jewish Agency's lack of support for his Irgunists. In May 1948, he complained that if support had been provided before the regular Arab armies had become fully engaged in the fighting, "we should have smashed the enemy in the central front in the first stage of his invasion, instead of only after the first truce. And the Jewish forces would have been free in the second stage for a full attack on the 'Triangle.' In a word, we should today have held the Western bank of the Jordan—at least."[13]

Israel finally realized its objectives in this area in the 1967 war. Nadav Safran, a pro-Israel historian, inventories Israeli gains on this central front in this later military campaign: pushing back the border in the Jenin region, putting the Valley of Jezreel beyond the range of Jordanian artillery, control of the Latrun-Ramallah road, securing and widening the Tel Aviv–Jerusalem corridor, forcing a link between west Jerusalem and the Mt. Scopus enclave. He concludes, "As may be readily seen, the achievement of these objectives would automatically cut off East Jerusalem and place the Israelis in an excellent position to move on against the nodal sectors of the mountain spine in pursuit of the maximal objective of capturing the entire West Bank and routing or destroying the Jordanian army in the second phase."[14]

Growing intimate coordination of U.S. tactics and strategies (if not yet of policy) with Israel made the Americans at least accessories after the fact of Israeli expansionist aspirations. This is confirmed in a long urgent and secret telegram dated March 23, 1949, from Wells Stabler, the U.S. chargé in Jerusalem, to the secretary of state. Stabler had been asked by Abdullah to meet him at Shuneh where the king reported in detail on another of the secret meetings on the twenty-second, in Jerusalem, between the Israelis and senior officials and confidants of the king. The Israelis had demanded "Arab withdrawal up to 10 miles from present front lines" in the central area. After "many hours" of bargaining, the Israelis "modified demands" somewhat but told Abdallah's representatives that "Transjordan must agree and sign formal agreement within 24 hours or Israel would withdraw its consent for Arab Legion to take over from the Iraqis" (*FRUS* 6 [1949], p. 860).

The telegram informed Acheson that the Israelis "proposed this agreement remain secret," but "as soon as armistice agreement signed at Rhodes, secret agreement (although still remaining secret) would immediately be regarded as agreed in mutual revision of armistice terms." The explanation for this sleight-of-hand diplomacy was that there would be an "adverse effect on Arab public opinion when this agreement became public unless Transjordan received compensation" (*FRUS* 6 [1949], p. 860). The telegram continued:

> Israelis refused and said they would not agree any compensation.
> Transjordan representatives at meeting, with whom I talked at Shuneh, indicated atmosphere of meeting not friendly and that Israelis had taken very strong line. They had impression that if agreement not signed Israelis might take offensive action to make adjustments demanded. (It is understood Dayan told Member Consulate General Jerusalem on March 18 that if rectification not made by agreement, Israel would make them anyway.)

And, according to the U.S. chargé, the king added that

> he felt that if he refused to sign agreement, Israel would recommence hostilities and whole area might be lost. It would in fact be better to sacrifice another fifteen villages with additional estimated 15,000 refugees than to lose what little left of Arab Palestine. . . . He not entirely decided what his attitude would be and it would depend on circumstances of tonight's meeting at Shuneh. If he could be certain that US would take action prevent Israel from reopening hostilities, he would try postpone decision for another day or two and endeavor negotiate more reasonable adjustments. However, in absence this certainty, he felt he [was] almost forced into signing agreement tonight. (*FRUS* 6 [1949], pp. 859–61)

Three hours after the first cable, in a second message, Stabler called the Israeli "24-hour ultimatum . . . totally unreasonable and in nature of blackmail." Another meeting between the Israelis and Jordanians was scheduled that night of March 23, and Stabler urged that the

> Department give consideration making strong representations to Israel Government (if agreement not signed tonight) insisting that

matter of territorial dispositions and adjustments be left to peace settlement and that armistice negotiations at Rhodes be concluded at once on present *status quo.*

Transjordan is willing and ready reach peace settlement but it does appear to be rank injustice for USG to stand by while Israel at point of gun in forcing Transjordan into such an agreement. (*FRUS* 6 [1949], p. 862)

On March 24, Acheson saw President Truman and reported the substance of the cables from Amman. He also told Truman that in a conversation with Sharett, on March 22, he had raised the question of Israel's intentions with respect to the Iraqi front. In response, Sharett asked the secretary to "inform the President that policy of Israel was to seek to avoid hostilities." But despite this Israeli disclaimer, Acheson reported Stabler's description of the Israeli position as "unreasonable" and "blackmail." In a memorandum dated the twenty-fourth, the secretary noted that "the President was disturbed over the uncooperative attitude being taken and said we must continue to maintain firm pressure" (*FRUS* 6 [1949], p. 863).

Despite—or perhaps because of—this ring-around-a-rosy diplomacy, the agreement was signed the night of March 23. The State Department was informed with the full text (*FRUS* 6 [1949], p. 867). The agreement was essentially what the Israelis had demanded. The Arab Legion was to take over the Iraqi forces. Between five and fifteen weeks after the general armistice would be signed, and in three separate phases, the Israelis would take over the territory from which the Jordanians (and Iraqis) would withdraw.

Paragraph 4 stated, "Israel, for its part, has made similar changes for the benefit of Transjordan." Stabler's comment to this "concession" was, "This is clause without meaning but according to Transjordan representatives included for sake Arab public opinion. Transjordan representatives hope later to change 'has made' to 'will make'" (*FRUS* 6 [1949], p. 867).

Paragraph 8 stated, "In case of villages affected inhabitants entitled to full rights of residence, property and freedom. If they leave may take livestock and movable property and receive without delay full compensation for land they leave behind." Again, Stabler noted, "Transjordan representatives believe this also empty clause" (*FRUS* 6 [1949], p. 867).

Paragraph 11 codified the conspiracy of silence to which, for expedient political reasons, the Israelis and Jordanians had agreed. "Agreement not to be published without consent both parties nor shall it in any way prejudice an ultimate political settlement between the parties." By acquiescence, the United States became a co-conspirator in these commitments that the parties knew would not be fulfilled. The plan to conceal the facts deliberately from other parties interested in the problem of Palestine became part of the ongoing charade for "establishing peace." It is small wonder, therefore, that the peace that was to follow the armistices still eludes the world and the principals themselves.

Having signed the document under the pressure of "blackmail," there was one technical hitch in the agreement to which the Jordanians resorted. Paragraph 12 required the Jordanian prime minister to ratify the agreement, which was then to be communicated to Israel "not later than March 30. Failing ratification agreement null and void and without effect" (*FRUS* 6 [1949], p. 867).[15]

Abdallah's duplicitous intentions to betray the other Arabs and to plot with the Israelis to divide Palestine between them hardly qualifies him for the role of an innocent victim of Zionist blackmail. But of the parties to this witches' brew, the conduct of the United States is the most reprehensible and lacking in vision. For even then Washington was holding itself out as the great power best qualified to persuade both sides to proceed with the armistice talks in the spirit of the United Nations, which regarded these negotiations as the prelude to a comprehensive peace. It was at this period that Washington began to give more credence to Israeli advice than to the counsel of its own Foreign Service operatives in the area.[16] With justification it may be said—forty years after this waffling against the Arabs and in support of Israeli violations of UN decisions to which the United States had given public support— that the seeds were planted then for American appeasement of the Israelis' insatiable appetite for more and more territory. American indulgence of the more than twenty years of occupation of the Arab territories "acquired by war" in 1967 has a long precedent.

The growing Arab (and particularly Palestinian) realization of the duplicity between Washington's rhetoric and actions has intensified the jeopardy in which U.S. policy has placed its own interests. Fundamentalist religious influence in the Middle East has increased. Native nationalist resentment raises discordant notes heard by all who are not tone-deaf, threatening the traditional, smooth symphony so confidently orchestrated for years by the Israeli lobby with its loud instrumentalists stressing the reprise "Israel is the reliable defender of American and Western interests in the Middle East."[17] The perfidy of U.S.-Israeli conduct in 1948–49 has now come almost full circle. And, as then, the U.S.-Israeli combine of secrecy leaves most Americans, and probably Israelis also, uninformed of the deals involved and the imminent danger of major conflicts resulting from many years of treating the Palestinians as nonpersons and denying their national identity.

Given this tangled web of double-dealing, of bad faith diplomacy, of hypocritical circumventions of the UN mandates under which the armistices were supposed to be negotiated, of deliberately ambiguous evasions of basic issues, it is not surprising that the Israeli records offer no comment on the deletion of Article 12 of the secret agreement with Abdallah. For Israel to explain the means it had used to eliminate this possible veto of the agreement it desired, or for Abdallah to try to explain the clearly implied opposing view among his own important ministers, might well have opened a Pandora's box with unforeseeable international complications.

While this furtive charade-diplomacy was in process in Jerusalem and Shuneh, formal negotiations continued under Bunche's leadership on Rhodes. The Israeli team was prolonging them as much as possible while still maintaining a posture of reasonableness and respectability. They were hoping for a fait accompli in the secret talks and also waiting for Israel to consolidate its hold on all of the southern Negev, where Abdallah still entertained visions of controlling at least the eastern part.

Having received no genuine support from either the United States or Britain on the issues on the Iraqi front, Jordan's prime minister, in what Stabler called "a somewhat better frame of mind," confessed that on Jerusalem, "Transjordan would have to accept almost any terms which Israelis demanded." He presumed that "Bunche would draft a compromise which Jordan would be obliged to accept" (*FRUS* 6 [1949], p. 874). The prime minister said he had informed the British chargé that "in future Transjordan, while remining friend and ally . . . and willing to receive advice from the British or anyone else would act as it saw fit in its own interests. Transjordan would no longer feel obligated to follow British advice." The kingdom's "own interest" may still have included Abdallah's dream of a "Greater Syria," for the minister also confided to Stabler, "He [was] no longer concerned about attitude Arab states or others, that his principal concern was welfare Transjordan and Arab

Palestine and that he must now act, regardless of cost, to prevent complete disaster" (*FRUS* 6 [1949], pp. 873–74).

Fait Accompli Diplomacy

At a meeting with Acheson and senior staff members of the State Department on March 28, Dean Rusk informed the group that "it would be necessary to bring pressure to bear" if the basic American policy, set forth in a paper on November 10, 1948, was to be made "effective" (*FRUS* 5, part 2 [1948], pp. 1565–67).[18] But, of course, by late March 1949 the situation that had existed on November 10 had been radically altered. Fixing the armistice line with Lebanon at the international border for all practical purposes foreclosed any Israeli territorial concessions in western Galilee. Operation Uvda, in violation of the truce, represented another example of Israeli fait accompli diplomacy and established Israeli control of the entire Negev. So even as Rusk urged the president to reaffirm the principles of the territorial recommendations of November 10, 1948, with wisdom born of experience, he added that to do so "would cause the President considerable heartburn before it is over" (*FRUS* 6 [1949], p. 875).

Acheson agreed to discuss these questions with the President but "thought he should advise the President to call in his political advisors to talk this over." That meant Clark Clifford and David Niles, among others. Undaunted by this prospect, Rusk offered that "if the President exercises reasonable firmness now, we will likely get a reasonable solution to the problem" (*FRUS* 6 [1949], p. 875).

The *if* in Rusk's closing observation was the operative word. It was not the first time—nor would it be the last—that the informed, specialized, intimate knowledge of the professional experts was filtered through the political advisors in the White House. The filter device was, to use Rusk's word, the "heartburn" of the president, meaning the politically indigestible composition of the Israeli lobby's threat of political reprisal. So, on March 28, Truman informed Abdallah that the United States believed that "Israel is entitled to the territory allotted in the November 29 General Assembly Resolution but if Israel desires additions in territory allotted to the Arabs, it should offer territorial compensation." The president added that he "understood" the "secret agreement . . . shall not in any way prejudice an ultimate political settlement between the parties" (*FRUS* 6 [1949], pp. 878–79). The pro-Israeli tilt is something more than subliminal. Truman allowed for—perhaps even encouraged—an Israeli initiative for territorial changes exceeding the partition-recommended boundaries.

The gratuitous advice that the secret agreement should not prejudice a final, political settlement was pure boilerplate. Everyone kept insisting publicly that the armistice negotiations were only military in purpose, designed to bring a halt to the fighting. The tenacity with which all parties to the Egyptian, Lebanese, and now the Jordanian negotiations fought over almost every inch of territory—and the strategic locations of the territory over which the disputes occurred—strongly suggested that the armistice lines would be generally regarded as de facto frontiers. There is no explicit evidence indicating that any of the parties realized then that even forty years later there would be no peace. But the passions and intensity of the negotiations must have suggested to the more imaginative and perceptive participants that many of the most hotly disputed places on the armistice lines offered potential advantages for future fighting rather than contributing to a final peace.

Despite these ambiguities Truman concluded his message to Abdallah with the same ritualistic promise of future American firm commitment, "even-handedness," as Acheson had used in his instructions to Stabler on March 25: "Your Majesty may be assured that the United States Government, as a member of the Palestine Conciliation Commission, will regard any attempt at a major breach of the provisions of the secret agreement between Transjordan and Israel as a serious obstacle to the progress being made toward peace in Palestine, and that the United States Government would be prepared to make strong representations against such action to the party attempting it. I send Your Majesty my best and most cordial wishes" (*FRUS* 6 [1949], p. 879).

The Israelis and Jordanians met on the evening of March 30 to sign the ratified secret agreement. The prime minister and the king were both present. In a last desperate effort to prevent the Israelis from acquiring "the areas . . . not allotted to Israel under partition," the Jordanians proposed that they "should become no-man's-land under UN until a final settlement." The Israelis rejected the idea and declared the question of partition did not enter into discussions (*FRUS* 6 [1949], p. 886). This is another example of Israel's whipsawing the Arabs, invoking the authority of the partition proposal when it was to their advantage and insisting on their claims to "territory [beyond the partition borders] acquired by war" when *that* served their interests. They strenuously opposed every proposal that might provide even interim authority for the United Nations over territory they coveted but that had not been designated for them by the partition. To avoid adding to the swelling numbers of refugees, it was agreed that neither side would deploy military forces in the Arab villages in the disputed territory. They would "remain 'enclaves' " (*FRUS* 6 [1949], p. 886).[19]

In his cable to Acheson reporting the March 30 Israeli-Jordanian meeting at Shuneh, Stabler also noted the commitment of both parties to secrecy until the armistice agreement would be signed at Rhodes. The details would then be sent as instructions to the two official delegations, which would then include the terms of the secret agreement in the general armistice agreement. The Jordanians announced they expected the agreement to be signed at Rhodes on April 4 and the Arab Legion would then replace Iraqi forces on the central front on the fifth. The armistice was actually signed at 7:30 P.M., April 3 (*FRUS* 6 [1949], pp. 886–88).

The atmosphere of conspiracy that had shrouded the secret agreement persisted to the final moment. Last-minute disagreements persisted over definitions of military equipment and deployment. Shiloah was afraid the details of the secret agreement might leak. If that were to happen before the signing, he anticipated "possible reactions in the Arab world . . . might impel the King to go back on the agreement" (*C.V.*, p. 91). The matter came finally to Ben-Gurion who "instructed Eytan" "not to postpone signing because of these more, or less technical differences over armaments and their deployment" (*C.V.*, p. 183).

Jerusalem II: "Who Shall Ascend the Lord's Mountain?" (Psalm 24)

While the under-the-table deals of the secret agreement were being worked out, Bunche and the delegates to the official negotiations at Rhodes were struggling with the fate of Jerusalem. The details of Bunche's compromise efforts, the virtual abandonment of the UN resolutions calling for internationalization of the city and its demilitarization, are too complicated and, without constant study of relevant maps in great detail, too bewildering to reproduce here. On March 12, at the fourth meeting of the negotiating teams, both sides submitted detailed maps, identifying holy places, road crossings, and the elevation of various hills which might offer an advantage if occupied by one military force or the other. The Israelis assigned high priority to Mt. Scopus, where the Hadassah

Hospital and the Hebrew University were located, and to the Tel Aviv–Jerusalem railroad. Also, for the Israelis, the water pipeline and pumping station at Latrun that had been cut by the Transjordanian forces during the fighting was vital. The major considerations of the Transjordanians were numerous holy places, transit between areas predominently inhabited by Arabs but separated from each other by Zionist settlements or Israeli military forces, and concern that civilian violence would erupt if the two peoples were permitted freely to move back into homes that had been evacuated during the fighting.

The claims of the two sides were virtually irreconcilable. The obstacles were not so much ill will as fear and the fact that the city had become a rabbit warren of intersecting streets, a profusion of holy places, and, particularly in the Old City, such an intermixture of people from both parties that it seemed impossible to draw any rational geographical borders to determine recognized, acceptable armistice lines to separate the military forces.

Significantly, during two long sessions on March 12, neither party demonstrated any interest in invoking the Security Council resolution that called on both parties in the Jerusalem area to take steps looking toward the demilitarization of Jerusalem. Bunche reminded them: "As you know, there have been some ineffectual talks. We have encountered obstacles which are well-known here. That resolution, adopted originally in May of 1948 was reiterated in July, August, and October" (*M.V.*, p. 401).

Bunche then attempted to break the stalemate by suggesting a no-man's-land, between the belligerents. It was an idea that had been on the table. The mediator, however, added that this area should not be "barren" because "trouble might arise as a result of [civilian] incidents." He suggested "widen[ing] the area between the lines in such a way that there could be a reasonable normal use of that area by the civilian population" and "a clear-cut scheme for policing the area on civilian levels" (*M.V.*, p. 402). He reminded the negotiators that the ultimate objective of the armistice talks was a permanent and comprehensive peace: "There is no reason why the civilian population should continue to suffer on either side once an armistice liquidating the war on the military level is achieved." And he mildly upbraided both sides for thinking in military terms rather than "liquidating the war" (*M.V.*, pp. 402–5):

I think the difficulty in the proposals made today is that they are thinking too much in terms of military positions—each side maintaining lines which are at least as good as those maintained presently—with a tendency for the burden of withdrawal to be placed on the other side. . . .

I think, Colonel Dayan, that is true of some of the proposals you made this morning—I must confess I have some concern . . . [that your suggestion] is likely to create areas of friction, as you indicated. It is not an entirely happy solution.

In the Transjordan proposal this afternoon the difficulty is of course that one side is asked to withdraw and the other remains pretty much where it is. That is fine if the other side is willing to withdraw. In a situation of this kind, where there are two equal partners—I hope they will be partners—the normal procedure is to take the existing lines in working out an armistice, but we hope to get an agreement which would be much better than would be obtained by maintaining the existing lines because, from experience, we see potential trouble in the existing lines. (*M. V.*, pp. 401–2)

But the two sides failed to reach agreement on withdrawal or on the definition and regulations for the proposed no-man's-land. The sessions were resumed on March 13. Early on, Colonel El-Jundi, speaking for Transjordan, declared that "the Transjordan delegation here will not deal with the points of discussion between Colonel Dayan and Colonel Tell" (*M. V.*, p. 411).

This reference to the secret negotiations (no longer unknown to Bunche, apparently) raises the question of the good faith of the Rhodes negotiations. The Israelis had been aware of the secret negotiations. But El-Jundi's refusal to accept the Dayan-Tall blueprint suggests that the Transjordanians at Rhodes may have been "cut in" only recently. The rejection may have been the result of the divided authority representing Transjordan. Or, because of their secret character, the Rhodes contingent may have felt it could not trust an Israeli version. Or the El-Jundi reaction may have been a bold lèse-majesté. None of these explanations—or any other—or El-Jundi's rejection is provided in the available texts. But it can be assumed that the secret talks toughened the Israeli bargaining position and weakened the Transjordanian delegation. To this extent Bunche's efforts to construct some agreement for untangling the involved mix of military, demographic, and geographic problems in arranging a viable armistice for the Holy City foundered. The impasse on Jerusalem, so critical to any possibility of an armistice formula that could be a step toward peace, demonstrates the political tragedy that so often accompanies disregard for the law.

Dayan's reaction to the El-Jundi veto is recorded in a message he sent to Yadin, in Tel Aviv. Absolving Israel of guilt as a coconspirator in the secret deals impeding progress for an armistice, "Dayan notes the shortcomings of the Jordanian delegation; its members have difficulty understanding the topics under discussion, and they are not permitted to deviate from their instructions. Because of this limited independence the Israeli delegation feels that for the time being no advantage can accrue from direct contacts" (*C.V.*, p 73). Because Dayan was a participant in the behind-the-scenes diplomacy, his cynicism and denigration of the Transjordanians would be plausible—and not entirely undeserved—if they had been offered by a witness with cleaner hands.

El-Jundi proposed that Bunche offer a proposal to break the deadlock. Reluctantly Bunche agreed, observing with a touch of forlorn hope and irony, "I hope that neither delegation will expect too much. We are dealing with the Holy Land, but it has been a long time since miracles occurred, even in the Holy Land." Ruefully, he added, people in the UN Secretariat "are quite accustomed to having our ideas thrown unceremoniously out of the window. . . . Horrible things have happened to papers we have produced in various places" and, more plaintively, he again reminded the negotiators that the preference of the United Nations was demilitarization of Jerusalem. As he put it, "As a peace-loving man, I should like to say 'Settle it by completely de-militarizing the place, and then there is no problem'; but I realize that things cannot be done so simply" (*M.V.*, p. 412). He sadly reviewed the failed efforts to realize the UN goal: "It was tried, I am afraid, half-heartedly, and in a jerky way. I never have had a really clear picture as to what did transpire as regards the efforts to de-militarize Jerusalem. I remember back in August we had talks with Arab representatives in Beirut and Israeli representatives in Tel Aviv, and at the time I thought there was some sort of real possibility—and Bernadotte did too. However, hitches were encountered, and I never have been clear about just how the effort bogged down so completely. What was it?" (*M.V.*, pp. 411–12).

If Bunche expected his mild criticism to elicit any remorse or to encourage greater flexibility from either of the delegations, he was immediately disappointed. Dayan lost no time in responding. "Oh—there were just maps and schemes. I think the latest was Neuville's[20]—and then they came to the conclusion that all the schemes were no good and Neuville suggested more or less dividing Jerusalem up into an Arab Zone and a Jewish Zone, and then they gave up the scheme of internationalizing Jerusalem and having a unified town" (*M.V.*, p. 412).

Bunche tried again to lead the discussion around to an admission that the armistice talks had drifted from simply stabilizing the existing military situation, to total demilitarization of Jerusalem: "The de-militarization scheme immediately merged into the political questions" (*M.V.*, p. 412). Dayan unapologetically confessed that the Israelis, at least, were thinking not of armistices and demilitarization but of some form of permanent occupation and state boundaries. He replied, "Yes. On the border of every state it is necessary to have some kind of defense line. There would be the questions of customs and taxes and everything else, as it is the border of a state. You cannot leave policemen with clubs, especially as we haven't signed a peace yet. The other thing is that you call Jerusalem an international city and have a defense line somewhere else but everyone gave this scheme up, as I understand it." Transjordan added nothing more. Bunche therefore proposed adjourning the session until "sometime before lunch" the next day (*M.V.*, p. 412).

Without much conviction, Bunche offered his proposals on March 15. As he presented them, he said to both delegations, "I cannot say that I am in any sense satisfied with the results." He confessed there was "as much difference of opinion" among members of his staff "as there was between the two delegations." He described his proposals as "only tentative ideas." He listed four major difficulties: "Secure use by the Jews of the road from the Latrun sector; secure use by the Arabs of the Bethlehem road; secure use by the Jews of the Mount Scopus road, over and above the present arrangement, which is a convoy arrangement and not fully secure or free; and the question of the operation of the railroad" (*M.V.*, pp. 424–25).

Again he offered a mild rebuke to both parties because both insisted the "existing lines would be the best arrangement" and "that underlying any consideration of armistice lines is the anticipation by both sides of what may be the final arrangement in Jerusalem, which would involve territorial questions" (*M.V.*, p. 425). In other words, both sides were less interested in ending the fighting than in speculating how Jerusalem would be divided between them in any ultimate peace.

Bunche divined their motives but he was powerless to alter them. The best he could do was to offer another restrained rebuke. He reminded them, "Obviously the best approach would be complete de-militariza-tion of the city. That would eliminate lines. It would satisfy the Security Council's demand. It would simplify the entire problem very greatly." But even as he spoke, he yielded, admitting, "conditions in Jerusalem today would probably render any such scheme impracticable and unac-ceptable by me or the other side, or by both."

According to Bunche, the existing conditions militating against the Security Council's legislation were the inflexibility of the adversaries' positions and "a disparity in the size of the two populations." There were also "irregular and terrorist elements" and "the civilian popula-tions themselves might remain armed and capable of fighting unless there were some very effective system of policing" (*M. V.*, pp. 425–26).

The two delegations met again in plenary session with Bunche on March 16, to offer comments on his proposals. The Jordanians responded first. They agreed it would be impractical to try to demilitarize the city and establish a neutral corridor at the present time, but with minor exceptions they accepted Bunche's proposals. They also recommended the introduction of UN personnel for policing several points at which roads intersected or where existing lines of military forces had the capa-bility of interfering with traffic on roads that were considered essential to both sides (*M. V.*, pp. 434–36).

The Israelis, however, held to their consistent opposition to any UN presence. They argued instead for the Jerusalem formula of the secret negotiations, which by this time were secret to Bunche only in the sense that he knew none of the specifics, and they may not have been much better known to the delegation of Transjordan in Rhodes. Shiloah put the Israeli objection to a UN police action to Bunche:

> We all know the final status of Jerusalem is under discussion somewhere else. We do not know whether the parties concerned will agree to the idea of internationalization or what degree or form of internationalization there should be. What you have suggested is a step towards this.
>
> The business of introducing more and more international super-vision—I shall not say it is not acceptable in principle—but we are not here to decide the ultimate fate of Jerusalem. We will studi-ously avoid any arrangement which might prejudice the delibera-tions now taking place about it. . . .
>
> We prefer settlements which do not involve any third party super-

vision. . . . The introduction of a third party, even with the best intentions, might lead to confusion, unless it is accepted as a permanent regime. . . .

   If it were accepted by all concerned that the way to solution would be de-militarization and international supervision, then your suggestion would be a step in the right direction. (*M.V.,* p. 436)

But demilitarization and internationalization were farthest from the ambitions of those occupied with the back-room plans for dividing the Holy City between themselves, so that neither could have the whole.

   Still exercising restraint, Bunche outlined the logic of using his UN team as a transition. UN personnel would provide an insulating force between the two hostile parties, not yet psychologically prepared for a formula in which direct contact might cause frustrations and tempers to surface, which could easily ignite in renewed battle. Bunche explained, reasonably:

> We did not see this as a step towards internationalization at all. Quite the contrary. We felt that in those places where you might have policing of the road, UN participation or intervention would be necessary only if direct joint control were premature. In other words, it would be merely a temporary step until the two parties were willing to deal with it themselves. . . . The only way they could be dealt with was to remove them from the dangerous situation by United Nations intervention. This was considered only a temporary stopgap arrangement until the two parties could arrange something better. In that sense only have we suggested United Nations participation. The next step would be a reduction of it precisely as the parties themselves could agree to take it over jointly without our assistance. (*M.V.,* p. 437)

Shiloah conceded that Bunche's intentions might have been as explained, but "the practical result might be some form of perpetuation of a machine." "We are not scoffing at the United Nations. . . . I think," he added, "we should try to find solutions to each of the specific difficulties which do not require any third party. That is our general approach" (*M.V.,* p. 437).

   The Transjordan delegation argued for Israeli withdrawal from most of the places the Israelis considered vital to security. And Abdallah's representatives insisted they would not relinquish either to Israel or to the United Nations important points that they held. Commenting on El-Jundi's response to Bunche's proposals, Shiloah said, "Colonel El-Jundi suggests that we evacuate our positions in the south of Jerusalem. He suggests also that we evacuate all the line to Mount Zion—denuding our defenses in the south. He is extremely generous about the King David and the YMCA, which he is willing to hand over to the United Nations. I have not heard of one point—one line—one building—now held by Arabs which he suggests should be handed over to us or to the United Nations authorities." Considering Israel's own inflexible posture, Shiloah added with what must appear as a bit of cynicism and hypocrisy:

> The approach of the Transjordan delegation, to put it mildly, seems to us very far away from the actual state of affairs. I don't feel it could serve as a basis for discussion.
>
> When we opened our discussion on Jerusalem, we suggested that both sides submit a plan, taking into considerations the problems of the other side. Here we see no such attempt. (*M. V.*, p. 438)

Bunche put the best face possible on the impasse. His own efforts, he said had served "a very useful purpose," an "informal agreement of both parties" that the armistice lines in the Jerusalem area "would be based upon existing lines." All "existing arrangements" covering Mount Scopus and Government House areas "would be part of the draft agreement" for the Jerusalem area. The UN resolutions allowed the acting mediator some latitude for negotiating strategies or tactics to resolve the problems of both territory and military strength. In Jerusalem, the ultimate goal was demilitarization. Bunche rationalized his compromise by calling the agreement "informal." His acceptance of the existing lines, contrary to the language and intent of the UN resolutions, he explained, would expedite concentrating negotiations on the "reduction of forces" within the "existing lines" (*M. V.*, p. 439). Regarding the UN order to demilitarize Jerusalem, Bunche settled—for the moment, he thought—for half a loaf as better than none.

Some desultory discussions followed over where the existing lines should be fixed and whether Latrun should be included in the Jerusalem area settlement or dealt with as a separate item. Questions were also raised—without providing answers—about the line from Hebron to the Dead Sea. Should "the existing fighting lines, as certified by United

Nations observer" become "the basis for demarcation of the armistice lines" (*M.V.*, p. 441)?

Bunche reminded both parties that at "virtually every position in the Hebron area," their positions were "outside what was understood to be the truce lines, at the time of their establishment." Neither side had respected the UN truce. He urged both negotiating teams to agree between themselves or face the probability that the UN chief of staff would conduct an investigation of the disputed points. The result, he speculated, would be that both sides would be ordered "to return to the previous truce lines" (*M.V.*, p. 441). Both sides had violated them, and both probably considered them unsatisfactory.

The March 16 session failed to resolve these problems. The meeting was adjourned, with delegates agreeing to reconvene the following day to try to spell out specifically how to bring about Bunche's chief objective, "the reduction of forces" within "the existing lines" (*M.V.*, pp. 439–41).

If Bunche thought that problem would be comparatively easy, he soon learned the contrary. He first listed the subjects to be considered under the heading "reduction of forces." Shiloah, for the Israelis, immediately raised the question of whether British forces at Aqaba should be included as part of the defensive forces on the Transjordan side of the existing lines. Shiloah's question was "If we both agree that there may be two battalions of each force on their respective sides of the determined lines, will this mean that on the Transjordan side the British at Aqaba will be included in the Transjordanian battalions, plus whatever number of troops the British may maintain at Aqaba?" (*M.V.*, p. 447). The Transjordanians argued that the British were at Aqaba under a treaty arrangement, and discussion of the terms of the treaty would be a political matter that had no place on the agenda for negotiating a military armistice. The place for such discussions would be London, not Rhodes.

At Bunche's suggestion, John Reedman, a special representative on Palestine for the UN secretary-general, reported that the question of the British at Aqaba had been raised during the negotiations with Egypt. Reedman had queried London via the British representatives at Lake Success. He reported, "Within two days we received a firm and definite written assurance that these forces would in no circumstances be used for offensive purposes and would in no circumstances be used in Palestine" (*M.V.*, p. 448).

This did not satisfy Shiloah. The Israelis, he said, regarded the British with more than "suspicion." He added, "Relations between us and Great Britain are not the best. It is not as if this is a force with which we have never had any relations and with whom we should not feel uneasy. We know where we stand with the Arab Legion; we don't know where we stand with the third party" (*M. V.*, p. 452).

Bunche finally recommended that instead of a reduction of forces, both sides should agree "to remove their forces entirely from that [the Aqaba] area. I am sure the British can be induced to leave." He proposed to proceed at Rhodes. If agreement were reached there, he would then tell "the British at Lake Success that I have been instructed by both delegations at Rhodes to inquire whether if all forces are removed from all sectors of the line, would the British remove their forces?" Shiloah responded he would "like that Transjordan delegation put the formula to their delegation to produce a formula which would satisfy us" (*M. V.*, pp. 443–53).

Shiloah's hair-splitting with the Transjordanian, El-Jundi, and with Bunche is hardly to be explained by the assurances Bunche offered to meet the Israeli objections. Nor can it be entirely justified in the light of Bunche's repeated admission that the Israeli-Transjordanian negotiations to establish armistice lines and reduction of forces were complicated by the problem of Jerusalem and the presence of Iraqi troops in the area north of the city. Shiloah's persistent negativism was focused not on Jerusalem but on the southern front, "from the Dead Sea south to the Gulf of Aqaba" (*M. V.*, p. 446), where British troops were present. Both the Israelis and the Transjordanians agreed that because of its size and the terrain, it was difficult to establish a line and a reduction of forces in the south to provide only defense and to prevent offense. A kind of "mobile control" would be needed. In a word, therefore, the real explanation for Shiloah's delaying tactics was the continuing secret negotiations in which Dayan, Tall, the king, and various of his confidants were busily engaged.

These negotiations had expanded to include contacts between the king and Shertok, who was attending the special session of the General Assembly at Lake Success. A channel of communication had been opened via Paris. Abdallah transmitted messages to Elias Sasson, director of the Middle East Division of the Israeli Ministry of Foreign Affairs, for forwarding to Tel Aviv. No explanation is offered for Sasson's presence in Paris. But a letter dated March 21, from him to Walter Eytan in Tel Aviv, reveals some facts about the secret diplomacy and, by strong implication at least, offers a partial explanation for Shiloah's inquisitorial challenges to Bunche at Rhodes. The king had informed Sharett that Operation Uvda—the Israeli seizure of the Negev—was "superfluous" because "he always intended to recognize" Israeli rights to Um Rashrash (Elath) "at the time of the final political negotiations." The king also advised Eytan that "he needs an outlet to the Mediterranean—Gaza or Jaffa for instance. . . . An outlet to the sea for Transjordan as a guarantee of a durable peace between Transjordan and Israel" (*M.V.*, p. 463).

In the same letter, Sasson reproduced a telegram from the king. The first paragraph confirms the suspicion that Shiloah's fencing with Bunche was an effort to prevent the acting mediator from introducing any UN authority into the armistice negotiations to resolve the question of the British forces at Aqaba. The king's design for undercutting Bunche had even broader objectives and was definitely in conflict with the UN resolutions for demilitarizing Jerusalem. "Like you, we also want to protect our rights in Jerusalem, and we are ready to discuss directly the rights of both sides. (The King means thereby that he is ready to reject any proposal which Dr. Bunche may make to create de-militarized zones under UN supervision, in case we reach an agreement with him)" (the words in parentheses are Sasson's interpretation of the king's intentions; *M.V.*, p. 463).[21]

Abdallah also agreed to meet the Israelis "halfway to rectify the lines in the Triangle," provided the Israelis agreed the Transjordanians "should take over this region from the Iraqis." The king explained the reason for the deal was that, because of internal conditions in Iraq, "the government there could not enter direct negotiations" with Israel. If it did so, "the Government would fall and the life of its members would be endangered" (*M.V.*, p. 463).

The final paragraph of the king's telegram, according to Sasson, urged the Israelis to continue the secret talks: "The King begs us not to make mistakes and to be patient in order not to complicate matters further and give him time to deal with the matter in his way, so that he can convince both the Arabs and the British to adopt his point of view" (*M.V.*, pp. 462–63).[22]

The next day, March 22, Sasson sent Eytan a longer letter, confirming—and amplifying—important points in the March 21 communication. In this second letter, Sasson told Eytan "I have the impression that if we persist in our present attitude of toughness with regard to our rights and demands, *we will manage to obtain everything we want from Transjordan*. It seems to me that the King is anxious to conclude an armistice with us at any cost and that the British are not giving him much backing" (*M.V.*, p. 465; emphasis supplied). Obviously, both parties were hoping to complete the details of what would finally amount to peace, rather than merely an armistice, and then to confront all other parties, particularly "the Arabs and the British" and, no doubt, the United Nations, with a fait accompli.

Syrian Intermezzo

The Israelis were further encouraged on March 22, also by word from Sasson, that Syria was prepared for "military and political negotiations." According to Sasson, Syria's prime minister was threatened by internal problems and wanted "to normalize the situation in his country." And "the Americans exerted strong pressure on the Syrians" (*M.V.*, p. 466).

The stage was set, therefore, for Israel to take advantage of internal Arab weaknesses. The Israelis knew how to make the most of the situation. They initiated a press campaign of a mixture of truths, half-truths, and disinformation. Sasson reports actions that apparently required some collaborators in Lebanon and Syria.

> As far as we are concerned, we managed by various means, during the past ten days, to bring to the knowledge of the Syrian Government the information that hostilities would be resumed between our two countries if the Syrians persisted in their refusal to negotiate. We also managed to bring to their knowledge the fact that it was to the interest of Syria to enter into military and political negotiations with us as soon as possible. . . . We insinuated that Transjordan was ready to start political negotiations with us to settle the fate of the Arab areas of Palestine and the future of the Greater Syria plan. We also managed to get many stories about this published in Beirut and Damascus papers. (*M.V.*, p. 466)

Sasson's final advice to Tel Aviv was that he had learned the "[Palestine] Conciliation Commission has started working and does not see things as we do." He therefore urged Eytan to discuss future strategy with Ben-Gurion and to take advantage of the situation in which Israel was able to call most of its own shots. With the back-room support of the United States, Eytan should try to win Ben-Gurion's approval for a procedure in which "the cause of peace" would be expedited, even if less effort and attention were devoted to the tactical and strategic advantages the Israelis had concentrated on in the negotiations so far (*M.V.*, pp. 466–67).

Concluding with Transjordan

While stalling and confusion hobbled the meetings at Rhodes, the secret negotiations were proceeding apace. In a letter dated March 23–24 to Sharett, still in New York, Eytan wrote from Tel Aviv to inform him that the king had exhibited "a receptive frame of mind" to the Israeli demands for resolving the problem of the Iraqi troops (*M.V.*, p. 468ff.). Abdallah, however, still insisted "the agreement be kept secret" and that it "include a clause for face-saving purposes in case the agreement ever leaked out, to the effect that Israel had handed over to Transjordan comparable areas elsewhere." (In fact, Israel had agreed to nothing of the kind [*M.V.*, p. 471].) The king also rejected the idea "that he would be willing to have this arrangement included in the General Armistice Agreement now being negotiated in Rhodes" (*M.V.*, p. 468).

On Tuesday, March 22, there had been a meeting between the Israeli secret negotiators, including Eytan, and their counterparts from the king's side. The meeting, at the Mandelbaum Gate in Jerusalem, had lasted six hours. Eytan warned Shertok that the event was kept "a close secret in the office [of the Israeli Foreign Ministry], where only people whose knowledge of the matter was essential were informed of what was happening." Eytan continued to Sharett, in New York, "It is urgently requested that you observe similar secrecy at your end." By 1:00 A.M. Wednesday the secret negotiations had produced an armistice line and a draft text (*M.V.*, p. 470). The map and the text were to be taken to the king that same day. Eytan's communication to Sharett is another example of how the Israelis wore down the Arabs, who were lamentably unprepared. "According to Abdullah Tell, the King had never realised that he would have to give up so large a tract of territory. (As a matter of fact, it has been stressed throughout, beginning with Dayan's visit to Shuneh on Saturday night, that the King is not so much concerned about territory as about villages, i.e., the potential increase in the number of refugees. It appears that the line finally agreed upon by us last night leaves some 30 villages, including a number of large ones, in our area, and Abdullah Tell thought that the King might be rather appalled when he saw this)" (*M.V.*, pp. 470–71).

On Thursday, March 23, the Israelis went to Shuneh to make it easier for the king to attend. After a sumptuous dinner and exchange of pleasantries in which the king took a leading role and after he had retired at his usual time to go to bed at 9 o'clock, the business of the session began at "nearly 11 o'clock." It concluded with the signing of "the agreement" at 2:00 A.M. (*M.V.*, p. 471).

Eytan rejoiced to Shertok, "In a sense, this agreement is too good to be true," adding, "I shall not believe in its reality completely until I see what happens when the time comes for it to be implemented. It gives us in respect of territory—nearly all of it highly strategic—far more than we should ever have contemplated taking by military action" (*M.V.*, p. 472). Ratification by the prime minister still had to be obtained (*M.V.*, p. 498).

The significance of this Eytan celebration is apparent in all that has already been recorded here: the "good faith" of the Israelis' negotiating strategy, their utter cynicism, their objectives of strategic advantage in contemplation of a future war rather than peace, and the tacit admission that they were prepared to fight for this strategic advantage if it could not be gained in negotiations are all so crucial for what was still the tortured future of Palestine that it merits editorial comment. The duplicity in the conventional negotiations at Rhodes and Bunche's faltering effort to preside over them within the parameters of law inscribed in UN resolutions is apparent in Eytan's final paragraph: "In conclusion I should like to emphasise once again the need for secrecy. We have guaranteed, under Article II, not to publish the agreement, and it is obviously in our interest to get its provisions implemented before they become generally known in the Arab world, where they would be sure to produce an outcry, perhaps on a scale that might make their execution impossible. All the cables I have sent you on this subject have been ciphered by Efrat himself, so that even in the code room the matter is not known" (*M.V.*, p. 472).[23]

Eytan, of course, could not foresee the tragic consequences of this secret diplomacy. It was impossible for Abdallah to cede these territories so cavalierly and still maintain secrecy. Nor could the displacement of Arab Palestinians be forever concealed. Eventual Arab awareness of these humiliations, compounded with Israeli arrogance and attitudes of superiority, destroyed any atmosphere in which the armistice agreements might have been nourished into the enduring and comprehensive peace that was the goal of the United Nations. A hindsight study of the impressive Israeli military and diplomatic victories reveals all of them to have been flawed by short-term perspectives. If indeed—as the Israelis with continued U.S. support still maintain—Israeli policy has always been in the interest of peace and security, those goals could not have been worse served by the back-room maneuvering. The still-lingering aftermath gives a frightening sense of accuracy to the description of the Palestine conflict by the late secretary-general of the United Nations, U Thant, who predicted it might become a new "hundred years war."

Ratification of the agreement by Abdallah's prime minister proved somewhat more complicated than anticipated in Eytan's letter to Shertok on March 24. On April 3 Eytan wrote again to Shertok, in New York, to inform him of specific changes in the final agreement, before ratification of the final document on the thirty-first. But another meeting at Shuneh was necessary for this formal signing, which was accomplished only after "the argument went on right through the night," until 4:00 A.M. Eytan notes that the king "did not go to bed . . . but stayed up till four o'clock in the morning" (*M.V.*, p. 498).

In his April 3 letter, Eytan observed that the Transjordanian delegation at this Shuneh meeting showed "a distinct rise in level" of "rank and individual ability" over the team that had met with the Israelis in the secret negotiations. The textual changes made during this marathon session were material. Some increased the already considerable number of pressure points that would lead, eventually, to obstruct any transition from the armistice agreements to permanent peace. First among these was abandoning the secrecy to which both parties had agreed. The provisions of the amended agreement were to be up front, in the general armistice agreement still in negotiation at Rhodes (*M.V.*, p. 498).

The Transjordanians now insisted on this change. The concern about public opinion in the kingdom and among the other Arab states, should the secret become public property "by leaks," suddenly disappeared. It is possible only to speculate about the reasons. Had the members of the higher-ranking delegation realized that the British and Americans knew about the secret negotiations, although they may not have known all the details? Was the pretense of secrecy therefore no longer credible? Or was there a more sinister motive? Were the more sophisticated Transjordanian negotiators reasoning that if the rest of the Arabs learned the specifics of the agreement, the indignation and resentment would be sufficient to scrap the already concluded armistice agreements with Egypt and Lebanon and, perhaps, lead to a renewal of warfare? Or did the British have a hand in this turnaround? Did they hope, somehow, to begin to undo the process that began with the Balfour Declaration? As early as 1922, the British had already shown clear signs of regretting that ambiguous grant to Zionism. Later British governments were often irritated at growing U.S. influence in an area once regarded as a British preserve.

Neither Israeli nor American documents provide answers to these legitimate questions. The answers might shed light on the wearying persistence of warfare over the same old issues and the deliberate ambiguities with which almost all would-be peacemakers continue to confront them. About all that can responsibly be said at present is that there was enough guilt to be generously portioned out for all parties to these earliest armistice negotiations.

A second alteration made in the final version of the secret agreement left some 32,000 Arabs in villages in the Triangle in Israeli hands. Even Eytan confessed some moral qualms about this (*M. V.*, p. 476). But neither his personal misgivings nor any modification of policy in Tel Aviv sufficed to end the conspiring with which the Israelis and Abdallah's sycophants hoped to finesse both the other Arabs and the United Nations. A final, lengthy paragraph in Eytan's April 3 message is highly instructive of the monarch's mind-set, at least according to Tall. And Eytan apparently raised no objection to an Israeli role in the plot. As he tells the story:

For the sake of record I shall add here a few lines about the conversation we had with Abdullah Tell in the car which took us from Shuneh to Jerusalem in the early hours of March 31st. Abdullah Tell began by saying that he hoped to be the first Transjordanian officer to enter Syria, and that in any case he was due to go to Damascus in a day or two to carry the King's good wishes to Colonel Hossni Zaim. He asked what our attitude would be if the King marched to Damascus and hinted that our air force might play a useful part. Nothing would be easier than to paint our aircraft with the colours and markings of Transjordan. If we were interested, he would be able to let us know in two or three days time whether the King intended to carry out his plans. This provided for the unification of Syria and Transjordan under a single Government, whose seat would be in Damascus. The King would rule from Damascus, while the Prince Talal would remain at Amman as Prince of Transjordan. He hoped we would not take advantage of the King while he was engaged with the bulk of his forces elsewhere, and asked point blank what our attitude would be, to which we replied that we should not interfere. Abdullah Tell said that even if marching into Syria meant killing fellow Arabs, the King would not hesitate. He was anxious to rid himself of the British, and this provided a golden opportunity. (*M. V.*, p. 500)

The Israelis' response was, to say the least, something less than a contribution to peace. As early as March 20, Bunche had informed the Israelis that "the Syrians had agreed to begin the talks on 1 April, and that they wanted to sign a cease-fire agreement before the beginning of the negotiations. Bunche invited the Israeli delegation to Metulla on 1 April and urgently requested: notification of the delegation's composition; a reply to his invitation to negotiations; and an undertaking to clear the Metualla-Marj Ayun road of mines" (*C. V.*, p. 91).

The leak was obviously deliberate. It involved personalities who had been engaged in Abdallah's designs against his fellow Arabs. The episode nourishes suspicions of early Israeli interests in continuing internecine warfare among the Arabs. The Israelis may have speculated that if Abdallah moved quickly, with the armistice and a cease-fire on Transjordan's long border, the Syrians might be an easier negotiating party; or, if Abdallah quickly realized his goals in Syria, the Israelis would have a more compliant opponent. But whatever were the similar or separate motivations of the secret negotiators, Israel's acquiescence—perhaps even collaboration—in Abdallah's plot raises serious questions about the good faith with which Israel began the Syrian negotiations. The suggested deal was hardly a statesmanlike, prudent decision in view of the Zionist state's proclaimed interest in peaceful accommodation with the Arab world.

Refugees and the Erosion of the U.S. Position

Throughout the protracted Transjordanian negotiations the United States gradually altered its position in favor of the facts on the ground. This change really meant support for Israel's fait accompli diplomacy and the flouting of the international consensus expressed in UN resolutions. On March 23, Abdallah had invited the U.S. chargé in Amman to Shuneh to inform him of the developments in these talks (*FRUS* 6 [1949], pp. 798, 859), so the State Department had been aware of the secret negotiations for some time.

On numerous occasions—and as early as February 8, 1949—Israel had informed the United States, directly or through the Conciliation Commission, that it would not agree to repatriation of the refugees (*FRUS* 6 [1949], pp. 709, 737, 761, 855, and passim). Consequently, although the United States continued to support General Assembly Resolution No. 194 (1948) in the United Nations, including the important paragraph 11, its less public diplomacy concentrated on attempting to organize international refugee aid and to "liquidate" the refugee problem through resettlement in the Arab states (*FRUS* 6 [1949], pp. 828–42).[24] The United States was abandoning its commitment to the principle of repatriation, the internationally agreed formula for resolving this crucial issue of the Palestine conflict.

Egypt had raised the refugee problem during its armistice negotiations, and the Arab League had called for a "beginning of a solution of [the] refugee problem as sine qua non of discussions of other questions." But the State Department acquiesced in the Israeli argument that because of "the scale [of] preemption of Arab lands and housing by Jewish immigrants, who are entering Israel at the rate of 23,000 monthly, it would be wholly unrealistic to expect Israel to agree to the repatriation of all those so desiring" (*FRUS* 6 [1949], p. 831). The U.S. shift from the "right to return" to international funding of resettlement and relief programs showed little concern for the human or political rights of these earliest victims of Zionist exclusivism and territorial expansion. The Israelis reinforced—probably inspired—this disregard by asserting that "emotional and moral values should not be taken into consideration in international settlements" (*FRUS* 6 [1949], p. 946).

The State Department's March 15 policy paper stated prophetically that a continuation of the refugee problem might well provide motivation for the overthrow of certain of the Arab governments, would provide "the likeliest channel" for Soviet exploitation, and "would create a permanent source of friction between Israel and the Arab states" (*FRUS* 6 [1949], p. 833). On January 25, 1948, Acting Secretary of State Robert Lovett had sent Secretary of State George Marshall, in Paris, a telegram from Secretary of Defense James Forrestal. In his own words, Forrestal wanted "to advise" Marshall "of the considered views of the

Joint Chiefs of Staff on the urgency of taking definitive action" for "early provision of general assistance to the Arab refugees from Palestine." Forrestal concurred in the advice (*FRUS* 6 [1949], p. 1427). The secretary of defense, on January 25, 1949, in a letter to Congressman Sol Bloom, described the "presence of the refugees in the Near East as a serious threat to the political, economic and social stability of this region, and a serious threat to the health and welfare of the peoples of the Arab states and Israel" (*FRUS* 6 [1949], p. 833, n. 9).

These were expert, professional judgments. But a major obstacle to effective U.S. support for the free choice between repatriation and compensation, recommended in paragraph 11 of Resolution No. 194, was the almost total ignorance of the refugee problem on the part of the American people.

United States Public Attitude toward the Problem

The American public, generally is unaware of the Palestine refugee problem, since it has not been hammered away at by the press or radio. Aside from the *New York Times* and the *Herald Tribune*, which have done more faithful reporting than any other papers, there has been very little coverage of the problem. . . . Wire service stories, if filed, have not been used. Editorial comment is still more sparse. . . . Most of the news articles and editorials have had a friendly slant, except for the *New York Post*, which was violently opposed to helping the Arabs. While some of the articles have addressed . . . the question of . . . repatriation or resettlement, none of them have [*sic*] raised the question of continuing aid. Consequently one may conclude that, barring any dramatic developments which would arouse prejudices or create new issues, a continuing but not spectacular aid program would probably be supported by the enlightened few, and would not, in all likelihood, run into strong opposition. (*FRUS* 6 [1949], p. 838)

No one in the executive branch of the U.S. government had "hammered away" at this refugee problem and its perceived dangers for the United States and peace, either.[25]

Congress had been asked for authorizing legislation for the United States to contribute $16 million to an international fund for relief of the refugees. The appropriate committees in the House and Senate had recommended enactment of the legislation to provide "relief over a limited period of time on the basis that aid was essential to contribute to the peace, settlement and stabilization in the Near East," as the State Department put it. Out of the other side of its mouth, the department "stressed [to the Congress] the General Assembly resolution declaring the right of refugees to return to their homes should be recognized." None the worse for this double-talk, the Senate and the House adopted a joint resolution supporting the U.S. contribution. Bald-facedly, the department's March 15 policy paper notes the equivalent of functional illiteracy prevailing in the Congress: "The only hitch to passage through both houses" occurred in the House Rules Committee, which "postponed action . . . to report the measure because its members, *with one exception, never heard of the Arab refugee problem*" (*FRUS* 6 [1949], p. 839; emphasis supplied).

The March 15 policy paper admits, "It is the present policy of the Arab states to insist upon the re-patriation of all the Palestinian refugees and none of the Arab states with the exception of Transjordan contemplates the *permanent* settlement of any refugees within its own territory" (emphasis supplied). The paper continues, "Active cooperation of the Arab states for any solution to the refugee problem, short of the right to repatriation, could be obtained only with a number of financial and political considerations." Not the least of these was "evidence that Israel was prepared to cooperate effectively in the liquidation of the refugee problem" (*FRUS* 6 [1949], pp. 837–38).

Chronologically, the March 15 policy paper is the last reference in the U.S. records pertaining to the armistice agreements with Egypt, Lebanon, and Transjordan. That paper, however, may be called a watershed in U.S. policy about the Palestine problem. The United States had elected to surrender to Israel on the crucial question of the rights of the displaced Palestinians. The available documents suggest the little-publicized shift had more to do with domestic political considerations and avoidance of political confrontations with Zionists than with the State Department's awareness of the unanimous position of the Arab states or compliance with UN resolutions.

None of the inconsistencies disclosed in the official record prevented the department from stating in the same policy paper that its "present position" was that

We should use our best efforts, through the Conciliation Commission and through diplomatic channels, to insure the implementation of the General Assembly resolution of December 11, 1948;

We should endeavor to persuade Israel to accept the return of those refugees who so desire, in the interests of justice and as an evidence of its desire to establish amicable relations with the Arab world;

We should furnish advice and guidance to the governments of the Arab states in the task of absorbing into their economic and social structures those refugees who do not wish to return to Israel. (*FRUS* 6 [1949], p. 833)

The exact language of these paragraphs is reminiscent of the promise made by the British in the Balfour Declaration. "Best efforts" was also the phrase used then to describe what the British would do to ensure that "nothing shall be done which may prejudice the civil and religious rights" of the indigenous Arabs of Palestine "or the rights and political status enjoyed by Jews in any other country." The State Department's 1949 paper uses the noncommittal "should" rather than the definite "will." The significance will not be missed by semanticists and others who take seriously the importance of words to convey ideas and intentions. The deliberate use of less than precise language suggests that the United States would continue its thinly veiled pro-Israeli partisanship, repeating the tragedy that had already led to the dismemberment of Palestine and the displacement of its indigenous people.

For less than sophisticated observers this formulation of U.S. policy deserves amplification. First, although Egypt—and later Syria—insisted that repatriation of the refugees should be stipulated in the armistice agreements, the United States supported the Israeli contention that the refugee problem belonged in negotiations for a final peace and not in armistice talks. Later, the Israelis were to hold that the refugee problem could be addressed only as part of a *completed* comprehensive peace settlement. U.S. support for this strategy was a clear threat to the recognized inalienable "right of return" of the refugees.

Second, the U.S. government made no consistent, serious "endeavor to persuade Israel to accept the return of those refugees who so desire." Nor is there any published evidence of serious efforts to advise or guide the Arab governments in the "task" of absorbing the refugees who elected not to return. Third, U.S. support for the Israeli formulas for determining armistice lines beyond the borders specified in the partition recommendation increased the numbers of refugees, particularly in the Jaffa, Beersheba, and Triangle areas. Fourth, the emphasis of the March 15 policy paper was on international humanitarian relief for the refugees rather than on their right to return.

Whether all this was part of a cynical, calculated policy to support Israeli expansionism and demographic discrimination or simply ignorance of the long-term Zionist aspirations, going back to Theodor Herzl and Vladimir Jabotinsky, for the largest possible state with a built-in, guaranteed Jewish majority, is not clear from the available evidence. But Israeli policy in 1948–49, easily discernible in the armistice negotiations, should have been recognized by knowledgeable foreign policy officials to be an extension of declared, historic Zionist policy. That it was not recognized as such—or that the declassified, official U.S. documents provide no clue that any U.S. policy makers recognized this history—reflects the superficial knowledge about Zionism prevailing in Washington.

Finally, the March 15 paper indicates a diminution of American interest in the armistice-making process and a shift of attention to the Conciliation Commission. Examination of the records of the commission are beyond the scope of this study. But references in the 1949 volume of *FRUS* indicate that U.S. participation in the Conciliation Commission's work was little, if any, more respectful of international law, or of respect for the Arab sense of injustice than American contributions to the armistice negotiations had been. The frequently expressed disillusionment of Mark Ethridge, the American representative on the Conciliation Commission, is proof of this conclusion (*FRUS* 6 [1949], pp. 880, 936, and passim).[26]

The consistent U.S. acquiescence to Zionist-Israeli demands and flouting of Arab rights stipulated in UN resolutions planted the seeds for the protraction of the Palestine conflict. The continuation of these policies obstructs the prospects for peace. Armed with tacit or overt American support, Israel flouted international law. As a member-state and a charter member of the United Nations, the United States has failed its obligation, under Article 2 (4) of the charter, to "give the United Nations every assistance in any action it takes in accordance with the present Charter, *and shall refrain from giving assistance* to any state against which the United Nations is taking preventive or enforcement action" (emphasis supplied).[27]

With the United States shifting its focus from the Bunche efforts at

Rhodes to the Palestine Conciliation Commission (although on the Syrian front there was not yet a cease-fire, much less an armistice), the UN's expressed hope that the armistices would lead to a permanent peace was dead in the water. Two other U.S. documents support this assessment.

On April 4 Ethridge cabled the Department of State from Beirut "that the Arabs had made a real concession in agreeing to go ahead with peace talks and that 'if Israel would make concession now on refugees we would be on our way' " (*FRUS* 6 [1949], p. 895). Ethridge and the Conciliation Commission had yet to meet with Ben-Gurion to learn the Israeli government's positions on the issues, the resolution of which were indispensable to peace. That meeting was held on April 7 and lasted two and one-half hours. On the ninth, Ethridge sent his report to Acheson (*FRUS* 6 [1949], p. 902ff.).

On March 29, the Israeli cabinet had announced its intention of moving the "Ministries of Health, Education, Religion and Social Welfare and War Sufferers to Jerusalem together with departments of additional ministries." The Jerusalem Committee of the Conciliation Commission concluded that "this constitutes a *fait accompli* and part [of the] process establishing [its] capital [in] Jerusalem." This view was conveyed in writing to Ben-Gurion and to Washington (*FRUS* 6 [1949], p. 883, n. 1).

The atmosphere for the April 7 meeting with the Israeli prime minister was therefore not conducive to much progress. By contrast, at meetings with the Arabs in Beirut, the Conciliation Commission had persuaded them to modify their demands to allow peace talks without prior Israeli commitment to a solution for the refugee question. This major concession was reported to Ben-Gurion by Huseyin Yalcin, the Turkish member of the PCC and its chairman. The PCC had "requested Israel for [a] conciliatory statement on refugees without result. Would Israel now be willing to accept *principle* of repatriation, resettlement and rehabilitation as stated in paragraph 11, GA resolution [194 (III)] December 11th?" (emphasis supplied).

Ben-Gurion simply stonewalled the question of whether Israel would accept the principle of the resolution. He repeated the standard Israeli position that "peace has not yet been achieved and it was not yet clear Arabs wished to live at peace" (*FRUS* 6 [1949], p. 902). In plain language, Israel was insistent that the Arabs agree to peace without any Israeli commitment—even in principle—to meet the UN formula for resolving the refugee problem. Sharett had given Acheson the same answer on April 5. The prime minister's answers to questions about the internationalization of Jerusalem and borders were also almost identical with those Sharett had given Acheson in New York two days earlier.

After this discouraging exploratory meeting of April 7, Ethridge informed President Truman on the eleventh that his optimistic telegram of the fourth no longer represented his personal observations. The text of this April 11 message provides a suitable conclusion—and a sad prophecy—with which to move to the armistice negotiations with Syria and, indeed, to the ensuing years of tragedy: Dear Mr. President, Ethridge wrote, inter alia:

> This is by far the toughest assignment you have ever given to me. The Arabs are shocked and stupefied by their defeat and have great bitterness toward the UN and the United States. The Jews are too close to the blood of their war and their narrow escape, as they regard it, from extinction, and too close to the bitterness of their fight against the British mandate to exercise any degree of statesmanship yet. They still feel too strongly that their security lies in military might instead of in good relations with their neighbors. That is fantastic, of course, for so small a country and I have tried to point out to them that by not making peace quickly they are endangering their own security by stimulating Arab irridentism, and the security of America and the Western World. . . .
>
> The Arabs have made what the Commission considers very great concessions; the Jews have made none so far. I appreciate greatly the help you have given along that line and will of course be grateful if you will keep the pressure up. (*FRUS* 6 [1949], p. 905)

Ethridge concluded with an appeal to the president to persist in support of a refugee program incorporating the free choice offered in the December 11, 1948, resolution, plus generous assistance for the economic development of the Arab states to encourage them to contribute toward the resettlement of the refugees who elected not to return to their homes.

Whether Washington recognized the prophetic character of Ethridge's personal frontline observations, this was the atmosphere in which the State of Israel was born.[28] In a climate permeated with Arab frustration, Israeli arrogance, and studious American duplicity and ambiguity, the armistice negotiations with Syria began.

chapter 9

SCORNING SYRIA

The Coveted Waters

Several important differences appeared between the three concluded armistice negotiations and the one with Syria. First, the political climate had soured. Israel's successes in the earlier negotiations—assisted by American support—had made it confident of achieving more in negotiations than might have been possible in war, as Eytan had boasted to Sharett. And, as Ethridge had reported to Truman, the Arabs were bitter and had little hope for progress toward peace. Second, these attitudinal differences were exacerbated by internal, political disruption in Syria. Just before the start of talks, in a military coup on March 30, the Syrian chief of staff, Colonel Husni al-Zaim,[1] "appointed himself President, Prime Minister, Minister of Foreign Affairs and Minister of the Interior" (*C.V.*, p. 184). The governments with which armistices had been completed were either corrupt (Egypt), weak and corrupt (Lebanon), or duplicitous (Transjordan). But they were established governments. The Syrian coup, however, raised doubts about the authority of the new government, the credentials of Syria's negotiating team, and the durability of any agreements that might be reached (*M.V.*, pp. 516–17). Third, without minimizing the importance that Israelis attached to the Negev, to the Litani River waters, or to Jerusalem and the Triangle, the territory in the northeast, where the military forces of Israel and Syria had fought, had to be discussed in determining the armistice line. It was of particular significance to the putative Zionist state.

The difference in the negotiations with Syria was, therefore, one of a kind. In the three earlier negotiations, it was Israel that had insisted that the armistice lines be where the fighting had stopped. In each the advantage was always to Israel, for its forces were occupying Arab state territory. But the situation in the negotiations with Syria was the reverse. The Syrians were occupying territory that had been allocated to the Jewish state. More than mere acreage was involved. The map and the memorandum that the Zionists had presented to the Paris Peace Conference in 1919 explain the importance Israel attached to the then-Syrian-occupied territory. It included Lake Huleh, the Sea of Galilee, and the headwaters of the Jordan River. To use the language of the 1919 Zionist plan, "The economic life of Palestine . . . depends on the available water supply. It is, therefore, of vital importance not only to secure *all* water resources already feeding the country, but also to conserve *and control them at their sources*" (Hurewitz, p. 48; emphases supplied). The following chronology illuminates the critical importance the Israelis attached to this strip of land.

On March 20, Bunche had informed Shiloah at Rhodes that the Syrians were prepared to "begin talks with Israel." On the thirtieth, the day of the Syrian coup, Bunche advised the Israelis that the Syrians wanted the talks to begin on April 1. The new government, however, began to place conditions on opening the talks. It wanted a cease-fire before beginning negotiations for an armistice, and it wanted "to be among the first to negotiate for a peace." Bunche told the Syrians to prepare to evacuate "the Syrian positions in Palestine." The Syrians "prefer to hold the armistice talks on the Palestine-Syrian border rather than in Rhodes" (*C.V.*, p. 91).

Also on March 30, the Israelis met with Bunche. They gave him Israel's position on locating the armistice line and "pointed out that Israel's main concern was . . . a Syrian withdrawal to the international border." Bunche asked the Israelis' reaction to a "possible proposal" by the Syrians to withdraw from the territory beyond the proposed partition boundaries and to demilitarize "the evacuated area." The Israelis objected "in principle." The new Syrian government requested a "short postponement" of the armistice talks. The Israelis accepted the Syrian suggestion for "the location of the meetings." They informed Bunche that "if no other government recognized the new Syrian regime, Israel might have to postpone the negotiations." Bunche told the Israelis that "he would not pressure Israel to agree to the Syrian demand for . . . a cease-fire before beginning the negotiations," but that if the Syrians insisted, "Israel would have to agree in order to produce a congenial atmosphere for the negotiations." Bunche inquired "whether Israel would agree to a Syrian withdrawal unaccompanied by an Israeli advance." The Israelis refused. Bunche advised them "not to expect quick results in the first meetings and to be patient with the Syrians" (*C. V.*, pp. 91–93).

Bunche appointed Henri Vigier, who had chaired the Israeli-Lebanese negotiations, to supervise those with Syria. The venue for the talks was to be in a no-man's-land near Mishmar Hayarden, in territory occupied by the Syrians but allocated to the Jewish state (*M. V.*, p. 514). This was another Israeli success over the Syrian preference for the recognized Palestine-Syrian border.

The talks began on April 5, 1949. On April 3, Vigier had handed the Israelis "a cease-fire proposal" to be signed by the Syrian army, not the government. Rosenne, who was still at Rhodes, advised Eytan that the Israelis should "refuse to sign and to object to the letter of credentials brought by the Syrians because it is signed by Zaim as Commander-in-Chief of the Syrian armed forces" (*C. V.*, p. 93; *M. V.*, p. 516).

The Israelis were still concerned about gaining admission to the United Nations. On March 3, the Security Council had recommended approval (*C. V.*, p. 185). According to the charter, the General Assembly had still to affirm that decision. Qualifications for membership were that the applicant-state must be found to be "peace-loving" and "accept the obligations" of the Charter and be "able and willing to carry out these obligations."

On April 6, the UN secretary-general told Eban of his "grave concern" about Israeli "troop movements" on the Syrian frontier. The Israeli UN delegation was apprehensive because Bunche had certified that Israeli forces had crossed the frontier. Eban urgently contacted Eytan in Tel Aviv, advising him that Sharett was "utterly shocked [at the] irresponsibility" and was "awaiting [Eytan's] full explanation and measures to correct" (*M. V.*, p. 521).

That same day, Eytan confirmed that Israeli troops had "occupied two points Syria yesterday, one unnoticed, other causing row." Bunche was "very excited" and "threatens [to] report [to the] Security Council, blaming us for any fighting that may ensue." Eytan added that there was no sign of any fighting at "the present," but the U.S. ambassador, McDonald, and the U.S. military attaché were "also on [the] warpath" (*M. V.*, p. 521).

This generated another message from Sharett in New York to Eytan. The foreign minister said if the Israelis were to continue to work for admission to the UN, he "cannot tolerate such self-defeating tactics," adding ominously that he was "certainly not prepared to carry on both." The "both" apparently referred to a defense of the Israeli aggression and lobbying for admission (*M.V.*, p. 522). The alarms from New York appear to have made only minor tremors in Tel Aviv.

On April 6, Rosenne, in Tel Aviv, informed the delegation in New York and Eliahu Sasson in Paris that, at the first meeting with the Syrians, the Israelis had objected to signing the cease-fire agreement. Whether this was related to the Israelis' aggression at the Syrian frontier is not clear. The Israelis maintained the demand that Syria withdraw to the international frontiers. Vigier reminded the Israelis that cease-fire agreements had preceded all the previous armistice negotiations. The Israeli reasoning and rationale for "hanging tough" with the Syrians reflect the general attitude with which they approached the substantive negotiations. This, from the official summary of Rosenne's April 6 telegram to New York and Paris:

> The Israeli representatives argued that the Syrians were different from the other Arab nations and Israel feared that once a cease-fire agreement was signed, the Syrians would discontinue the armistice negotiations. . . .
>
> The delegation's instructions were to refuse to sign a cease-fire agreement as long as it could do so without damaging Israel's standing prior to the voting on its admission to the UN. The argument about the powers of the Syrian delegation was intended to gain time pending clarification of Israel's status in the UN and of the future of the new government in Syria. Since Vigier and Riley were urging the Israeli representatives to sign the cease-fire—they had even threatened them with an appeal to the Security Council—the delegation proposed that the next meeting discuss a non-aggression declaration, similar to that which appeared in the first article of the armistice agreements with Egypt, Lebanon and Jordan. The Syrians promised to reply at the next meeting. (*C.V.*, pp. 93–94)

In fact, this next meeting never took place because the Syrians did not show up. They "were not sure Israel had completed the evacuation of the recently occupied territory." The real issue was that the Syrians were still insisting on a cease-fire agreement while Israel was equally insistent on refusal "unless the Syrians agreed to withdraw to the international border." The Israeli documents, however, note that the refusal this time "was couched in milder terms in order to prevent the Mediator from submitting a censorious report to the Security Council before the General Assembly vote on Israel's admission to the UN." The Syrians continued to insist that "the present fighting line" should be the armistice line, leaving Syria in occupation of territory that partition had assigned to the Jewish state. Rosenne, in Tel Aviv, informed the delegation in New York and Sasson, in Paris, that "negotiations with the Syrians will be difficult and that there is little hope of agreement on the delineation of the armistice lines" (*C. V.*, pp. 94–95). Whether the Syrians' insistence on occupation of Jewish state territory was in reprisal for the Israeli occupation of Arab state territory in the Egyptian and Jordanian negotiations is not clear.

Foreign Relations of the United States (6 [1949], pp. 918–19) reports for April 16 that Bunche notified the Security Council on April 13 that Israel and Syria had signed "identical declarations" that were tantamount to a cease-fire. The Israeli documents contain no reference to this action. Both declarations stated the issuing party "accepts and confirms" the July 15, 1948, Security Council resolution, "which forbids any recourse to military force of any form" and "obligates the interested parties to grant every facility to United Nations observers . . . to allow them to ensure a complete and effective supervision of the cease-fire." The way was now cleared for the next meeting in no-man's-land on April 21 to address the substantive issues of an armistice.

At Vigier's invitation the Syrians opened the meeting by stating their goal was "consecration of the decision of the Security Council on 15 July 1948." They then offered the narrowest possible interpretation of the Security Council resolution of November 16, 1948. The present negotiations, they asserted, should be "limited to consideration of military questions," to create "mutual security between the forces of both sides" and to prevent "all contacts between those forces" to "prevent accidents." They argued these principles could be implemented "by the submission of both parties to the resolution of the Security Council," which would "prevent either of the parties from having at its disposal any means for threatening the other party." Avoiding potentially dangerous contacts could be realized by the "drawing of armistice demarcation lines" (*M. V.*, pp. 528–29). With this statement of the obvious—and no provisions for procedural details—the conciliatory atmosphere evaporated. The Syrians also presented a map proposing each party "shall return to the position held by it on 17 July 1948 at 1800 hours" (*M. V.*, p. 530).

Rosenne replied immediately that Israel was not "buying." Picking and choosing among UN resolutions, he mentioned the one adopted by the Security Council on November 16, adding, "We are concerned with that resolution alone." He then explained "the only criterion we admit for the establishment of armistice demarcation lines, except where special circumstances exist, is the re-establishment of the international frontier." He did not explain whether by "the international frontier" he meant the partition-recommended boundaries or the historic boundaries of Palestine. He argued that where Egypt and Transjordan were concerned, there were "deviations" from the international frontier because "special circumstances" existed. "I am unable," he added, "to see how the Syrian delegation is following any equitable principle whatsoever when it puts forward a proposal which is not based on the principle of the international frontier. I cannot see what considerations of equity can be brought to justify a Syrian advance beyond the international frontier" (*M. V.*, p. 532).

Rosenne then proceeded rather pedantically to lecture the Syrians on the difference between an armistice and a truce: "I would like to remind the Syrian delegation that the main purpose of an armistice, and this is how it differs from a truce, is the establishment of a permanent demarcation line." The definition was self-serving as it reinforced the Israeli argument that the armistice line and the international border were immutably synonymous terms. This rigidity was inconsistent with a standard clause in all the armistice agreements that "rights, claims, or interests of a non-military character . . . may be asserted by either Party" and these, "by mutual agreement being *excluded* from the armistice negotiations, shall be, at the discretion of the Parties, the subject of later settlements" (*M. V.*, p. 690).

The Israelis were pressing a legal claim legitimated in the partition recommendation. But by the accepted terms of reference for the armistice negotiations, that claim belonged in negotiations for a permanent peace, if and when they would be held. The Syrians were attempting a tactical maneuver to position themselves better in the armistice talks.

They also had the precedents of the Israeli demands in the Egyptian and Transjordanian armistice talks for basing the armistice lines where the fighting had been stopped. The Syrians may also have thought that if they prevailed in establishing the armistice line at the fighting line, they could move the border to their advantage in any final peace negotiations.

The territory in this dispute was of vital importance to Israel because of the water resources that had been noted in the 1919 Zionist memorandum. Rosenne cleverly did not continue with more strategic or tactical fencing. He resorted instead to historic precedent and to some implied appeal to international law—a departure from Israeli strategy in the previous armistice talks in which the Israelis had argued vigorously for denigrating whatever law was acknowledged to be inscribed in UN resolutions. So, Rosenne continued, "The international frontier is the only permanent line which has ever existed between Syria and Palestine so long as those two countries had a political existence, i.e., the frontier existing since the end of the First World War. There is no other line. When in November 1947 the General Assembly made its proposals regarding the future of Palestine, it based its proposals so far as this part of the country was concerned on the international frontier" (*M.V.*, p. 532). Further stressing the point, he added what amounted to an ultimatum:

> I am now going to make a statement which reflects the considered view of the Government of Israel. . . . [I]t was conveyed to me yesterday. The Government of Israel gave this delegation firm instructions, *from which it will not deviate at all.* The only demarcation line which is to be inserted into an armistice agreement is the international frontier. That is to say that all forces of one country found to be over the international frontier as it was existing on 14 May 1948 are to be withdrawn to that international frontier. That being so and having regard to what has been discussed here during the recent weeks, my delegation feels that it would not serve any useful purpose in taking this proposal back to our Government in Tel Aviv. (*M.V.*, p. 532; emphasis supplied)

And in the unlikely event anyone was still uncertain of the Israeli position, Colonel Mordechai Makleff, head of the delegation, weighed in with "the position just stated by Mr. Rosenne is a rigid position. *This is*

*not a position for bargaining, it is the last word of the Israeli delega-
tion"* (*M. V.*, pp. 531–32; emphasis supplied).

Recognizing the impasse, Vigier suggested the Syrians might want
to postpone further discussion until the next meeting. But Mr. Tarazi,
legal advisor to the Syrians, felt the Israelis had oversold or, at least,
overargued the point. Ignoring the geographic specifics of the partition
recommendation and implying possible Syrian rejection of partition in
its entirety, Tarazi adroitly tried to play the Israeli game of showing
respect for UN resolutions that were advantageous to Syria and ignoring
those that favored Israel. He put it this way:

> It is understood that the armistice negotiations are strictly lim-
> ited to military questions. In military conversations there is no
> room for questions of international law or international frontiers.
> The demarcation of armistice lines is based on military considera-
> tions and cannot depend on political considerations. When the
> Israeli delegation asks us to go back to the international frontier, it
> is because it considers that such a frontier must exist between us.
> Consequently, and since the resolution adopted by the General
> Assembly on 29 November 1947 has been quoted by Mr. Rosenne,
> it means that he wishes to take this resolution as a basis for discus-
> sions and that he considers that, in order to begin these armistice
> negotiations, it is necessary to take the partition plan as a starting
> point.
>
> Consequently, I would like to ask two precise questions and I
> hope that Mr. Rosenne or Colonel Makleff will give the Syrian
> delegation answer[s]. (*M. V.*, p. 533)

Tarazi then invited the Israelis to make his point for him by answer-
ing his questions:

> (1) Does the Israeli delegation consider itself bound by the parti-
> tion plan and [therefore] puts as a condition the return to the politi-
> cal frontier? If the Israeli delegation considers itself bound by the
> partition plan, we do not see why the Israeli forces are stationed in
> certain parts of Palestine, for instance [w]estern Galilee, not to
> mention other sectors.
>
> (2) If the Israeli delegation does not consider itself bound by the
> partition plan, we do not see any connection between the reference

which the Israeli delegation has just made to the political frontier and the armistice talks.

On the other hand, Colonel Makleff said that the position stated by Mr. Rosenne was a rigid position which did not permit bargaining. [This] apparently [means] the Israeli delegation does not wish to reconsider its position, and the situation as regards the armistice talks seems to be difficult. (*M.V.*, pp. 532–33)

But Rosenne was not so easily trapped. Having tried and failed to make his stand on the partition recommendation, Rosenne retreated. He now declared the recommendation was irrelevant in the present situation. And yet, perhaps not quite. If the Syrians thought the partition recommendation supported their present position, the place for adjudication was the General Assembly or the Security Council or—most interesting of all—with the Arabs of Palestine: "The questions just asked are entirely irrelevant. Any question about the present validity of the partition resolution of 29 November 1947 might concern the relations of Israel with the General Assembly or the Security Council or be a matter of discussion with the Arabs of Palestine. It is not a matter of discussion for any foreign State *per se;* those questions have to be raised at the General Assembly" (*M.V.*, p. 533).

Considering the territories beyond the partition boundaries occupied by Israel and claimed as necessary to security, it would have been difficult for them, in any general UN debate, to demonstrate clean hands in their contention with Syria. But the strangest alternative Rosenne suggested was "the Arabs of Palestine." Was this a preview of contemporary statesmen of the United States and Israel who are still looking for Palestinian Uncle Toms to sanctify some scheme or other for betraying *some* Palestinians while foreclosing Palestinian *national* claims for a sovereignty and self-determination on their native soil?

Rosenne ignored the double standard Israel had pursued in negotiating the previous armistices and shifted to the language of self-righteousness that has become a familiar ingredient of Israeli diplomacy in following years. With only slightly concealed contempt he went on: "Therefore, I do not propose to go into any discussion concerning the resolution of 29 November 1947. I want to know on what right, moral, legal, political or otherwise, the Syrian forces have advanced beyond the international border of Syria. Whatever happened inside of Palestine does not give right to Syria to be across its border. If the Syrian delegation does not like the date of 29 November 1947, we can recall that of 14 May 1948 or even go further back, at the end of the European War in 1945" (*M. V.*, p. 533).

Conveniently ignoring the Israeli occupation of western Galilee and Israel's rejection of Bunche's original proposal to bring all of the Arab states and Israel together to negotiate armistices and then to proceed to negotiations for a comprehensive peace, Rosenne finally advised the Syrians that if they were "quite serious in raising any question about Galilee, I would suggest that its correct addressee is not the Government of Israel but the Government of any Arab State which has come to an agreement with Israel concerning Galilee" (*M. V.*, p. 533). Tarazi broke the impasse, saying, "Our negotiations can continue, but no delegation should take a rigid standpoint which proceeds from purely political considerations" (*M. V.*, p. 534).

Rosenne, still mindful of the vote on Israel's UN membership, suddenly discovered that instructions from Tel Aviv had not been as immutable as he and Makleff had first represented them to be. The "formal proposal of our Government," he confessed, "regarding armistice demarcation lines does not appear in our written document." But the written document to be submitted to the Syrians did read, "Armistice demarcation lines shall follow the international boundary between Syria and Palestine." He also said that Israel agreed the demarcation lines are "a military matter" and the Israeli proposal "will be a provisional measure." This clarification closed the gap between the two parties. He added, however, "that this delegation will not sign an armistice agreement which leaves Syrian troops on the Palestine side of the border which formally existed between Palestine and Syria" (*M. V.*, p. 534).

This review of the substance of the April 21 meeting is warranted because, in many ways, it is typical not only of Israeli techniques in these armistice negotiations but of their strategy in subsequent years. It was not—and is not—a unique strategy. The Israelis had doggedly adhered to Eytan's recommendation in the Egyptians talks to wear down their Arab adversaries. Rosenne followed the same tactic as the Syrian talks began. The Israelis' legal position, vis-à-vis the Syrians, was probably stronger than it had been with the earlier Arab states, for Syrian forces were occupying Jewish state territory. In addition, the Israelis felt the internal governmental weakness in the new Syrian government could be exploited. Thus, as the talks began, the Israelis were obviously probing the extent of the weakness by adopting a rigid, arrogant, and even scornful attitude. They attempted to steer the armistice negotiations into geopolitical issues that properly belonged on the agenda for final peace negotiations.

Despite their internal turmoil, the Syrians presented a more determined and better informed resistance than had been offered by the other Arab states. And, to avoid embarrassment in Israel's campaign for admission to the United Nations, Rosenne conceded that the armistice negotiations should be confined to purely military matters. In short, Israel yielded a tactical matter to further an important policy objective, and they did so without surrendering the commitment that the international border be accepted as the armistice line.

This sophisticated differentiation between tactics and strategy, on the one hand, and long-range objectives involving vital interests to Israel, on the other, dictated the methods by which the Israelis added "dunam to dunam" for consistent territorial expansion. With the same tactics and strategy Israel established on the ground facts, gradually eroding the viability of the Palestinians' right to return and denying them territory in which Palestinian self-determination and sovereignty might be exercised.

The Long Way from Mishmar Hayarden to Lausanne: Between Armistice and Peace

The narrative of the negotiations must be interrupted at this point to note that early in April, under the authority of the Palestine Conciliation Commission, talks had been convened at Lausanne, Switzerland, intended to move beyond the armistices to the issues involved in a final peace settlement.[2] The Lausanne discussions are not an integral part of the armistice negotiations. But the convening of the belligerent Arab states and Israel was a development that, because of world opinion, none of the belligerents could ignore. As the frustrating armistice discussions continued, both sides used that fact whenever it was to their advantage.

The Israelis and Syrians had agreed the armistice talks should be limited to military considerations. Vigier closed the April 21 meeting, cautioning that "the armistice agreement must be negotiated" and "political questions should be referred to Lausanne" (*M. V.*, p. 535). But this was easier said than done. On the twenty-seventh, Eytan sent Paul Mohn, Bunche's personal representative, a lengthy letter from Sharett, complaining that "the Government of Israel is much concerned at the course taken by the armistice negotiations with Syria. It has unfortunately become clear that the Syrian Government is unwilling to agree to the withdrawal of its forces occupying Israeli territory." Sharett noted that in the Lebanese negotiations Bunche had given strong support to Lebanese demands for Israeli withdrawal to the international border. Israel continued to occupy western Galilee, which partition had designated as Arab state territory. Sharett, therefore, may have had this in mind when he added, "The Government of Israel hopes the principle will receive equally strong support now, although its principle may not be convenient to the Government of Syria" (*M.V.*, pp. 536ff.).

Sharett also complained that Syria intended to mobilize 20,000 additional troops immediately. According to Sharett, the explanation was that Syria felt that "a dangerous situation exists on the frontier between Syria and Transjordan." In light of Eytan's April 3 report to Sharett about Abdallah's plot to march on Damascus with possible support of the Israeli air force, Sharett's official irritation with the reported Syrian mobilization to defend its border with Transjordan appears a bit theatrical. To Bunche he confided that the Israelis thought the Syrian explanation "may be merely a cover for new aggressive action contemplated against Israel," and he protested that the mobilization was "a serious violation of the terms of the truce" (*M.V.*, p. 537).

"Under these circumstances," Sharett concluded, "the Government of Israel sees little profit in discussing a final settlement with the Syrian delegation at Lausanne." As long as the Syrian government refuses "to accept the political boundary as the armistice demarcation line, the Israeli delegation to the Conference at Lausanne will be instructed not to enter into conversations, formal or informal, with the representatives of Syria" (*M.V.*, pp. 537–38).

That same day, Sharett advised Eban at the United Nations that the negotiations with Syria had "reached virtual deadlock." He informed Eban that from Lake Huleh northward the Syrians had "agreed [to] restore [the] international boundary." But in the rest of the territory they occupied they were "insisting [upon the] waterline" as the armistice line. It is not clear whether Sharett's concern was that Syrian interest in access to the waters of Lakes Huleh and Tiberias (Sea of Galilee) and the tributaries of the Jordan was for themselves, or if they were trying to deprive Israel of these water resources that the Zionist proposals at the Paris Peace Conference had identified as critically important to their then-proposed Jewish state. In a postscript, Sharett added to Eban that General Riley had said that the "Syrians [were] aiming [at] permanent change [in the] frontier" (*M. V.*, p. 539).

On April 28, Eban reported that Bunche, for the first time, had proposed for "both northern southern sectors" of the disputed territory a "demilitarized strip and zones for defensive forces only on either side" (*M. V.*, p. 539).[3] Also on the twenty-eighth, the Israelis discussed the impasse with the U.S. delegation at the United Nations. John Ross, deputy to the U.S. representative, told the Israelis that the United States thought Bunche's proposal was "reasonable, acceptable" and added that the United States was not "ready to press" the Syrians "so shortly after recognition" of the new government (*M. V.*, p. 540). When Sharett was informed of this American position, he instructed Elath in Washington, "We must turn tables on State Department's view" that the time was inopportune to "pressure Syria" (*M. V.*, p. 543).

Elath saw the State Department's director of the Office of Near Eastern and African Affairs, Joseph Satterthwaite, on May 3. From the Israeli viewpoint, the conversation was less than satisfactory. Elath advised Sharett that Satterthwaite had told him that "Zaim [was] interested in reaching [a] settlement" but was "anxious" to show his people some gains. But no encouragement was offered the Israelis about the placement of the armistice line or the Syrian occupation of Jewish state territory. Elath could only "strongly underline" Israeli "demands for complete Syrian evacuation [of] Israeli territory" and reiterate the Israeli refusal to negotiate with Syria at Lausanne until an armistice was signed (*M. V.*, p. 546).

Foreign Relations of the United States suggests that the rather cool reception given Elath at this May 3 meeting represented a modest alteration in American strategy. Neither U.S. nor Israeli documents explain this apparent shift. But it is important historically—and may help explain American policy making in the succeeding years—to speculate on the reasons, mindful that no hard, documented evidence is available.

Probably, a major consideration was that by the time attention focused on the Syrian negotiations, the 1948 presidential election was over. This facilitated the State Department's assertion of policy-making leadership, reducing the influence of Truman's White House political advisors Clifford, Niles, and Josephus Daniels.[4] The department's professionals had consistently opposed the imposition of the Zionist political formula on the indigenous Palestinians. They were concerned about

American access to Middle East oil and the possibility the Soviet Union would exploit the Arab hostility that American support for Jewish statehood was certain to arouse.[5]

A second factor was the department's optimism that a final settlement might be reached in the Lausanne meetings. U.S. interest in the narrower objectives of the armistice negotiations gradually became desultory. The Americans wanted to dispose of these as expeditiously as possible so as to move on to the substantive business of a final peace. The less-than-adequate attention paid to some territorial and technical military details of the armistices produced no profound soul-searching among the American diplomats, although they had been consulted frequently by the Israelis and occasionally by Arab ambassadors. Each armistice agreement contained the provision that the armistice lines were without prejudice to claims that the several parties might advance in final peace negotiations. That diplomatic "safe-house," however, was now threatened—together with the peace process itself—by the intransigence of the Syrians and the Israeli ultimatum refusing any talk with the Syrians at Lausanne while Syrian troops continued to occupy Jewish state territory. There was, therefore, a sense of urgency among the State Department's professionals to break the deadlock, to bring the Syrians and Israelis to Lausanne, and, together with the other three confrontation states, to proceed to a comprehensive peace (*FRUS* 6 [1949], p. 957, particularly n. 2).

There were also—most important—some political facts influencing the modest shift of U.S. policy. They are part of the history of the protracted Palestine problem but have had little exposure to the public, still often confused about the fundamental issues. This record and analysis of the attitudes with which the parties to the armistice negotiations began efforts to resolve the problem by diplomacy would be incomplete without some value judgments about these fundamentals. They remain unaddressed and unresolved, continuing to nourish hostility and distrust and obstructing even promising approaches to a settlement.

One difference between the United States and Israel was the paramount importance of General Assembly Resolution No. 194 (III) of December 11, 1948, particularly paragraph 11 calling for a free choice for the refugees between repatriation and compensation. The United States had been emphasizing formulas that would require the Arab states to contribute to the "resettlement of those not desiring (or permitted) to return [to] Israel"/Palestine. In a telegram sent on April 29 to Saudi Arabia, Egypt, Iraq, Syria, Lebanon, and Transjordan, as well as to London and Israel, Acheson said that the U.S. government

> continues support principle of *repatriation* of refugees so desiring in accordance GA res of Dec. 11. On Apr 5 Secy made strong representations to Israeli Fon Min [foreign minister] re Pres' [Truman] conviction of necessity for early Israeli agreement to *repatriation*; Pres on Apr 25 took occasion Weizmann's visit to press him *repatriation*; Secy made similar approach to Israeli Amb Apr 26. USG will continue use best efforts vis-à-vis Israel this regard. However, USG is in full agreement with PCC's second progress report to UN, which emphasizes likelihood that not all refugees will decide return to their homes and consequent necessity obtaining agreement in principle by Arab states to *resettlement* those not desiring repatriation.
>
> Unrealistic and intransigent attitude of both Israel and Arab states re agreement to repatriation and resettlement, respectively, of Arab refugees has created problem of serious concern to USG and major obstacle to PCC's task of implementing Dec 11 res with respect to refugees. Coincidental with PCC meetings Lausanne, Dept considers it essential that strongest diplomatic approach be made to both sides in endeavor to soften their respective attitudes this question and to support PCC in its task. (*FRUS* 6 [1949], p. 959; emphasis supplied)

The United States, Acheson continued, "considers both Israel and Arab states have significant responsibility for cooperating with PCC in obtaining agreed settlement this problem, and avoid its perpetuation as threat to peace, stability and development of all Near Eastern states" (*FRUS* 6 [1949], pp. 959–60).

On the same day, April 29, President Truman sent a personal letter to Mark Ethridge.

> Dear Mark: I appreciated very much your letter of the eleventh and I was particularly interested in the attitude of the Arabs with regard to the present situation.
>
> I am rather disgusted with the manner in which the Jews are approaching the refugee problem. I told the President of Israel in

the presence of his Ambassador just exactly what I thought about it. It may have some effect, I hope so. (*FRUS* 6 [1949], p. 957)

Obviously, the United States was waffling on the issue. Sharett had made it clear that Israel was opposed to repatriation in any degree that would threaten a Jewish majority in territory that it might eventually govern. The American efforts to persuade the Arab states to agree to resettlement plans, however, provided the leaders of Israel with an escape hatch.

The Arabs, for their part, saw any surrender of the *right* of Palestinian repatriation as tacit endorsement not only of territory loss but as acquiescence in Zionist-exclusivist, anti-Arab policies. They were being asked to recognize with friendly terms a neighbor-state with an active policy of denying Arab fundamental rights. Territorial compromise was something with which the Arabs might live. But yielding territory on which "brother Arabs" would suffer official degradation of their rights was another matter.[6]

A Syrian Peace Proposal

The sudden flurry of U.S. policy makers—including the president's personal intervention and his revelation of displeasure with the Jews—may be partially explained by a cable, dated April 28, from James Keeley, U.S. minister in Damascus, to Acheson (*FRUS* 6 [1949], p. 962, n. 3). The message is of sufficient importance to warrant full reproduction:

> [Syrian Prime Minister Zaim had] intimated willingness as part general settlement including realistic frontier adjustments accept quarter million refugees if given substantial development aid in addition to compensation for refugee losses.
>
> [The Prime Minister] reiterated his earnest desire to liquidate Palestine debacle by pursuing henceforth policy of give and take provided he not asked to give all while other side takes all. [It concluded that there was a] real opportunity for rapid settlement of Palestine problem if only US Government will exert itself to bring Israelis to face situation realistically and in spirit of fair compromise.[7]

On April 29 Acheson sent an identical telegram to most U.S. diplomats in the Arab world, including Keeley in Damascus and presumably the consul in Jerusalem. The American diplomats were ordered to inform the governments to which they were posted that the "unrealistic and intransigent attitude of both Israel and Arab states re agreement to repatriation of Arab refugees has created problems of serious concern to U.S.G. and [a] major obstacle to the Conciliation Commission's task of implementing the December 11 resolution with respect to refugees" (*FRUS* 6 [1949], p. 959).

Acheson instructed his diplomats to make the "strongest diplomatic approach to both sides" and added that the United States was asking the British to make "a similar approach to Arabs." The secretary added that on April 5 he had made "strong representations" to Sharett, informing him of Truman's "conviction of [the] necessity for early Israeli agreement to repatriation" and that on April 25, Truman, personally, had pressed Weizmann "on repatriation." Acheson, however, did not inform his colleagues in foreign posts of the generally negative reaction of Sharett or of Weizmann's vague and noncommittal response to the president (*FRUS* 6 [1949], p. 959).

On May 2, Keeley cabled Acheson again. The most important item was reiteration of Zaim's offer to resettle refugees, adding some conditions for which Zaim requested consideration. Keeley reported that Zaim was responding to Keeley's relay to him of Acheson's instructions in his round-robin message of April 29. The Syrian reminded Keeley that

> several days ago he had expressed his desire speed solution Palestine problem and had stated his willingness to accept as part comprehensive settlement of Palestine conflict quarter million or more Arab refugees for resettlement provided they are compensated for their losses and Syria is given adequate financial aid necessary to resettle them. He reiterated his sincere desire for prompt agreement with Israel and his willingness to enter direct negotiations with Israel to that end. . . . As Syria, Transjordan and Egypt are Arab states most directly concerned in Palestine problem, he is willing meet with Abdallah and [King] Farouk in effort to reach common basis for realistic approach to Israel.

> He emphasized that unless Israel also manifests spirit of compromise stalemate will continue since Arab states cannot be expected to make all the concessions.

> He laughed at Sharett's fear that mobilization 20,000 recruits

could be immediate threat to Israel. Call up is internal measure to take potential trouble makers off streets. . . . Israel has, he added, nothing to fear from Syria if it comes to reasonable terms. (*FRUS* 6 [1949], pp. 965–66)

Acheson's telegram of April 29 also brought replies from Cairo and Beirut. Cairo responded that the Egyptian prime minister insisted the principle of repatriation should be reaffirmed by all participating in the "Lausanne conversation; Zionists in particular." Once "the principle of repatriation shall have been established as basis of conversations," the prime minister believed all the Arab states "would at once get down to [the] study of practical aspects of the problem." The Lebanese response was realistic, considering the country's internal problem, but less encouraging for the peace conversations at Lausanne. The "Minister" told the American chargé that Lebanon "is already overpopulated and is organized on confessional lines so delicately balanced that acceptance [of the proposal for] permanent settlement any refugees . . . would be impossible" (*FRUS* 6 [1949], p. 966 n. 2).

No longer harassed by White House interference or domestic concerns about the election, and with indications of some possible cooperation by the major Arab adversaries, the U.S. shift of focus from the armistices to the peace negotiations at Lausanne becomes understandable. The dispute over placement of the armistice line in the Syrian theater assumed less importance in Washington. And the State Department was encouraged to resist the Israeli demand to pressure Syria.

The Israelis were surprised. Their confidence in consistent American support was shaken. They were confused by the Syrian offer to move quickly to the substantive issues of peace. Their response was to stall for time. The only complication was their application for UN membership. To expedite the General Assembly vote and ensure active American support, Elath and Eban had had a long session with Acheson on April 26. The secretary offered less than certain reassurance. In a "Memorandum of Conversation" dated April 26, he recorded:

I said that I felt that the Israeli Government itself was in a much better position to facilitate its entrance into the UN than we were. I recalled that I had suggested to President Weizmann at the White House luncheon yesterday that if Israel would only make some conciliatory gesture or statement along the lines that we have suggested, we would then have some basis on which to talk to the other nations in the General Assembly.

Frankly, I continued, I had been very disappointed in my failure to obtain any results from the two long talks I had with Mr. Sharett. Not only had my suggestions not been acted upon but in some ways it seemed that we were farther away from a solution than when I had talked with Mr. Sharett. The three questions, in order of importance, which appeared to call for some explanation by the Israeli Government were the refugees, Jerusalem and the boundaries.

With reference to the refugees, I had never suggested that Israel accept a specified number now. I had only suggested to Mr. Sharett that Israel first announce that it would accept the principle of repatriation. Next, at least half of the refugees had come from areas outside the Israeli boundaries fixed by the UN Resolution which were [now?] under Israeli military occupation. Surely it should be possible to allow a good number of such refugees to return to non-strategic areas. . . . [W]hen the final peace settlement had been reached, or shortly before, it should be possible to determine the exact number which could be repatriated. Mr. Sharett, in spite of my two talks with him, had flatly rejected this thesis and had even gone so far, when I had suggested the emotional and moral values that my proposals might have, as to suggest that *such values should not be taken into consideration in international settlements.* . . . [But they were an important part of Israel's campaign. Au. note.]

As to the boundaries, I was disappointed to learn from Mr. Ethridge's telegrams that Mr. Ben-Gurion was apparently adamant in clinging to the view that *Israel was entitled not only to the territory allowed it by the UNGA* [General Assembly] *resolution but to all the rest of the territory it occupied militarily.* Since, in writing at least, I understood the Government of Israel to accept the position that it was willing to negotiate on the basis of the November 29, 1947 resolution, it seemed to me that this was a very unwise position to take. . . .

The U.S. had supported Israel's application for membership and would continue to do so. Unless, however, the Israeli Government were willing to make its position known on these important issues, it would be difficult for the U.S. Delegation to go to the other nations at Lake Success and endeavor to persuade them that they should also vote for Israel's admission at this session. (*FRUS* 6 [1949], pp. 945–46; emphasis supplied)

The American Embassy in Tel Aviv was informed of the substance of Acheson's remarks and instructed to emphasize them to Israel's prime minister and foreign minister "in the strongest terms" (*FRUS* 6 [1949], p. 967, n. 2).

The next meeting of the Israeli and Syrian delegations discussing the armistice did not take place until May 10. Vigier began with a statement reflecting the discouraging trend of the discussions. "Unfortunately," he concluded, "we must also envisage a possible failure." But he hastened to add that "in that case . . . a report will be submitted to the Security Council by Dr. Bunche" (*M.V.*, p. 551).

The Syrians then presented a detailed proposal, complete with a map that, they explained, took into account "several military considerations" that, in the spirit of the Security Council resolution, "would prevent all contact between the forces of the two parties." It would also, they asserted, in contrast to Sharett's dismissal above, "respect the national feelings of both sides," and, in addition to these military considerations, it would "give all possible guarantees to the two parties for the safeguard of their respective rights, interests, claims and position" (*M.V.*, p. 552). The proposal provided detailed suggestions for drawing the demarcation line but added a new idea: the precise line would be drawn "on the spot" by "a mixed sub-commission" of Israelis and Syrians. A no-man's-land would separate reduced forces of both sides, with the mixed subcommission determining "on the spot the strength of forces and the places where they would be stationed" (*M.V.*, p. 556).

A final item was a political-territorial problem that was of greater importance to the Syrians.

A last point would be the demilitarisation of Western Galilee under United Nations supervision. The military occupation of this area constitutes, I shall not say a threat, but a rupture in the equilibrium between the forces of the two parties, and renders possible a concentration of troops, which the other party might consider as a possible threat to its security. As that area would be placed under United Nations supervision until a final peace settlement is concluded, there would, I think, be no prejudice to the rights of the party occupying it at present [Israel]. I would like to repeat that the establishment of demarcation lines which would have to be delineated on the spot would be without prejudice to the rights, position, interests and claims of the parties. (*M.V.*, p. 553)

The question of western Galilee belonged more logically in the negotiations with Lebanon. But there can be little doubt that the Syrian attempt to make it an item in *their* negotiations was more complicated than the military considerations that they had been arguing should be the only subject of armistice negotiations.

Western Galilee was, first of all, one of Israel's most extensive expansions into Arab state territory measured by the partition formula. Second, it was heavily populated by Arabs. Third, although the armistice line had been established at the international Lebanese-Palestine border, the Syrians may have been aware of the 1919 Zionist blueprint that anticipated the Litani River as a part of the water system of the Jewish state. They could well have reasoned that the Galilee was a good strategic base from which Israel could later advance on the coveted water source. If Syria could create doubts about the legitimacy of Israeli claims to the Galilee, they might set a precedent for challenging Israeli claims to the territories beyond the partition boundaries occupied by the Israelis after the armistices with Egypt and Transjordan had been signed. And, finally, they might establish a rationale for their own continued occupation of the territory they were holding in the Jewish state partition boundary.

Whatever the Syrians had in mind, the Israelis refused the bait. A detailed Israeli interrogation of the Syrians followed. The objective was to clarify where the armistice lines would be drawn and what rights might be reserved in some of the disputed territory for the Israelis. Three of these questions appear to have had special significance. Would "normal civilian life" be permitted inside the so-called no-man's-land? "Are the Israelis going to be allowed to live and work there?" And "Who is going to have the right to fish" in Lake Tiberias?

Whether the Syrians knew the answers to these questions but did not want to reveal them, or whether they had not thought through the implications of their proposed armistice line, is not clear. Their answer to the understandable Israeli probing was that they would have to consult their government "to obtain the requested clarification" (*M.V.*, pp. 554–55). The morning session on May 10 adjourned on this note.

The following acerbic exchanges opened the afternoon session. Colonel Selo of the Syrian delegation is speaking.

Mr. Rosenne has mentioned fishing in Lake Tiberias. Of course, it is a question of vital importance for both parties. This will be kept in mind when submitting the question to our Government and in future discussions.

Mr. Rosenne: I deny that the question of fisheries on the Lake of Kinnereth is a vital question for Syria. I would like to know since when it is a vital question for the Syrians.

Mr. Tarazi: This question will be discussed at a later date and we will see then how it will be settled. The two parties have rights.

Mr. Vigier: Are those rights the result of international agreements?

Mr. Tarazi: There are agreements.

Mr. Rosenne: Which one?

Mr. Tarazi: Between the two High Commissioners.

Mr. Rosenne: What is the date of the agreement in question?

Mr. Tarazi: This question will be discussed later. I would like to ask Mr. Rosenne the following question: What is the fishing right he wanted to discuss?

Mr. Rosenne: We raised questions but received no answer. We were told that the fishing rights depended on an agreement between two High Commissioners, but we received no answer as to the date when such an agreement was signed. All the questions we put forward arose out of the Syrian proposal; we have not made any proposal. We were trying to clarify the Syrian proposal. I suggest that the question of fishing rights be dropped; obviously we will get nowhere at the present stage.

Mr. Vigier: I agree that it is impossible to discuss this question now. We could do it only if we had the texts on which those rights are based. Even then, as this Conference must draft an armistice convention which is a purely military convention, I would suggest merely to reserve these rights in the Armistice Convention.

Colonel Nasser: We do not have on hand all the data required to give an immediate answer. However, we do not intend to prevent fishing. (*M.V.*, p. 556)

The Israelis rejected the Syrian placement of the armistice lines and then found the proposal for who might live and work in the no-man's-land vague, if not deliberately evasive. They did not however, object in principle to the idea of a no-man's-land. But because the Syrians had recommended the idea, the Israelis complained "the no-man's-land is only in Israeli territory and it includes at least ten Israeli villages which were not affected by this war." Continuing the unfriendly atmospherics, the Israeli spokesman said, "We do not understand why the Syrian delegation cannot include Tel Aviv in this no-man's-land." With some logic, not consistently applied where it complicated their strategy, the Israelis added, "A no-man's-land in principle should be applied on both sides of a line." In sum, all that the Israelis were willing to accept from the Syrian proposal was the "reduction of forces." Then "it will be ready to meet the Syrian delegation on any proposal and, of course, determine the areas where these defensive forces will be" (*M.V.*, p. 558).

The Israelis dismissed out of hand the Syrian effort to have western Galilee included in the negotiations with the following comment: "As regards Western Galilee, we do not see what it has to do here. This question has been settled when an armistice was signed between Israel and the Lebanon. . . . As to the influence that forces may have on a demarcation line, I think that forces stationed in Damascus or in Tel Aviv may have the same bearing on the demarcation line as the forces stationed in Western Galilee. I would ask the Syrian delegation to drop the matter altogether, because as I mentioned it before, it was settled when an armistice was concluded between Israel and the Lebanon." The Israeli concluded, "Therefore, I am very sorry to say that this proposal does not appear to serve any satisfactory basis for the drafting of an armistice agreement" (*M.V.*, p. 559).

The Syrians repeated the necessity to submit the Israeli objections to their government, although they indicated an interest in pursuing the question of reduction of forces. "What would this reduction of forces consist of and what would be the demarcation line based on that reduction?" they asked (*M.V.*, p. 559).

The Israelis rejected the suggestion that the questions of forces and the demarcation line might be separated. Colonel Makleff responded for them: "The reduction of forces has a bearing on the demarcation line and the demarcation line has a bearing on the reduction of forces. If you know where your line is, then you know how many forces. . . . The Israeli delegation did not change its mind and it is the Israeli Government's opinion that the demarcation line between Israel and Syria should run along the international frontier" (*M.V.*, p. 559).

Vigier, by now, despaired of any progress. In another effort to separate a peace settlement from the military considerations relevant to an armistice, he reminded both parties that "the international frontier cannot be changed by an armistice convention" (*M.V.*, p. 557). As all the armistices stated, it would be possible to establish an armistice line while reserving the "rights, positions, interests and claims of both parties for peace negotiations." Neither side was responsive to this effort, but neither offered reasons for ignoring the standard formula. The Syrians may not have been free to move beyond their stated positions without further consultation in Damascus. But given the Israeli record, they may have decided that they were not interested in any peace negotiations involving fixing final borders. If this were their strategy, the armistice lines would stand as borders for an indefinite period. That strategy had gained them territory in the three previous armistice agreements.

Considering the vital importance they had attached to water resources in their 1919 proposal to the Paris Peace Conference, the territory in dispute with Syria, between the truce lines in the west and the international boundary line to the east, was of much greater critical, economic importance to the Jewish state than the territory beyond the partition borders in the Negev, or in the Triangle on the Transjordan front, or even their penetration into Jerusalem. And their claims to the territory in dispute with Syria had more legal legitimacy. It was the Syrians who were occupying Jewish state territory.

These considerations may explain the silence with which the Israelis greeted Vigier's compromise; with hindsight, it now becomes apparent that their unusual inarticulateness may be explained by their military campaigns in the 1967 war when they not only crossed the international boundary but occupied and—in 1981—annexed the Golan Heights. Israeli partisans may, with justice, complain this is ex post facto reasoning and the introduction of circumstantial evidence at this point. But, to paraphrase Santayana, if the value of learning history is to avoid the doom of repeating it, there is some justification for attempting here to explain this stalemate in negotiations with Syria in the continuum of history.

Israel: The 1919 Map Still Operative

With such hindsight, the Israelis' goal at the time of the armistice negotiations can be stated clearly. They agreed reluctantly to partition. Almost immediately they embarked on actions designed to incorporate *all* of mandated Palestine into the Jewish state.[8] The first assault on territory that had been allocated to the Arab state was the terrorist campaign, led by Menachem Begin's Irgun forces in the late months of 1947 and early months of 1948 *before* the scheduled, formal termination of the mandate. The Jewish Agency and other official Zionist bodies *publicly* maintained a hands-off policy and occasionally reprimanded the terrorists for these campaigns. But as Begin later recorded in his autobiography, *The Revolt*, the Jewish Agency, in fact, combined acquiescence with active encouragement or concealed support.[9] The Irgun irregular forces attacked Jaffa and moved on to western Galilee. They also penetrated the Negev and, on the eastern front, the area of the Triangle and Jerusalem. After May 15, 1948, and the official Zionist "Declaration of Establishment" of the State of Israel, the regular Arab forces joined the fighting with the objective of regaining the territory beyond the partition lines that the irregular Israeli campaigns had occupied. Many of these points became the subjects of dispute and negotiations in establishing armistices with the Egyptians, the Lebanese, and the Transjordanians.

In most of these negotiations the Israelis prevailed. They had been required to withdraw to the international border with Lebanon, but they retained western Galilee. They failed to gain their objective in Gaza. In the Negev, they held Beersheba, and that, contrary to the Bernadotte proposal, facilitated campaign Uvda to take over the rest of the Negev. On the Transjordan front the Israelis counted on holding the Triangle and some toehold in Jerusalem while hoping for more in the secret deals they were cutting with Abdallah. But on the north-central front the ragtag army, which had been trained in Syria, had entered Palestine territory in February and March 1948.

Between April 1 and July 15, the Security Council had adopted seven resolutions ordering a truce, or an extension of truces already ordered, but they were ignored by one or another of the belligerents. The texts of these resolutions specified no particular party as culprit. In the main, they called on "all Governments and authorities concerned" to cease "all acts of force" (*UN Resolutions*, p. xvii). Generally speaking, "authorities" was intended to refer to the Jewish Agency and the Arab Higher Committee as parties other than governments which presumably had some control over irregular forces engaged in the fighting.

During those two and one-half months of UN failure to stop the fighting, the Zionist-Israeli forces, both terrorist (before the actual declaration of establishment of the state) and the Israeli forces (after the establishment), occupied "790 square miles of territory . . . on all fronts" which the partition had allotted to the Arab state. "The Arabs continued to hold parts of Galilee, nearly all of eastern Palestine, and most of the Negev. Syrian units, after throwing back an Israeli offensive south of Lake Huleh, actually gained some ground at the expense of the Israelis."[10] Reluctantly, in leaving Gaza to the Egyptians, Israel insisted on maintaining defensive forces along the lines where the fighting had been halted, although they "never admitted the right of the Egyptian army to be in that area at all" (*M.V.*, p. 178).

The Gaza area, the territory held by the Syrians, the West Bank, and the confusing divisions in Jerusalem were the only parts of Palestine that Israel had not occupied. The Syrians had refused to discuss an armistice as part of the negotiations with Lebanon. The Syrian forces occupying Lebanese-Palestinian territory were therefore referred to as "the forces of a third party not covered" by the armistice agreement with Lebanon, although Lebanon agreed that no military activity against Israel would be permitted from its territory.

These Syrian forces, on May 10, remained the bone of contention. Their presence in Jewish state territories explains the Israeli insistence on establishing the armistice line at the international border. Longer range, beyond the armistice, the headwaters of the Jordan River and Lakes Huleh and Tiberias were involved. And the partition had assigned this part of Palestine to the Jewish state.

At the conclusion of the second session of the talks, Vigier, with Bunche's approval, had proposed that "existing truce lines" become the "permanent armistice lines, with such modifications as the Parties may find mutually agreeable" (*M.V.*, p. 559). Eban notified Bunche at Lake Success that the Israelis found this proposal unsatisfactory. It would permit defensive forces of *both* sides in a zone between the truce lines. Eban observed this would be different from a "demilitarized zone" which, apparently, the Israelis were prepared to accept *provided the Syrian forces withdrew to the "frontier."* Eban told Bunche, "There is neither real withdrawal of Syrian forces to the frontier, nor facilities for the return of civilians with suitable protection to any villages or settlements in the demilitarized zone" (*M.V.*, p. 561).

The Israeli repeated that Israel would not agree to any armistice that did not require Syrian withdrawal to the international boundary. "Our delegation is prepared, provided these two principles are maintained, to be quite flexible and lenient with regard to the technical procedure. Of one thing, however, *I have certain knowledge: that any scheme which does not take Syrian forces back to the frontier*, irrespective of where the armistice line is deemed to be, will not furnish the basis for an armistice agreement" (*M.V.*, p. 561; emphasis supplied).

But in the Lebanese situation, Israel's withdrawal to the international boundary left it in occupation of western Galilee, contrary to the partition plan. This fact haunted the Israelis. Nevertheless, Eban tempted the fates by reminding Bunche that Israel had complied with his insistence on withdrawal to the border in that situation: "You will recall the insistence of the mediation staff during the Israeli-Lebanese negotiations on the immediate and unconditional restoration of the frontier. We remain as convinced as ever that this would be the only just and equitable solution in this case, a solution simple and clear-cut, and easily understood by public opinion everywhere" (*M.V.*, pp. 561–62).

One of Ben-Gurion's rare direct interventions in the armistice negotiations emphasized the importance Israel attached to Syrian withdrawal to the border. On May 12 the prime minister wrote Bunche in New York, repeating and emphasizing Eban's arguments. He stressed that as Bunche—"rightly"—had insisted on Israeli withdrawal in the Lebanese negotiations, so now it "was the duty of your representatives to insist on the withdrawal of the Syrian forces to the international frontier on the Syrian border." Professing that "peace . . . is very close to my heart," Ben-Gurion added, "Chances for it are not hopeful . . . unless the Syrians agree to withdraw from any part of our territory which they seized during their willful aggression against our country" (*M.V.*, pp. 562–63). On May 14 Sharett, still in New York, cabled Tel Aviv that Bunche "emphatically agreed" the Syrians "must withdraw completely" and "our civilians must return" accompanied by police protection (*M.V.*, p. 564).

But the problem was not yet resolved. On April 27 Sharett, now back in Tel Aviv, cabled Eban in New York that the Syrians, at a meeting on the twenty-sixth, attempted to buttress their case for fixing the armistice line—from Lake Huleh southward—at the "waterline." They based their claim on an "earlier Anglo-French commitment." But they were unable to produce the agreement for the Israelis to examine. The Israelis, understandably, rejected the proposal as "irrelevant" (*M.V.*, p. 538). Nevertheless, reflecting the thoroughness with which they prosecuted their case, the Israelis obtained a copy of the "Anglo-French Convention" dated December 23, 1920. Somehow, Rosenne, in Tel Aviv, had obtained the copy and, on May 15, had sent an extract to Eytan who was in Lausanne (*M. V.*, p. 566).

This convention was part of the British-French division of the Asiatic parts of the Ottoman Empire, after World War I. The French obtained the mandate for Syria (and Lebanon) and the British the mandate for Palestine. The 1920 document established "the general principles" for determining the boundary and, according to Rosenne, could be said "to have taken the place of the Sykes-Picot agreement in this respect."[11] An exchange of notes followed on March 7, 1923, in which the frontier was actually delineated.[12]

Whether the Syrians had located the original document is not clear from the Israeli records. But now, confronted with this discovery, they claimed the British had deceived the French and had moved the boundary from the water line to the boundary lines. But, for the intervening years, from 1923 on, apparently, the "new" line had been recognized by Syria without protest.

In the same May 15 message, Rosenne outlined the history of fishing rights on Lakes Huleh and Tiberias. He instructed Eytan that "if in fact Syrians used to work now and then on the lakes, they did so as employees of Palestinian contractors and for a short season, without licence from the Palestine Government and with a nod from the Police. There also exists a private partnership between a Jew named Goldzweig and a Syrian named Shehadeh el-Khouri for the exploitation of fishing in Lake Tiberias for the benefit of Palestine and not of Syria. This partnership employed many Syrians. I assume that any arrangements which might be reached with the Syrians regarding the frontier will not affect such a private contract" (*M. V.*, p. 567).

The Israeli research apparently had discovered that there had been a dispute about Lake Huleh between the government of Palestine and an organization called the Palestine Jewish Colonization Association (PICA), founded in 1882 by Baron Edmund de Rothschild as part of his personal philanthropic effort to establish colonies for Jews (largely from eastern Europe). In 1900 he transferred the administration of the colonies to the Jewish Colonization Association (JCA), an older organization that had been established by Baron Maurice de Hirsch to resettle Jews, mostly from Russia, in Argentina. With the grant of the Rothschild colonies in Palestine, a Palestine Commission was established, and in 1924 PICA became a separate organization.[13]

Given the essentially Jewish or Zionist history of these lakes—at least as Rosenne's research presented it—his conclusion to Eytan was that "even the disputed zone" in Lake Huleh "was included entirely within the frontiers of Palestine." Therefore, in practice the Syrians had no rights on Huleh, whatever the theoretical position might be (*M.V.*, p. 568). Also on May 15, Ben-Gurion instructed the Israeli delegation at Lake Success "to break negotiations . . . unless [the] Syrians accept complete withdrawal [to the] international frontier" (*M.V.*, p. 569).

The next joint meeting, the eighth, was held on May 17. Vigier began by asking both if they were ready to start "the debate" of Bunche's proposals that Vigier had presented on May 10. An "Alphonse and Gaston" act followed, obviously intended to divert attention from the rejections by both delegations. Each wanted the other to make the first confession. Vigier tried to end the charade by asking if "the delegations [could] reply by yes or no to the question whether they accept the proposals." He followed that question (to which he received no answer) by suggesting the proposals be examined "paragraph by paragraph," avoiding direct responses to the proposals as a whole. Still, neither side offered a cooperative reaction. Vigier then recessed the session to hold separate and private talks with both delegations.

When the joint session resumed after an hour and fifteen minutes, the Israelis had apparently been persuaded to speak first. Colonel Makleff announced that Israel was prepared to "accept" the Vigier/Bunche "proposal as a basis for further discussion" but only on condition "the implementation of the proposal carries with it a complete withdrawal of all Syrian forces from the non-Syrian territory which they occupy." Further, Makleff added as a condition, "Also, as far as the no-man's-land is concerned, on the understanding that the proposal guarantees complete restoration of normal civilian life and activities under Israeli civil authorities. As regards the no-man's-land area, the opinion of the Israeli delegation is that it would be inequitable for the entire zone to be on the Israeli territory. Therefore we demand that a part of the zone be on the Syrian side of the border" (*M.V.*, pp. 571–72). The Syrians countered that Makleff had introduced conditions contrary to Vigier's instructions for the two delegations to give a "yes" or "no" answer to the principle of the proposal.

In the long circular argument that followed, the Israelis phrased and rephrased their questions in different ways, hoping the Syrians might be led (or misled) into conceding that the frontier would be an important marker in establishing an armistice line. Just as circuitously, the Syrians evaded answers. After each side had offered conditional agreement to a no-man's-land with only defensive forces of both sides allowed "on each side of the permanent demarcation line," Rosenne finally put what the Israelis wanted to know in simple, direct language. "We would like to know if the Syrian delegation wants to maintain troops in the area west of the frontier. Our understanding is that no troops will be maintained west of the frontier. Does the Syrian delegation understand, as we do, that all troops will be withdrawn to beyond the frontier? This is a question that can be answered by yes or no" (*M. V.*, p. 575).

The Syrians responded: "Paragraph 1 of the proposal submitted by the Chairman states that 'the permanent armistice demarcation lines shall be based on the general principle of following the existing truce lines.' The border is not mentioned in this paragraph. The political border is not mentioned, but only permanent armistice demarcation lines" (*M. V.*, p. 575).

The summary of this sparring session illustrates again that the Israelis were attempting to insert into the armistice discussion agenda items for a final peace. This explains their determined resistance to the corresponding, rigid Syrian insistence on "forces in defensive strength only . . . in defined outposts" on both sides of the armistice demarcation lines. Rosenne cut through the impasse, asserting that "it is the intention of the Syrian Government to secure our agreement to maintain Syrian troops west of the international frontier, and it does not matter what the strength of these forces will be. In our estimation . . . there is no reason why the exception should be brought into use and it is a thing which our Government is unable to agree to" (*M. V.*, p. 577).

Colonel Muhammad Naser,[14] representing Syria, attempted to separate an issue relevant to an armistice (the demarcation line) from the question of the international border, which the Syrians considered a subject to be determined in a final peace: "Mr. Rosenne has said that according to Colonel Selo's statement the Syrian Government's intentions were this or that. The Syrian Government's intentions are not being discussed; what is being discussed is the acceptance of the proposal by the Chairman. We have accepted the principle of the proposal. Mr. Rosenne's statement [that] the Government of Israel would be unable to agree to an armistice convention which would leave Syrian forces, in any strength, during the armistice, west of the international border, completely ruins the proposal" (*M. V.*, p. 577).

The different negotiating tactics of the sides are important. The Israelis' determination to make the international border the armistice demarcation was supported by the partition recommendation. Their case was weakened because, in the previous armistice agreements, when it served their long-range purposes, they had insisted on "existing fighting lines." But despite this lack of consistency, they refused to be moved in the negotiations with Syria. The record contains only passing references to the historic Zionist aspirations to possess the water resources of the disputed territory.

The frequent Syrian reminders of Israeli occupation of western Galilee clearly were meant to emphasize the Israeli inconsistency in giving priority to the fighting lines over the partition-recommended boundaries in the earlier negotiations but now objecting to Syria's resort to the same negotiating strategy. If this caused the Israelis any embarrassment, it was not enough to persuade them to yield ground in the present argument. The weakness in the Syrian case was that their refusal to withdraw to the border would leave their forces in Jewish state territory, a situation equally contrary to the partition plan as Israel's conduct in the Egyptian, Lebanese, and Transjordanian situations. This example of "two wrongs not making a right" dramatizes what a quagmire easily follows from a total denigration of international law, in this case the UN resolutions. The situation also illustrates the almost certain consequences when great powers, parties to the resolutions, fail to exercise their influence on and responsibility to support the law.

In a slip of the tongue—and perhaps an inadvertent lapse of security—Mr. Tarazi, legal advisor to the Syrian delegation, may have revealed the Syrian motivation for verbal fencing during the lengthy session. Responding to a Rosenne intervention, Tarazi said, splitting some legal hairs, "In the first place, as far as the international border is concerned, there is no such border between Israel and Syria. There was a political border between Syria and Palestine. . . . We have to sign an armistice convention not on the basis of any political border, but on the basis of a demarcation line" (*M. V.*, p. 579).

The Syrian lawyer, of course, implied Syria did not recognize the geography of partition and perhaps not even the existence of Israel. This argument may have reflected something of a fading, pre–World War I Syrian dream of a Greater Syria in which Palestine was called southern Syria.

These speculations, however, must remain unanswered by any evidence in the Israeli or American records. About all that can be said is that there were some grounds for the Israeli suspicions that the Syrians had no intention of withdrawing to the international frontier as part of an armistice agreement. Rosenne simply ignored Tarazi's "clarification" and reiterated that Israel "will not sign any agreement if Syrian troops are to be maintained west of the international frontier" (*M.V.*, p. 580). Tarazi matched rejection with rejection, saying the Bunche-Vigier proposal "has been entirely rejected, as the delineation of the armistice lines will not be based on the general principle of following the existing truce lines" (*M.V.*, p. 580).

The impasse remained unaltered for this long, unproductive session, compelling Vigier to announce he did "not think that it is useful to proceed with this discussion." He would, he said, report to Bunche and ask him "to send new instructions" from New York (where Bunche was undergoing medical treatment that he had long postponed so as not to interrupt the armistice talks). "No date should be fixed for the next meeting," Vigier added, until he had consulted with Bunche. Vigier then asked if the two delegations agreed to his suggestion, which they did (*M.V.*, p. 581).

On May 19 Rosenne reported other important developments in a telegram to Sharett and Ben-Gurion, both of whom were in New York lobbying the General Assembly for the vote on Israel's admission to the United Nations. The occasion for Rosenne's communication had been a "confidential talk" with General Riley on the seventeenth. Rosenne reported:

> Riley informed him that he had learned from unofficial sources that Hussni al-Zaim wanted to solve the Syrian-Israeli problems peacefully and to devote his energies to the development of Syria. Zaim feared a counter-revolution which would lead to a critical review of his activities, including the negotiations with Israel. He therefore wanted Israel to help him out of his quandary without his having to lose face. He had asked Riley to find out Israel's reaction to the following proposal: within the framework of the Lausanne talks, Syria would agree to settle some 300,000 refugees within its borders. The problem of the Israel-Syrian border would also be settled there. (Riley commented that the Conciliation Commission would probably press the Syrians to withdraw to the international border). In return, Syria would sign an armistice based on the pres-

ent military lines and with clear instructions regarding the reduction of forces on both sides. The agreement would be valid for three
months and would include a paragraph alluding to Israel insistence
on a Syrian withdrawal to the international border. (*C.V.*, p. 99)

The Zaim proposition was hardly airtight. But it contained sufficient
references to Syrian self-interests to have signaled that it was worth
serious consideration if Israel was really searching for peace. Rosenne's
immediate reaction was "negative," and "he told Riley that Ben-Gurion's
reaction would in all probability be the same." Candidly, he added that
"Israel was in no hurry and that Syria was in greater need of an agreement. . . . Moreover, Israel did not fear the Security Council's reaction
and felt that the time had come to exert heavy UN pressure on the
Syrians" (*C.V.*, pp. 99–100).

In New York, in the less parochial atmosphere of the United Nations,
Eban questioned Rosenne's summary dismissal of Riley's information.
He asked Rosenne to explain why "we [were] unimpressed" with the
prospect that Syria might "absorb 300,000" refugees. Eban noted that
Washington had news of the offer, adding, the "Syrian readiness [to]
accept large-scale resettlement seems to me of great importance" (*M.V.*,
p. 584).

In a long letter to Secretary-General Lie, Eban reviewed the entire
history of the negotiations with Syria (*C.V.*, pp. 585–88). The letter
emphasized the UN insistence on Israel's withdrawal from Lebanese
territory to the international border. Israel, Eban said, "was accepting
the principle of restoring the international frontier with Lebanon in the
hope that the same principle would be followed during armistice negotiations with Syria" (*M.V.*, p. 585). Then, with tongue-in-cheek pontifica-
tion, the Israeli ambassador added, "Principles cannot be selectively applied," implying that the principle of the "*international* frontiers" of
Palestine was sacred (*M.V.*, p. 586). But boundaries for the partition of
Palestine between Jewish and Arab states were up for grabs, and, in the
Israeli official minds, the recommended frontiers of the new states could
be determined by war and where the military forces had stopped fighting. (This double standard had paid Israel dividends in western Galilee,
the Beersheba area, the southern Negev, the Triangle, and the parts of
the jigsaw territory Israel held in Jerusalem after the cease-fire on the
Transjordanian front.) Through *their* selective application of principle
the Israelis held "some 780 square miles of territory from the Arabs," as

Khouri summarizes the military results that had preceded the armistice negotiations.[15]

Eban's letter to Lie confirmed that "the area in question [with Syria], though small, is vital for Israel since it commands important water resources essential both for the life of the Galilee [which Israel claimed by conquest] and for the execution of irrigation schemes affecting the country as a whole." Then the Israeli ambassador garnished his legal-political argument with the standard Zionist expression of "Jewish martyrdom"—this time inflicted by malaria-bearing mosquitoes! "This territory has been reclaimed for cultivation by the exertions of Jewish pioneers, who gave their lives in great numbers to overcome the ravages of malaria" (*M.V.*, p. 586). Eban continued, "The Syrian attitude, if maintained, as at present, has grave consequences. It prevents the completion of the armistice system, and thereby endangers results already achieved. It precluded peace discussions between Syria and Israel at Lausanne, thereby weakening the prospects of the conference as a whole. . . . For all these reasons this refusal by Syria to restore the international frontier should be regarded not as a merely local event but as a matter full of danger to the maintenance of international peace and security" (*M.V.*, pp. 587–88).

He concluded with the following paragraph, which, again mindful of the Israeli claims "by conquest" in the other negotiations, must have been added with at least a thin coating of cynicism. "My Government feels that the same international influence which was used to secure the restoration of the Israeli-Lebanese frontier by Israeli withdrawals, should now be used to restore the Syrio-Israeli frontier. This step would crown the United Nations armistice efforts with final success and open the way to swifter progress towards a final peace settlement" (*M.V.*, p. 588).

Whether there was any direct connection between Eban's letter and events that followed on that same date, May 23, is not clear. But Eban cabled Sharett that General Riley was proceeding to New York from Damascus, where he had discussed the armistice, and Bunche, also in New York, was preparing "draft proposals to be sent to Zaim and Ben-Gurion." The new proposals would "make it crystal clear" that the "demilitarized zone between the truce line and frontier is one from which all troops are excluded, but civilian activity [could be] fully resumed, with appropriate security measures" (*M.V.*, p. 588). The Israeli position was about to prevail.

Meanwhile, Sharett, in apparent disagreement with Rosenne and Ben-Gurion, had decided to meet with Zaim. In a May 25 message to Eban, the foreign minister said he attached "tremendous importance" to the "alleged" Syrian offer to "resettle 300,000" refugees (*M. V.*, p. 589). Israel had been admitted to UN membership on May 11. The admitting resolution recalled the partition resolution and the resolution of December 11, 1948, and noted "the declarations and explanations made by the representative of the Government of Israel before the *Ad Hoc* Political Committee in respect of the implementation of the said resolutions" (*UN Res.*, p. 18). Probably conscious of the critical importance of paragraph 11 of the December 11, 1949, resolution dealing with refugees in his message to Eban, Sharett added, "Our position inside the UN can only be strengthened by this initiative [on] my part" (*M. V.*, p. 589).

On May 26, Arthur Lourie, Israeli consul-general in New York, informed Sharett that, having received from Vigier a report of Zaim's proposal and the Syrian's interest in meeting Sharett personally, Bunche had decided not to proceed with his proposed compromise. Ben-Gurion had declined to meet Zaim. But Bunche wanted some meeting of an Israeli with Zaim, and to improve the possibility for such a meeting he had instructed Vigier to urge Zaim to accept an Israeli authority, even of lesser stature than the prime minister. "If necessary for protocol," the Syrian should "take along his Foreign Minister as counterpart Sharett" (*M. V.*, p. 590).

But on May 30 the Israeli documents report Zaim had reneged on his offer to meet personally with an authoritative Israeli, even if he were the foreign minister. Nor was Zaim willing to send his own foreign minister. He had informed Vigier he was willing to send only the undersecretary of the Foreign Ministry to meet Sharett at Kuneitra. The usually accommodating Sharett now stood on protocol and withdrew his offer to meet, describing the Syrian proposal "as gross impertinence." Sharett reasoned these new Syrian ideas were designed to pressure Israel to petition for another meeting of the delegations where Israel would "be expected [to] make new proposals." Sharett advised Eban that "this would completely distort [the] picture." He instructed Eban to tell Bunche to "go ahead" with his compromise proposal, which substantially reflected the Israeli positions on the international frontier and the status of civilians in the demilitarized zone. Moreover, Israel had now been admitted to membership in the United Nations, and, in this particular situation, its position was more consistent with relevant UN resolutions than Syria's. Under these more favorable conditions Sharett asked Eban's opinion about submitting the dispute to the Security Council "even without awaiting Bunche's new initiative" (M.V., p. 591).

The usually detailed Israeli record does not contain the text of the new Bunche initiative. But the U.S. record reports an urgent and confidential communication dated May 12 from Warren Austin at the United Nations briefing Acheson with a summary of the proposal, describing it as "along the following lines":

(a) Truce lines to be the armistice lines;

(b) A demilitarized zone to be established on Auja model in Egypt agreement. Syrians to withdraw to their frontier. Israelis also to withdraw. For those points on which it is not possible to persuade Israelis to withdraw, a radical reduction of forces to effective strength should be established;

(c) Demilitarized zone to be under UN supervision again on Egypt armistice model. Israeli civil officers to operate in zone;

(d) Syrians to withdraw by stages from demilitarized zone;

(e) If absolutely necessary, Israelis might be allowed one or two outposts in demilitarized zone. This would be last resort, however. (FRUS 6 [1949], p. 1000)

Austin added that Bunche was attempting to persuade the Syrians this was probably the best bargain they could hope for, even if the matter went to the Security Council. Bunche added that the Israeli withdrawal "or a drastic reduction of forces" offered Zaim "the essential . . . face-saving device" for which he had asked. Eban, however, objected to any Israeli "withdrawals or reduction of forces" and argued that the "possibility of Syrian outpost in the demilitarized zone should apparently be discussed in negotiations and would nullify [the Syrian] withdrawal." Bunche replied the plan would give Israel "their major point which is to get Syrians out of Palestine." Austin also relayed Bunche's hope for "any assistance possible" from the State Department (FRUS 6 [1949], pp. 1000–1001).

Acheson responded in a long telegram on May 12. He supported the Israeli claim, almost without reservation. "The Syrian position," he said, "is so difficult to defend within the principles of the Charter [of the UN] and of previous armistice practice that Israel would not hesitate to make a complaint to the Security Council. . . . All available international influence should be brought to bear in order to persuade the Syrian Government to give the same weight to an established international frontier as has been given in all similar circumstances before" (*FRUS* 6 [1949], p. 1003). And, on the same day, telegrams to Damascus and Tel Aviv urged both governments to "accept this compromise" and "immeasurably increase [the] possibilities of reaching [a] final settlement at Lausanne" (*FRUS* 6 [1949], p. 1004).

Bunche and the United Nations vs. Israel and the United States

The next day, May 13, according to Austin, Bunche reacted "very unfavorably" to the Israeli position. He accused the Israelis of "inaccuracies, half truths and unwillingness to withdraw or reduce forces and permit the Mixed Armistice Commission to control the demilitarized zone." Austin advised Acheson that instead of approaching the Syrians, Bunche "wishes the Department would urge on Israel acceptance [of the] compromise of May 12th." They "are the recalcitrants" (*FRUS* 6 [1949], p. 1006). Bunche's criticisms of Israel illuminate his opinion of how Israel had created the impasse.

First, he rejected the Israeli analogy between the situation with Syria and the Lebanese negotiations on the border question. He recalled that the Israeli withdrawal from Lebanon had come in an agreement between Ben-Gurion and Bunche as a "prior condition to negotiations." "Also, [the] Israelis were definitely outside Palestine invading Lebanon." Consequently, the Israeli representation to the State Department had misrepresented Bunche's position when it claimed that "during the armistice negotiations [he] insisted vigorously on this point and that Israel unilaterally had accepted withdrawal" (*FRUS* 6 [1949], p. 1006).

Second, the "basis for all armistice negotiations has always been truce lines." Israeli incursion into Egypt in October had been "a truce violation." Bunche asserted that he "had never heard of the alleged principle that whenever a truce line was in the vicinity of an international frontier the armistice line was based on the frontier and not upon truce positions." He pointed out that "this was not true in Gaza, Auja and elsewhere in the Negev, or in the Transjordan agreement." The "only Syrian violation" of the truce of which Bunche knew, he said, was one hill position from which they had withdrawn. Bunche told Austin that the "Israeli claim that they should have all [the area allotted them in the partition recommendation] *plus* what they have been able to seize" was contrary to the position of the United States, stated by Truman and also by the U.S. representative at the United Nations, that any "adjustments" of the November 29 recommended borders should be compensated with an exchange of comparable territory from the other party. Finally, Bunche informed Washington through Austin that "if the Syrian talks collapse and cannot be revived," he will place the "blame on Israelis" before the Security Council (*FRUS* 6 [1949], pp. 1005–7).

On May 13, the American minister in Damascus, James Keeley, sent a secret, priority telegram to Acheson advising Washington not to pressure the Syrians at this time. The minister's last paragraph substantially supports the editorial comment in this narrative so far. A further editorial comment reflects the recurring Washington pattern of ignoring—or at best subordinating—the professional, on-the-ground advice of Foreign Service specialists with experience in Arab capitals to the domestic political counsels of advisors to presidents or aides to members of the Congress. Justified by tested facts, or not, in U.S. policy in the Middle East, the *politically* perceived intimidation-power of American Zionists is a hobgoblin of gargantuan proportions to candidates for elective office.[16]

Keeley wrote Acheson, "Syria long ago became accustomed to its inability obtain justice in SC [Security Council]. For U.S. to remind Syria that this situation likely to continue if she fails accept Israeli armistice terms will not, I feel sure, be persuasive, particularly in light of favor currently being shown Israel by US re Israel's acceptance as UN member despite her continued disregard of resolution of December 11 and her failure otherwise fully to live up to standards of UN Charter" (*FRUS* 6 [1949], p. 1008).

If there are Americans who are still bewildered by the erosion of their country's credibility in the Middle East, the 1949 volume of *Foreign Relations of the United States* provides an official record that may clear their minds. The contretemps between Washington's professional diplomat in Damascus and what domestic political expediencies provided by Clark Clifford, David Niles, and the like were generating was the rule—not the exception. The difference was translated into political results evident in the benefits bestowed on Israel compared to the grudging acknowledgment of the human and political rights of the Arabs. The imbalance continues, as does the protracted potential for crisis and the paralysis of U.S. political influence to contribute to a settlement of the Middle East's most stubborn source of instability.

After consultation with General Riley on May 19, Keeley again telegraphed Acheson that "Everyone who has discussed [the negotiations] with Zaim is impressed by his sincerity and broad minded attitude toward Israel (far cry from stubborn intransigence previous Syrian Government) but his ardor is cooling in face of evident Israeli insatiability. . . . Unless Israel can be brought to understand that it cannot have all of its cake (partition boundaries) and gravy as well (areas captured in violation of truce, Jerusalem and a resettlement of Arab refugees elsewhere) it may find it had won Palestine war but lost peace" (*FRUS* 6 [1949], pp. 1031–32).

On May 23, Senator Austin, at the United Nations, informed Acheson that General Riley had returned to the United Nations and he and Bunche were drafting new proposals. Bunche would send the new plan "to the field" and suggest that Ben-Gurion and Zaim meet to "negotiate on this basis." If they refused to negotiate, "he will turn the matter over to the Security Council." Austin added Bunche's estimate that the Israelis "will be in a very weak position in that event" (*FRUS* 6 [1949], p. 1046).

This was not the first effort by Bunche to rein in the Israelis with the prospect of publicity generated by Security Council debate. On previous occasions the Israelis relied on an American veto, and, consequently, they did largely as they pleased, discounting any ephemeral public reactions with new, concrete facts on the ground. This time, however, there were some indications the United States might support Bunche's new proposals. With their conduits into the policy-making procedures in the U.S. government, the Israelis may well have been aware of this possibility.[17]

The Israelis may also have feared a U.S. veto if Bunche took the Syrian-Israeli armistice-line problem to the Security Council. The Palestine Conciliation Commission was already engaged in Switzerland with the Israelis and the Arab states (which, other than Syria, had already agreed to armistices), grappling with the substantive issues of a possible lasting peace. These talks were commanding prior U.S. attention over the armistice negotiations.

In the Conciliation Commission's forum the Arabs were proving tougher bargainers than they had been in negotiating armistices. The Arabs were still not unified on any comprehensive plan for peace. But they were in closer contact with each other, and discussions were involving all of them within a limited time-frame. This tended to frustrate the one-by-one strategy Israel had used for months during the armistice talks. Although Israel regarded the armistice talks as opportunities to stake out what it wanted as permanent, strategic territorial points, the Arabs did not regard armistice lines as unchangeable. Nevertheless, in final peace negotiations, under the auspices of the commission, the Arabs were less conciliatory about territorial changes that they considered might become permanent boundaries. And finally, the United States had been more than tolerant of the expansionist Israeli claims in the armistice talks, relying on the escape clause in each agreement that stated that territorial adjustments to separate the belligerent forces were *not* to prejudice claims in negotiating a lasting peace. For any or all of these reasons, in the Conciliation Commission's early efforts, the United States appeared to tilt toward the Arabs and to show greater respect for UN resolutions and international law.

In this context the following telegram from Austin to Acheson, on May 25, reveals something of U.S. wariness about the negative impact that Israel's negotiating positions might have on the peace that Washington still considered possible. "SECRET NEW YORK, May 25, 1949—7:05 P.M. Bunche and Riley were both of opinion last evening that disclosure of Israeli territorial aspiration to PCC will result in breakdown of Israeli-Syrian armistice negotiations. They also agree that this disclosure will probably wreck PCC talks and might also threaten armistice agreements. Austin" (*FRUS* 6 [1949], p. 1055).

Two other documents to the secretary of state within about twenty-four hours of Austin's message suggest the Ethridge draft-note. Acheson was in Paris at a meeting of the Council of Foreign Ministers. The note had been prepared for Acting Secretary of State Dean Rusk. It had been sent to Ethridge in Switzerland for comment. After approval by Rusk and the president, the note was to be handed to the Israeli ambassador in Washington. Salient paragraphs reveal Washington's apprehensions about Israeli negotiating positions. The draft-note made it clear that it was "the President of the United States . . . [who] has instructed me [Rusk] to inform the Government of Israel, as follows":

> The Govt. of the US is seriously disturbed by the attitude of Israel with respect to a territorial settlement in Palestine and to the question of Palestinian refugees, as set forth to Mr. Mark Ethridge by Dr. Eytan on May 19, 1949, at Lausanne upon instructions of His Excellency the Fon Min of Israel. According to Dr. Eytan, the Israeli Govt. will do nothing further about Palestinian refugees at the present time. In connection with territorial matters, the position taken by Dr. Eytan apparently contemplates not only the re-

tention of all territory now held under military occupation by Israel, which is clearly in excess of the partition boundaries of Nov. 29, 1947, but an additional acquisition of further territory both within and outside Palestine.[18]

The US Govt. has recently made a number of representations to the Israeli Govt. concerning the repatriation of refugees who fled from the conflict in Palestine. These representations were in conformity with the principles set forth in the resolution of the General Assembly of Dec. 11, 1948, and urged the acceptance of the principle of substantial repatriation and the immediate beginnings of repatriation on a reasonable scale which would be well within the numbers to be agreed in a final settlement. The US Govt. conceded that a final settlement of the refugee problem must await a definitive peace settlement. These representations, as well as those made concurrently to the Arab States concerning the resettlement outside of Palestine of a substantial portion of Palestine refugees, were made in the firm conviction that they pointed the way to a lasting peace in that area.

In the interests of a just and equitable solution of territorial questions the US Govt. . . . has supported the position that Israel should be expected to offer territorial compensation for any territorial acquisition which it expects to effect beyond the boundaries set forth in the res. of the GA of Nov. 29, 1947 [the partition recommendation]. The Govt. of Israel has been well aware of this position and of the view of the US Govt. that it is based upon elementary principles of fairness and equity.

The US Govt. is deeply concerned to learn from Dr. Eytan's statements that the suggestions both on refugees and on territorial questions which have been made by it for the sole purpose of advancing aspects of peace have made so little impression upon the Govt. of Israel.

The US Govt. and people have given generous support to the creation of Israel because they have been convinced of the justice of this aspiration. The US Govt. does not, however, regard the present attitude of the Israeli Govt. as being consistent with the principles upon which US support has been based. The US Govt. is gravely concerned lest Israel now endanger the possibility of arriving at a solution of the Palestine problem in such a way as to contribute to the establishment of sound and friendly relations between Israel and its neighbors. . . .

If the Govt. of Israel continues to reject the basic principles set forth by the res. of the GA of Dec. 11, 1948, and the friendly advice offered by the US Govt. for the sole purpose of facilitating a genuine peace in Palestine, the US Govt. will regretfully be forced to the conclusion that a revision of its attitude toward Israel has become unavoidable. (*FRUS* 6 [1949], pp. 1051–53)

On May 26, in a Top Secret telegram from Lausanne, Ethridge informed Rusk that "a note of this character would strengthen my hand at Lausanne" but cautioned that "Israeli views regarding refugees and territory have crystallized to such extent . . . both privately and publicly, that it may be difficult for them to change. I strongly recommend its despatch nevertheless." Ethridge also recommended that the phrase "both within and out [*sic*] Palestine" be deleted and the last sentence of paragraph 1 quoted above be amended to read: "possibly an additional acquisition of further territory *within* Palestine" (*FRUS* 6 [1949], pp. 1058–59; emphasis supplied). He was referring to territory Israel was occupying within the boundaries recommended for the proposed Arab state.

Ethridge added a comment that, with hindsight, is ominous for the still uncertain future of the Palestine problem. He said, "Reference to Israeli acquisition outside Palestine would not strengthen note and would cause controversy. Israel desires small part of Lebanon and Syria and possibly in Transjordan for economic reasons but will undoubtedly have to approach on exchange basis as international frontiers are involved." And, finally, he suggested "that Department might orally suggest to Israeli Ambassador that final settlement Palestine question would be facilitated if meanwhile, Israeli Government were able to take such conciliatory steps regarding Jerusalem as action indicating Israeli Government was temporary trustee for Arab land and property within Jerusalem area and postponement transfer Israeli Government functions to Jerusalem" (*FRUS* 6 [1949], p. 1059).[19]

For "Eyes Only" Truman

On May 27, the State Department sent Truman a memorandum that, inter alia, listed Israel's "full territorial demands" based on a report from Ethridge. These included "a portion of southeastern Lebanon . . . [for] Israeli development plans," for which it was willing to offer unspecified territorial compensation. The list also included the Gaza Strip. It would accept the international frontier(s) with Syria and Lebanon "with the proviso that if either state desires to open negotiations in the future for border rectification, this may be done." Israel "will make further demands on Transjordan for territory in Arab Palestine" for "Israeli development plans" and give Abdallah "a few villages in return." It would retain "Western Galilee and Jaffa, Lydda, Ramle allocated to the Arabs under the partition plan." It would "relinquish none of the Negev" although it "might make some compensation in the Negev in return for the Gaza strip." It would "do nothing more concerning the Arab refugees at the present time" (*FRUS* 6 [1949], p. 1060).

The memorandum also reported that the Conciliation Commission "has failed to obtain any concessions from the Israelis on a territorial settlement or the refugee question." It added the department's belief "that it is now essential to inform the Israeli Government forcefully that if it continues to reject the friendly advice which this Government has offered solely in the interest of a genuine peace in the Near East, this Government will be forced with regret to revise its attitude toward Israel." If the Israeli government did not respond favorably the United States would find it "necessary to take measures" such as adopting "a generally negative attitude in the future toward Israel," including refusing Israel's request for "technical advisors and for the training of Israeli officials in the United States" as well as "withholding approval of the $49 million as yet unallocated of the $100 million earmarked by the Export-Import Bank" for a loan (*FRUS* 6 [1949], p. 1062).

The department's memorandum strongly recommended that the president approve "this suggested course of action." But it recognized that it "would arouse strong opposition in American Jewish circles" and therefore suggested the president "ask your advisors to give careful consideration to the possible implications of the above procedure." It added, "The Department hopes that it will receive your reply on a most urgent basis if this Government is to achieve a modification of the Israeli attitude in time to save the Lausanne meeting. Mr. Ethridge informed the Department by telephone on May 23 that he does not believe the meeting can last much longer than a week under the present circumstances. Dr. Bunche and General Riley concur" (*FRUS* 6 [1949], pp. 1060–63).

All the drafts of this recommended message to the Israeli government were unusually strong, but there is no record of any demurrer from Truman. On May 29 the final text, incorporating—virtually unchanged— the original draft, including Ethridge's modest language changes, was sent by the most urgent routing to the U.S. Embassy in Israel. It was marked "Top Secret" and "Priority" and instructed James McDonald, the U.S. ambassador, to deliver it immediately to Ben-Gurion (*FRUS* 6 [1949], pp. 1072–74).

The final version refers frequently to the partition recommendation of November 29, 1947, and to General Assembly resolution No. 194 III of December 11, 1948. The American attitude about compliance with these two basic resolutions had been fairly casually expressed during the negotiations. But with the Palestine Conciliation Commission's efforts to translate the armistices into a lasting peace, the United States began to adopt a more respectful posture toward the UN's decisions. Perhaps also because the Israelis more than the Arabs had abused earlier American lenient interpretations of these decisions, Israel was now subjected to a more demanding U.S. line.

Using such language as the government of Israel "should entertain no doubt whatsover" and "the U.S. Government must state with candor," the president's message warned Israel that if its "rigid attitude" led "to a rupture" of the talks at Lausanne, it "would place a heavy responsibility upon that Government and people." The president's note further warned that if the Israelis continued "to reject" the "basic principles" of Resolution No. 194 III and "the friendly advice" of the United States, "the United States Government will regretfully be forced to the conclusion that a revision of its attitude toward Israel has become unavoidable" (*FRUS* 6 [1949], p. 1074). But, as usual, no U.S. government action followed.

The president's note was handed to the Israeli chargé in Washington on May 30. On the thirty-first, the Israeli ambassador called on the acting secretary of state before leaving for Israel. A footnote to the text of the note describes the reaction of the ambassador: "With strong emotion in his voice the Ambassador said he prayed to God that the United States Government would not underestimate Israeli determination to preserve the security of Israel at all costs. It would be a tragic thing, he said, if the friendly relations between our two countries should be altered because the United States Government insisted on a course of action that would threaten Israeli security" (*FRUS* 6 [1949], p. 1074).

It was a familiar refrain, invoking God and parading the image of a threatened Israel. But there was no mention of exploring the alternatives, already on the table, for negotiating for a formal peace beyond the armistices. The acting secretary of state replied to the ambassador's comment by saying that he "was sure the Israeli Government realized that the United States Government would not send such a note without prior and careful consideration of all the aspects involved. I referred to the friendly relations between our two countries, and to the United States desire to see these relations continue, and I said that it was out of the deep friendship of the United States for Israel that we had made the recommendations which we believed would lead to a lasting peace in the Near East" (*FRUS* 6 [1949], p. 1074).

Israel took the note seriously. Sharett read it in the presence of the American ambassador in Tel Aviv and said, "This grave note calls for [a] considered answer which we shall prepare." But, at the same meeting, Ben-Gurion observed that the "note ignores two fundamental facts": Neither the United Nations nor the United States nor the Middle East states took "any strong action . . . to enforce the partition recommendation [or] to prevent aggression by Syria, Egypt, Lebanon and Iraq." (Interestingly, Ben-Gurion omitted Transjordan from this list.) He continued, "Israel was established not on [the] basis [of the] November 29 [resolution] but on that of a successful war of defence. Hence note's suggestion is today unjust and unrealistic for it ignores [the] war and continued Arab threats which make [the] November 29 boundaries impossible" (*FRUS* 6 [1949], p. 1075).

Ben-Gurion stated that the refugee problem could be considered only as part of a peace settlement, and the Arab states refused to make peace. As he put it, "As long as this attitude persists [the] refugees are potential enemies of Israel." Defiantly the prime minister concluded by declaring, "We do not intend to commit suicide by accepting [the] November 29 settlement in today's fundamentally changed conditions" (*FRUS* 6 [1949], pp. 1075–76).

It cannot be repeated too often that Prime Minister Ben-Gurion showed by this response that he either believed his own propaganda or had been persuaded by Israel's previous ability to influence American policies to favor Israel. Impartial observers such as Bunche, Ethridge, and U.S. diplomats were persuaded that the Arabs were eager for peace. Abdallah, of course, was an exception, as he nursed his (and Israel's) conspiratorial plans for Greater Syria. And Iraq had never been a significant factor. With obvious relief, it had abdicated to Abdallah its place in the deployment of Arab forces against the Israelis on the eastern front.

Furthermore, Ben-Gurion knew of Zaim's offer to resettle a substantial number of the refugees and the Syrian's interest in making peace. The prime minister's reaction to the Truman note, therefore, was more consistent with the Israeli strategy of defying the UN framework for peace than it was a reflection of any serious pursuit of peace. It may be problematical if any or all of the signals from the Arab side could have been carefully and diplomatically nurtured to attain the ultimate goal. What is significant is that at this crucial point the Israeli prime minister showed no interest in the exploration.

It is also important that Bunche had never agreed with the Israeli characterization of the Arab states' military intervention as "aggression." On the contrary, the UN mediator, attempting to persuade the Syrians to withdraw from the Palestinian territory they had occupied, had told Zaim on May 25 that he

> had in mind the stated fact that the armed forces of the Arab states entered Palestine for the sole purpose of protecting the rights and interests of the Arabs of Palestine. . . . The desperate plight of the vast number of Arab refugees and the extensive territory now under the control of Israeli forces give you grave concern and is a strong factor in determining your position as regards Palestinian territory now occupied by Syrian forces. But I submit that the provision for UN responsibility over the territory in the proposed demilitarized zone gives more than adequate protection to your interests and is much more consistent with the letter and spirit of the SC resolutions. (*FRUS* 6 [1949], p. 1054)

The Israelis did not reply to Truman's note until June 8. Seriatum, the Israeli response rebutted each of the points in the president's message. It acknowledged the great contribution of the United States in the enactment of the General Assembly's partition recommendation and declared this "will never be forgotten." But the response also deftly played hide-and-seek between that resolution and the one of December 11, 1948, and the concessions the president's May 28 note urged Israel to accept. For example, for the reasons Ben-Gurion stated to the American ambassador on May 29, the partition recommendation was held to be no longer relevant. The Israeli response also said that the American position "does not represent a UN policy" when it called on any state seeking territory beyond the boundaries recommended in the partition proposal to compensate by yielding other territory. To support this contention, the Israelis cited paragraph 5 of the December 11, 1948, resolution, calling it the resolution's "cardinal injunction." It called on "the governments concerned 'to seek agreement by negotiations, conducted either with the Conciliation Commission or directly, with a view to the final settlement of all questions outstanding between them.' This course the Government of Israel has consistently pursued," the Israeli note asserted. If the Lausanne talks were stalemated, the Israelis charged, "this is due entirely" to the concerted attitude of "the Arab states concerned" (*FRUS* 6 [1949], p. 1103).

The Israelis argued further that the recommended partition boundaries were based on "a series of assumptions which failed to materialize."[20] "The war," they continued, "has proved the indispensability to the survival of Israel of certain vital areas not comprised originally in the share of the Jewish state." And "in any case the Government of Israel cannot agree that the act of aggression committed by the Arab states in defiance of the charter and of the General Assembly calls for a territory reward" (*FRUS* 6 [1949], p. 1105).

In their own minds, the Israelis' rejection of U.S. criticism of their occupation of territory in the Arab state was a fait accompli. But this attitude did not inhibit them from saying they were perplexed by the U.S. concern over Israel's "rigid attitude" that the United States said endangered the possibility of a peaceful settlement.

The Israeli response to Truman's emphasis on the refugees put virtually all of the blame on the Arab states: "What produced the Arab exodus was the war on Israel."[21] "The exodus," the Israelis continued, "was partly spontaneous, partly decreed from above by Arab leaders and commanders." These explanations are largely fabrications. There was undoubtedly some flight of civilians from areas where fighting took place, although whether it could be described as spontaneous is debatable. But the myth that Arab leaders and commanders urged the Palestinians to flee and to return with the victorious Arab armies has been demolished by responsible research, now recorded as history.[22] Without even a hint of responsibility, the Israeli note reported, "The Arab economy lies in ruins." The note added smugly that "all the energies of Israel are focused on the absorption of the large-scale immigration [of Jews] now in progress. . . . The wheel of history cannot be turned back"[23] and that "it is inconceivable that the Government of Israel should find itself able to undertake in one and the same breath the absorption of mass Jewish immigration and the reintegration of returning Arab refugees. . . . The double burden is far more than Israel can bear" (*FRUS* 6 [1949], p. 1105).

And so, with a mixture of finely tuned selectivity among UN resolutions and some polite expressions of regret to the United States, whose "friendship" the Israeli government considered "an asset of Israel's foreign relations than which none is higher in value," the Israelis rejected both of the specific criticisms in the Truman note: territorial expansion by war and failure to comply with the General Assembly resolution on refugees. (For the full text of the Israeli reply, see *FRUS* 6 [1949], pp. 1102–6.)

The acting secretary of state handed the president a memorandum on June 9, noting that the Israeli reply "in effect rejects the cardinal points of the United States note." It "repeats the familiar arguments blaming the Arab states for the plight of these people [the refugees] and states the reasons why, in the opinion of the Israeli Government, it is impossible for a large number of the refugees to return to their homes." The memorandum, drafted by Dean Rusk, added that, "although firmly rejecting the points made in the United States note the Israeli note is not aggressive in tone and concludes with the hope that consideration of the Israeli reply will restore the 'sympathetic understanding of the United States Government for the problems and anxieties facing Israel.'" Rusk concluded his memorandum with his opinion that "there is no reason for the United States to abandon the firm position it has taken as regards Israel." He noted that "the Department will immediately consider what steps should next be taken and will shortly make recommendations to the President as to a possible course of action" (*FRUS* 6 [1949], p. 1107).

Acting Secretary of State James Webb had delivered the memorandum to the president on June 9. According to Webb, Truman had "expressed satisfaction that the Israelis appeared to be reacting well to the essential objectives which he and the Department are trying to achieve. He informed me that he had let it be known by a number of Jewish leaders who had called on him that unless they were prepared to play the game properly and conform to the rules they were probably going to lose one of their best friends" (*FRUS* 6 [1949], p. 1109).

This diversion from the Syrian negotiations is based primarily on U.S. records. But it fills a gap about which the Israeli records are virtually silent. In a sense, that silence is justified, for much of the American record is more concerned with the Palestine Conciliation Commission's efforts to bring about a permanent, comprehensive peace than with the seemingly intractable quarrels over the demarcation lines and the regulations for the demilitarized zones proposed for the Syrian armistice. Also, the attitude of the United States toward both Syria and Israel was a major consideration for both parties.

They were both to blame for the impasse because they were both guilty of ignoring—or attempting to circumvent—the relevant resolutions of the United Nations. This assessment is supported, at least indirectly, by both parties' concern with Bunche's repeated threat to take the whole problem back to the Security Council. Acheson's note of June 24 cited Israel's transgressions in the southern Negev, in western Galilee, and in the Jerusalem area. Abdallah had been a party to violations in the obscure deals in the secret agreement. And Syria had resisted withdrawal of its troops from Palestinian territory allotted to the Jewish state in the partition recommendation.

There was enough guilt to provide an abundant share for everyone, but it was not quite equally distributed. The United States had established a pattern of indulging Israeli violations of the UN truces. American Foreign Service officers in the field were aware of the violations and had kept Washington informed. An excerpt from a July 6 telegram to Acheson from the U.S. consul general in Jerusalem is typical: "Israel conducted the armistice negotiations with the intent that the boundaries fixed should be *minimum* frontiers of the new state and not temporary armistice lines" (*FRUS* 6 [1949], p. 1205; emphasis supplied).

As a further example, on June 11, from Damascus, James Keeley had advised Acheson that the Syrian foreign minister had told him the American interest

> in seeking cause of peace in Palestine might be more effective if weight [of] its influence were brought to bear upon Israel to respect its international engagements and thus help create atmosphere favorable to armistice and peace negotiations.
>
> Contending that as small area Palestine territory now occupied by Syria was taken in fighting against Israel before truce whereas Israel holds unchallenged vast areas occupied during truce, suggested demilitarization on Syrian front is scarcely equitable measure. (*FRUS* 6 [1949], p. 1119)[24]

The State Department's professionals in Washington were aware of such on-the-ground warnings and were inclined to act on them. This is reflected in the strong U.S. note of May 28. The president was finally persuaded to follow the department's advice. He approved its draft of the note and agreed to send it. But the United States failed to put these declarative policies into practice. An explanation for this gap between word and deed may be in Truman's reaction to the Israeli response on June 9, when he told "a number of Jewish leaders . . . that unless they were prepared to play the game properly and conform to the rules," they might "lose one of their best friends" (*FRUS* 6 [1949], p. 1109). What those "rules" were remains obscure. But the *subject* of a recorded conversation Webb had with the president only two days earlier may provide a partial explanation.

Memorandum by the Acting Secretary of State
Top Secret (Washington) June 7, 1949
Meeting With President, June 7, 1949
Israeli Propaganda in Palestine Case
   I informed the President of the activities of certain agents of the Israeli Government and he requested me to stand completely firm in the position we have taken. If necessary he is agreeable to the Department informing the Israeli Ambassador that, unless such activities cease, our note will be immediately released and the Department will take action to clear up any possible misunderstanding that has been created.

James E. Webb
(*FRUS* 6 [1949], p. 1092)

Again, there is no record of any follow-through. The pro-Israeli tilt of the United States, therefore, appears unchallengeable. It hardened the Syrian position, and, at the same time, encouraged the Israelis to believe they could ignore the so-called rules and still count on U.S. support for territorial expansion beyond the UN prescriptions for boundaries and refugees. More than forty years later, increasing numbers of observers see this ongoing pattern as a major frustration in the search for a still-elusive lasting peace. Bunche's reluctance to turn the problem over to the Security Council has been replaced in recent years by the near-automatic veto that Henry Kissinger promised the Israelis in the 1970s for any Security Council measure the Israelis considered detrimental to their interests.

   There was one other little-known development in 1949 that might have enjoyed greater efficacy had there been genuine and committed

U.S. support for UN efforts to lay the foundations for peace. On May 12, at Lausanne, under the auspices of the Conciliation Commission, Israel and the Arab states signed the Lausanne Protocol. At the insistence of the Arab states, the "rights and preservation of property" of the refugees was the first priority of talks with the commission. "Territorial talks" were assigned only a secondary importance. There was an "attached map showing [19]47 partition lines [to] be used as base for territorial talks." Israel was "willing to adopt [the] device [of the] protocol with map showing partition lines." After "several days delay" the Arab states "agreed [to] PCC formulation." The Syrians had "apparently [taken an] obstructive line, [but] finally agreed PCC formulation" (Cattan, pp. 108–9).

The Israelis qualified their agreement with the reservation that they "could not be a party to any exchange of views with Syria until an armistice agreement was concluded." They insisted no report of the protocol be made public; signing the protocol "in no way prejudiced" their right to express freely their position "on matters at issue" about which they entertained reservations. The commission did not object to the reservations but pointed out that "the protocol would be applicable to direct Israeli-Syrian talks whenever the governments wished to commence" (*FRUS* 6 [1949], pp. 998–99).

The various reservations probably neutralized the substance of the protocol. But it is worth noting that the Israelis had agreed to the map with partition lines that they had already violated in the Negev and western Galilee, and both Israel and Jordan had violated the map's lines in Jerusalem and at many other places on the Israeli-Transjordan front. Whether the Lausanne map was agreed to in good faith or not, the violations became de facto borders (until 1967) in the absence of any peace.[25]

The Israelis were so confident of the legal correctness of their position over placement of the armistice line that, in the confrontation with Syria, *they* threatened to take the matter to the Security Council. The Syrians were no less eager for a meeting between Zaim and Ben-Gurion to discuss the possibilities of a full peace, but Ben-Gurion consistently refused. Sharett had agreed to such a meeting, but as chief of state and head of the government Zaim had rejected the Israeli foreign minister as a substitute for the prime minister. The Syrian, however, was apparently amenable to sending a delegation headed by his undersecretary for foreign affairs to such a meeting. Sharett then rejected a meeting of the delegations, announcing he would meet "Zaim person-ally." Sharett called the Syrian shift "gross impertinence" (*M. V.*, pp. 591–92). Bunche, meanwhile, had postponed sending new proposals, hoping a direct meeting of high-level officials would eliminate the frus-trating impasse over the specifics of an armistice agreement.

No doubt prodded by Sharett's irritation and knowing that they were closer to compliance with UN resolutions than they had been in most other disputes in the earlier armistices, on May 31 Eban informed Bunche that "if he cannot devise means of getting Syrians out, we may go to [the] Security Council." According to Eban, Bunche was "shaken, con-fused." Eban thought he "let the cat out of the bag" because he knew "Riley believes Zaim would reject [the] Bunche compromise since it gets Syrians out of Israel completely" (*M. V.*, p. 593).

On June 1, Eban and Reuven Shiloah saw Bunche, Riley, and John Reedman, a member of Bunche's staff and a special representative of the secretary-general. Bunche told the Israelis he had submitted his latest proposal to Sharett and Zaim and emphasized to the Syrian that "total evacuation" of Syrian forces "from Palestinian territory [was] required." Bunche admitted that the Israelis would probably be unhappy over the "long duration" allowed for the Syrian evacuation and the "slowness" of "restoring civilian activity" in the demilitarized zones. But he also em-phasized that the Israelis should regard "the principle" of Syrian evacua-tion "as the most important element in his proposal." "Everything else is detail," subject to further talks and adjustment (*M. V.*, p. 594).

Eban and Shiloah then advised Sharett to enter discussion of the new Bunche proposal, "since UN commitment to Syrian withdrawal is valu-able whatever happens politically or militarily from now on." They described Bunche as "pessimistic" about Zaim accepting the proposal but claimed the Americans and French were both "pressing him to re-turn [to the] frontier." If all else failed, Bunche agreed to submit the matter to the Security Council. Finally, Bunche told the Israelis he and Riley believed that a meeting of Ben-Gurion and Zaim "could produce the first peace treaty between Israel and [an] Arab state" (*M. V.*, p. 594).

In view of the opinion of both Bunche and Riley about the possible suc-cess of a meeting of Ben-Gurion and Zaim, the Israelis were now fearful that a refusal would put the onus on them for obstructing peace. The diplomatic sparring now shifted to nit-picking about such a possible meet-ing rather than concentrating on the issues outstanding. Sharett informed Eban that the Israelis "will not, repeat not, meet [the] Syrians before

Bunche made his proposals." This instruction to Eban is dated June 4, although Bunche had reported he had submitted the proposal to Zaim on the first. Israel had not accepted the proposals either, so, also on the fourth, Sharett inquired of Eban whether Israel should reject the "distrustful features or accept [the] whole view [of the] tactical advantage [of] throwing [the] onus [of] rejection [on the] other side alone" (*M.V.*, pp. 595–96).

This jockeying continued for more than two weeks, with both sides employing their full repertoire of diplomatic evasions, fabricated excuses, and protestations of innocence. The Israelis skirted a meeting to talk peace probably because they were far from realizing the territorial aspirations of the 1919 Zionist memorandum. They were also unwilling to act on the problem of the refugees that, at this stage, would have required the repatriation of a considerable number and reiterated that they would address this problem only in the context of a final peace. The Israelis had exhausted virtually all their resources for continuing the war at that time and were in need of replenishing their weaponry. They were also war-weary. The major Western powers were maintaining an embargo on arms, and the Israelis wanted to consolidate their territorial gains. For these reasons the Israelis were prepared to negotiate only for an armistice, not for peace. The Syrians, on the other hand, were prepared to make concessions on the refugee problem as *part* of a formula for a final peace. But they now saw themselves as the leaders of the Arab cause and shunned a withdrawal from Palestinian territory in return for nothing more than an armistice.

Sharett confirmed this estimate of Syrian tactics to Eban in a message dated June 8. He instructed Eban to transmit to Bunche the following message, which Sharett had received from Vigier: The Syrians had "said question armistice is proper subject for armistice conference—if we [Israel] desire, should hold another meeting—whereas question future peace relations can only be discussed together with other Arab states" (*M.V.*, p. 597).

With some show of irritability and even bitterness—not entirely justified, inasmuch as Israel had done its own share of foot-dragging and obfuscation—Sharett added his comment on the Syrian position. Proposing an agenda for another meeting of the armistice negotiating delegations, he said to Bunche:

Apparently they assumed that we would list such subjects as medieval Arab poetry or Bedu lore or maybe Cartesian philosophy or

Japanese art. This new effrontery by self-styled Syrian Government is conclusive proof, obtained at cost more precious days and
impertinent snub, that all their recent reactions my proposal for
personal meeting been series of attempts at prevarication and deceit.
Only in deference your urgent request transmitted by Mohn and
out of confidence your judgment I reluctantly agreed adopt what
was to me distasteful procedure of indicating in advance and in
writing subjects for discussion at time when what I was anxious
obtain was chance free man-to-man talk untrammeled by formali-
ties. I must now urge you put end this inglorious chapter and com-
municate your proposals officially and immediately both parties
view hastening resolution deadlock and restoring prestige UN mediation in armistice negotiations, so badly shattered by way Syrian
business been handled throughout. (*M. V.*, p. 597)

The diplomatic shorthand is a little murky in spots, but its meaning is
clear. Convinced of their own advantage in law and unsure of the stability of the Syrian government at this time, the Israelis were prepared
to "go public," believing that the burden of obstructionism would fall
on the Syrians.

Whether there was any connection or not, on the same day, June 8,
Bunche's personal representative, Paul Mohn, submitted the acting
mediator's long-withheld compromise proposal for the armistice demarcation lines. It was little changed from earlier proposals. Where the
existing truce lines "run along the international boundary between
Syria and Palestine, the Armistice Demarcation Line shall follow the
boundary line." The compromise had something for everyone. It allowed
Syria to maintain some troops on the territory of the recommended
Jewish state and it acknowledged, tacitly at least, the Israeli position
that the recognized international boundary should be the site for the
interim arrangement of an armistice line. Bunche concluded his message to Sharett, containing this compromise, by asking that the armistice negotiating delegations convene again on June 10, when both parties would discuss the proposal (*M. V.*, p. 600).

On June 8 and 9 Eban cabled Sharett urging the Israeli government to
accept the compromise in "principle" while "reserving full right to argue"
the details. Eban's reasoning was pragmatic. In his message of the ninth
he argued that to reject the proposal involved great risks politically—
and even financially. If the compromise failed, Bunche was determined

this time to put the problem before the Security Council. Tel Aviv had been threatening military action against the Syrians if they refused to withdraw to the boundary. Eban predicted that if this course of action were pursued, the "political repercussions" would be "universal and profound." Furthermore, a "break" with the United States was almost certain to follow, "at least to [the] degree [of] certain stoppage [of] loan payments" and an "open adoption of anti-Israeli position." He warned that all members of the Security Council, including the Soviets, would be out of sympathy with an Israeli military action. The Arabs would "walk out" of the Lausanne negotiations, and Israel would be charged with the responsibility of sabotaging the putative peace conference. All existing armistices would collapse and it was possible the British would end the arms embargo—an act that would certainly be advantageous to the Arabs (*M.V.*, p. 602).

Eban's earlier enthusiasm for Israel to submit the impasse to the Security Council had apparently abated. There were, he said, two possibilities. The council would "support Bunche," he believed, and order the "total exclusion" of Syrian forces except, presumably, for minimal defensive forces at the perimeters of the proposed demilitarized zones. If the Syrians refused, Eban speculated, the consequences of "our direct action would have nothing like the consequences" he had listed if Israel resorted to such action without having the problem deliberated by the Security Council. And, finally, Eban considered the "possibility" the Security Council would "equivocate." In that event, he argued, if Israel took direct action, it would be "politically much easier" than direct action without having given the Security Council an opportunity to address the problem (*M.V.*, p. 602).

Therefore, Eban concluded, "prior reference" of the problem to the Security Council is "not, repeat not, a small question, but an enormously fateful decision [with] political [and] financial effects . . . overshadowing gain in time [or] money from premature action." Therefore, "prior reference" to the Security Council, he urged, was "indispensable if later action [presumably direct military force was] not to involve unnecessary and dangerous political perils." His long message concluded with a plea to Sharett to "cable your line of thought" (*M.V.*, pp. 601–2).

The French, meanwhile, were urging the Israelis to accept the Bunche proposal and the Syrians to "coordinate" with the United States. Sharett replied to Eban's request for instructions but made no direct reply about Bunche's proposals. He pointed out that the "main negative feature" is a "one-sided demilitarization" because "both areas" in which Israeli troops were "not to enter" or from which they had to be withdrawn, were "in [our] own territory." Also, the proposal was obscure about the "civilian authority [in the] demilitarized zone." Since both "civilian Jews [and] Arabs" would be "free to return" to these demilitarized areas, "we must insist they be under our jurisdiction" (*M. V.*, p. 604). Both in logic and in law, the partition-recommended boundaries, this time, were favorable to the Israelis.

On June 15, Eban told Bunche the Israelis would be prepared to resume meetings with the Syrians at the armistice negotiations in the no-man's-land near the Palestine-Syrian border. Eban informed Bunche that he had relayed to Tel Aviv Bunche's agreement, obtained several days earlier, granting Israeli jurisdiction in the demilitarized areas west of the "Syrian-Israeli frontier, with the obvious corollary of Syrian authority prevailing on the Syrian side." But Eban complained that Vigier appeared "to have no such understanding." "Swift and satisfactory conclusion [of] tomorrow's negotiations," Eban added, "would be greatly assisted" if Bunche made his representatives at the armistice negotiations "aware of your interpretation" (*M. V.*, p. 605).

With these preliminaries disposed of, the ninth meeting of the armistice negotiators convened on the sixteenth at the no-man's-land site. Both sides agreed that "the whole proposal be accepted as a basis for discussion." Immediately, the Israelis opened the discussion by asking whether this agreement meant accepting the proposal as a "basis for agreement, not just as basis for discussion." There followed another Alphonse-Gaston pattern of the earlier meetings. The Israeli spokesman, Colonel Makleff, announced he was ready to "make a statement" but added he wanted "to know if the Syrian delegation is also ready to make one." The Syrian response, offered by a Colonel Selo, was that although Makleff had made the suggestion, the Syrians did not know if the Israelis had "accepted the proposal as a basis for discussion" (*M. V.*, p. 607).

This kind of jockeying for position continues for nearly two pages of the record. It is illuminating only insofar as it permits us a glimpse of form rather than substance in diplomacy, as oral exchanges were used instead of a precise reading and understanding of written contractual agreements. The foreplay is not unique to Middle East modalities. Today, observers of international affairs can still recall the lengthy negotiations over the shape of a table during discussions seeking an end to the war in Vietnam.

Vigier finally terminated the verbal fencing by announcing the proposal would be "discussed paragraph by paragraph." Sensing that this implied acceptance of the draft, Mr. Rosenne, of the Israeli delegation, asserted that this did not mean "amendments cannot be proposed at a next meeting or at a later date" (*M. V.*, p. 608).

The Syrian, Mr. Tarazi, countered that "if amendments are to be presented, it would be better not to start the discussion today." He added, with some logic, that if an article is adopted, "no amendment could be brought at a later date." Then confounding that common-sense deduction, he added, "submission of amendments could be postponed to a further meeting," but again, neutralizing his own ruling, he added that "once an article has been adopted, it could not be amended at a later meeting" (*M. V.*, p. 608).

Vigier attempted to stop the verbal carousel by asking if Rosenne had meant the possibility of amending language or substance "at a later meeting." Rosenne did little to clarify, stating that if the text of one article, "for example paragraph 6," were to be changed, "it may be necessary to recast fundamentally another article accepted in a previous discussion" (*M. V.*, p. 608).

Vigier again attempted to break through the verbosity by declaring that, conceivably, important paragraphs might be subjected to "several readings, two or even three, if necessary," to offer amendments at any round. Thus, at last, the negotiating parties came to the agenda and the substance of the Bunche proposal (*M. V.*, p. 608).

But it soon developed that the haggling over procedure had not cleared the way for any expeditious disposal of the question of where to draw the armistice demarcation lines. Nor was the precise siting of the line the extent of this quibbling between the parties. There were also differences over the definitions of terms. What did demilitarization mean for the so-called demilitarized zones? What constituted defensive forces? Why was it necessary to destroy fortifications in the demilitarized zones if there were to be no military forces? And so, on and on, four solid pages of the Israeli record report a mixture of military expertise, geography, and demographics.

On one point Israel relentlessly pressed the Syrians: they could not claim any territory in the partition-proposed Jewish state territory. If—and when—negotiations progressed from armistice details to discussions for a formal, permanent peace, international law would support this Israeli position. In the disputed sector the Israelis had a weightier claim for establishing the international border at the armistice line than the Syrian claim for putting the armistice line where the truce had, at least temporarily, halted the fighting. So, for the fifth or sixth time at the meeting on June 15, Colonel Makleff said, "I want to know if the Syrian delegation understands . . . the withdrawal of Syrian troops [means] behind the international border." To which Colonel Selo replied for the Syrians that the reference to the part of the text of the Bunche proposal cited by Makleff "does not imply that Syrian troops should withdraw." And the Syrian then added the following equivocal comment, also quoting from the Bunche recommendation: "Where the existing truce lines as certified by United Nations Truce Supervision Organisation run along the international boundary between Syria and Palestine, the armistice demarcation line shall follow the border. There is a truce line separating the forces, which in this area is represented by the international boundary. Elsewhere, where the two lines are separated, it would be halfway between them" (*M.V.*, pp. 610–11).

The Israelis, of course, had no quarrel with the first part of the Syrian response. It was the final sentence that they found unacceptable. Makleff stated the objection, also quoting Bunche: "The area between the armistice demarcation line and the boundary, pending final territorial settlement between the parties, shall be established as a demilitarized zone from which the armed forces of both Parties shall be totally excluded. It is clear that the forces of both Parties will be out of this zone" (*M.V.*, p. 611).

This exchange led Colonel Selo to ask Vigier how to define a demilitarized zone from a military point of view. Both Vigier and General Riley gave technical answers stating that demilitarized meant removal of "fortifications, mines, obstacles and other military impedimenta used in defense of the zone." To this, Selo responded with the consistent Syrian position that "the draft we are now discussing aims at creating an armistice status and not a final peace status" (*M.V.*, p. 611).

This barely comprehensible dialogue makes clear that neither party had any respect for the other side's good faith. Their thinking was far removed from any earnest search for accommodation. Both willfully ignored the reservation that all the armistice agreements should be "without prejudice" to any resolution of issues in a permanent peace. Each side tried to manipulate the other for strategic advantage in a possible renewal of war or in fear that armistice agreements might evolve unchanged into a final settlement. Given such attitudes, after two and one-half hours of talk that resembled bickering more than negotiations, the meeting adjourned for five days, until June 21.

The Israeli documents have no detailed report of this scheduled meeting. It was, however, apparently held, and Rosenne from Tel Aviv cabled Eban that the "Syrians had confirmed they understood the proposals as implying their complete military evacuation." Also, according to Rosenne, "We interpreted restoration of normal civilian life" in all of the demilitarized zone "west of the frontier" to mean the "establishment of Israeli *civil* authority" (emphasis supplied). Rosenne than argued, with some kind of subliminal consistency, that this arrangement was "logical as the armistice deals with *military matters* only" (*M. V.*, p. 615; emphasis supplied). The interpretation gave Israel de facto what it had demanded all along—the withdrawal of all Syrian forces from the Jewish state territory and tacit admission of Israeli authority.

Therefore, in a somewhat different form, the deadlock continued. Faced with this Israeli interpretation, the Syrians countered again with one of their own. According to Rosenne, they now "saw lacunae" in the Bunche plan, and they recommended that the "community villagers" in the demilitarized zone should determine their own "civilian authority." Israel would then exercise authority in villages with a majority of Jews, and Syria would provide such authority in preponderantly Arab villages. The "whole area" would have "extraterritorial status" and be policed "under UN control" (*M. V.*, p. 615).

Rosenne announced that Israel "accepted" this Syrian "proposal" but asked Vigier to have Bunche clarify further the "status of the area." Both governments were to be sent clarifications. The next meeting of the delegations was fixed for June 28, which would be after elections for a new government in Syria. Rosenne believed that then the Syrians would "more easily swallow the bitter pill if pressurized sufficiently," because they were "unwilling to proceed to the Security Council" (*M. V.*, p. 615). On June 24, Eban informed Sharett that he, Reuven Shiloah, and Gideon Rafael (two colleagues of the Israeli UN delegation) had seen Bunche and John Reedman, Trygve Lie's special representative on Bunche's staff. The meeting, apparently, was to allow the UN people to "implore" the Israelis "not to raise theoretical aspects of sovereignty, citizenship, customs, since no armistice agreement can pronounce such matters." Bunche said he did not anticipate "any Syrian civil authority in any part of the [demilitarized] zone." He believed that the arrangements should "satisfy the substance" of the Israeli "desire to be the sole effective civil authority in the demilitarized area" (in which there were Arab villages). He was satisfied that discussion of the "reduction of forces" would result in an agreement of an even balance. The "only limitation" Bunche said he foresaw was that the demilitarized zone would be "supervised" by the chairman of the proposed Israeli-Syrian Mixed Armistice Commission. There would be no presence other than the Israelis in the zone. (*M.V.*, p. 618).

Bunche appealed to the Israelis "not to indulge in legalistic theories" and mentioned Rosenne several times in this context. Finally, he told the Israelis that Zaim had informed him, the United States, and France that he (Zaim) had "instructed Selo to behave and sign the agreement" (*M.V.*, pp. 616–17).

On June 26, Bunche sent a long letter to Sharett outlining much the same information that he and Reedman had covered in their meeting with the Israelis on the twenty-fourth. He added an appeal for Israeli cooperation. His major objective was to win Israeli support for his formula for the demilitarized zone, and he added, "I consider the meeting of the delegations on June 28th to be a most crucial one." "Agreement can be readily reached on the basis of the compromise proposal," he added, "if each delegation will come to this meeting determined to give every reasonable assistance to the United Nations effort to achieve agreement between the two parties."

Echoing the caution against either party overemphasizing "detail or tak[ing] a legalistic position," Bunche said, "I am confident that neither party will wish to bear responsibility for blocking agreement on any such specious basis." He repeated that "questions of permanent boundaries, territorial sovereignty, customs, trade relations and the like must be dealt with in the ultimate peace settlement and *not* in the armistice agreement" (emphasis in the original). Bunche then reviewed for Sharett the arrangements in the armistice agreements with Jordan and Egypt. Situations comparable to those still unresolved with Syria had been settled through compromises that had been proven satisfactory for the armistice period.

Finally, Bunche summarized. Using language somewhat more explicit than conventional diplomatese, he let Sharett know he regarded Israel as the hardliner. "From the beginning of these negotiations," he wrote, our greatest difficulty has been to meet Israel's unqualified demand that Syrian forces be withdrawn from Palestine. We have now, with very great effort, persuaded the Syrians to agree to this. I trust that this will not be undone by legalistic demands about broad principles of sovereignty and administration, which in any case would be worked out satisfactorily in the practical operation of the scheme.

In view of the foregoing, and my own firm conviction that the compromise proposal is reasonable and fair to both parties, may I present a strong appeal that the compromise proposal be accepted in essentials on 28 June without attempts at radical amendment.

I have the honour to be, Sir, Your obedient servant,

Ralph J. Bunche, Acting Mediator

(*M.V.*, pp. 617–19)

On June 27, Eban urged Sharett to accept the Bunche appeal and obtain a "swift armistice." To do so, he argued, would "consolidate [the] whole armistice system with good results [for] our overall territorial claims." Eban's messages support the preceding analyses of Israeli strategy. Israel regarded the armistice negotiations not as formulas for ending the fighting but as opportunities to stake out claims for expansion into the recommended Arab state and into the territory of Jerusalem. Eban underlined this strategy, adding, "[We] can continue pressing [the] details in [the] Mixed Armistice Commission" to be established as part of the armistice agreements. Its chairman would be assigned a kind of watchdog role supervising the armistice, particularly that part establishing the demilitarized zones. Besides, Eban counseled from the United Nations, the Security Council was "unlikely to regard us as aggrieved by my proposal which gets Syrians out, which [is] our main demand" (*M.V.*, p. 620).

There is no reference in the Israeli or American record about the meeting scheduled for June 28. But on the twenty-ninth, from Tel Aviv, Rosenne sent Bunche and Paul Mohn, Bunche's personal representative, still another gratuitous letter, which he claimed was at Sharett's request. It makes no reference to a June 28 meeting but refers to a meeting of the armistice negotiating delegations "fixed for Sunday," July 3. The burden of the legal advisor's message was that "no Israeli delegation will proceed" to the scheduled July 3 meeting "unless M. Vigier is able to confirm in good time before that date that the Syrian delegation will then be ready to proceed in a proper manner with the armistice conference" (*M.V.*, p. 621).

The acting mediator ignored the barely concealed disdain of Rosenne's "instructions." He simply cabled Vigier to be sure that for the July 3 meeting, the Syrians would "be fully prepared to undertake decisive action [on the] basis [of the] compromise proposal" and "carry on negotiations without intervening delays" (*M.V.*, p. 622).

Finally, the blizzard of words subsided. On July 3 the two delegations met for their eleventh joint session at the no-man's-land site, with Vigier again as chairman. The blizzard was over, but there were still a few short bursts of words and haggling over details. Rosenne demanded to know what "United Nations Representatives" meant in the context of supervision of the armistice. Did it mean the chairman of the Mixed Armistice Commission, or did it refer to UN observers attached to the commission? It was pointed out to him that the chairman, in principle, is the chief of staff of the UN Truce Supervision Organization and the observers serve under his orders, "therefore the problem is easily solved" (*M.V.*, p. 624). Rosenne was now satisfied.

Five points about timing the withdrawal of Syrian troops remained to be resolved. Ten weeks was proposed. The Israelis considered this "too long." For the Syrians it was "too short." This problem was deferred until the "powers of the Mixed Armistice Commission" would be discussed by a subcommittee composed of representatives of the two delegations. General Riley also felt that ten weeks was too long. It was agreed to have another subcommittee, identified as the "Military Sub-Committee," that would negotiate to "draw up the schedule of withdrawal" (*M.V.*, pp. 625–26).

The numbers of police (as differentiated from the regular armed forces) to be allowed in the demilitarized zone was referred to the Military Sub-Committee, and the rate at which civilians would return to the zone became a matter for negotiation between the Mixed Armistice Commission (MAC) and the Military Sub-Committee. The Israelis favored the sub-committee, the Syrians the MAC. The record reveals nothing of the strategy of either side, but, in general, the Israelis probably preferred minimal UN presence in implementing the armistice arrangements. The MAC would be integrally related to the UN. Consequently, the Israelis preferred the Military Sub-Committee, which would be composed only of Israeli and Syrian military specialists. For exactly opposite considerations, the Syrians preferred the MAC.

Vigier short-circuited the argument by the simple, if not entirely efficacious, suggestion that the Israelis present their case first to the

Military Sub-Committee. "If an agreement cannot be reached . . . in the Military Sub-Committee," the Syrian "proposal remains" (*M. V.*, p. 628). This completed the presentation of views of both parties on the first reading of Bunche's proposal at a joint session.

On their face, most of these points appear to be either tactical or at best strategic. But the vocalized opinions of both sides barely concealed considerable differences of long-range objectives and policies. That these motivations were so fundamentally different would not become apparent until the efforts to achieve a full peace moved to the Conciliation Commission. There the inability to reconcile these points and differences in the other armistice agreements finally defeated all efforts to negotiate a peace. The diplomatic technique of reaching stop-gap compromises on technical, tactical, or strategic differences and postponing decisions on the legal and substantive disagreements eventually aborted the negotiations that followed and thwarted efforts to reach a political solution for the Palestine problem.[26]

Having postponed any further exchanges or shunted the unresolved problems off to the MAC or subcommittees, the joint meeting of the two delegations agreed to move to the second reading of the Bunche compromise. Rosenne immediately raised a reservation about the first paragraph, which dealt with the "question of territorial settlement." He pointed out that this was one of the matters "before the UN Conciliation Commission at Lausanne." Then, consistent with Israeli strategy of trying to minimize UN participation in the armistice talks, Rosenne found "no necessity in bringing [this question] into an armistice agreement which is being concluded in compliance with resolutions adopted by the Security Council and the General Assembly." He suggested retaining only the part of Article I, paragraph 1 of the Bunche draft-compromise that stated, "arrangements for Armistice Demarcation lines" in the armistice negotiations "are not to be interpreted as having any relation whatsoever to ultimate territorial arrangements affecting the two parties to this [armament] agreement" (*M. V.*, p. 629).

Colonel Muhammad Nasser[27] objected, quoting Makleff who, at the June 21 session, had rejected a proposal made by Nasser, saying, "I am not at his disposal to cut out anything. Either we accept the proposal or we reject it." Vigier again resorted to a delay, recommending that whether Bunche's proposals "should be inserted in the [armistice] Agreement)" should be "referred to the Drafting Committee" (*M. V.*, p. 629).

Rosenne accepted Vigier's suggestion but argued that the question was "not merely a matter of drafting, it is a matter of substance." No one knew "what is going to happen at Lausanne," he continued. And "what will happen to this clause if we include a reference to the Lausanne talks? . . . [The armistice agreement] is only a provisional measure until a final settlement is reached" (*M.V.*, p. 629).

The point had been agreed over and over. It was an obvious, superfluous argument here. The Israeli lawyer probably raised it to conceal the real Israeli motive, which was to keep the Conciliation Commission, a UN instrumentality, at least at arm's length from the armistice agreement.

This time the Syrians apparently sensed the strategy, which had been used repeatedly by the Israelis. Tarazi, the Syrians' legal advisor, did not let the diversionary ploy pass without extensive commentary. In a lengthy reply he argued that siting the demarcation lines, any possible alteration, and established by any process, "emerges from the Security Council resolution of 16 November 1948 and the General Assembly resolution of 11 December 1948." The two resolutions, Tarazi continued, are "indivisible and cannot be dissociated." The rest of his intervention merits reproducing here: "The problem must be solved in three stages and the Lausanne Conference has been called only for the third stage. We are at present in the second stage. Our work is closely linked with the resolutions of the General Assembly and the Security Council, not only because the Security Council has called upon us to study this matter, but because the General Assembly, in accordance with the Charter, settles the essential problems with which the United Nations are faced" (*M.V.*, p. 630).

Having made his argument, Tarazi concluded, "I do not ask that this article be discussed now, but I have wished to reply to Mr. Rosenne. It is merely a matter of drafting." Probably with relief, Vigier then added, "I take it that the two delegations agree to refer the matter to the Drafting Sub-Committee. And Rosenne agreed" (*M.V.*, pp. 629–30).

Once again, behind the argumentative language, the long-term strategy of both parties was clear. The Israelis, seeking to capitalize on the momentum they had built up, so often supported by the United States, aimed to hold to a minimum any UN intervention that might decelerate that momentum by more deliberative debate of more complicated and permanent interests. The Syrians, on the other hand, with no great power supporters except occasional and timid assistance from France, attempted to counter such Israeli strategic moves by invoking the collective voice of the appropriate UN institution.

The joint discussion then tackled the problem of drawing the map that placed the demarcation line, pinpointing the area of the demilitarized zone. Three different maps were in circulation, prepared independently by each party "in company with United Nations [truce supervision] Observers." Agreement on one map to make final determination of the demarcation line was largely a responsibility for the Drafting Sub-Committee. Vigier finally ended the disagreement. General Riley had the map of the truce lines "certified by the UN Truce Supervision Organization." Vigier ruled that if the Israelis and Syrians could not themselves reconcile their separate maps, Riley, who would be presiding for the Military Sub-Committee, would "iron out" the difficulty (*M.V.*, pp. 630–31).

The last item discussed to complete the second reading of the Bunche proposal involved the temporary disposition of two areas—the Ein Gev and the Dardara sectors—that had been in dispute for most of the later sessions of the negotiations. Ein Gev was on the east bank of the Sea of Galilee and the Dardara sector about halfway between the international border and the Jordan River, both in territory that had been assigned by partition to the Jewish state occupied by Syrian forces during the fighting (*M.V.*, map facing p. 522). The Bunche proposal placed both of these territories in the demilitarized zone. Israel, relying on the partition recommendation, insisted there could be "no territorial claims about these two points" (*M.V.*, p. 632).

Vigier attempted to divide the problem into two parts, again postponing any decision at the joint session. First, he suggested that when the Military Sub-Committee drew the final map for the armistice agreement, the negotiators could "either accept or reject the map." Then, regardless of the armistice map, "nothing in the armistice agreement prejudices the rights, claims and positions of either Party." He emphasized that this language was taken from Article 40 of the UN Charter and "safeguards entirely . . . the rights of the Parties." This should "allow us to leave out of the discussion [of the armistice] non-military matters" (*M.V.*, p. 632.)

Tarazi objected, arguing that inasmuch as the two disputed areas "should be dealt with by the Military Sub-Committee . . . it should be decided now" (*M. V.*, p. 632). Colonel Makleff, the Israeli military expert, offered the Israeli response. Wherever the problem was decided, he said the Israeli reservation of no territorial claims (by the Syrians) would be applicable.

Vigier, totally frustrated in his efforts to begin the actual drafting of the final agreement, suggested that "we . . . not discuss this question now [but] wait for the consideration of the final text of the agreement. Should the Israeli delegation wish to reopen the debate then, it will be entitled to do it." He ruled that the two disputed territorial sectors should be included in the demilitarized zone, but the Israeli explanations and reservations would be included in the minutes. When the Israelis saw the final text of the agreement, they "would decide . . . whether it maintains [Israel's] reservations or not" (*M. V.*, pp. 633–34).

On this inconclusive note, it was agreed that Vigier would give each delegation a French and English draft of "an Armistice Agreement." He explained he "followed very closely the Agreement between Lebanon and Israel for all articles except Article V," which addressed the problem of siting the demarcation line. (For the text of Article V in the Lebanese-Israeli Agreement, see *M. V.*, p. 313.) It stated that because of the presence of "a third party" (the Syrians) in some sectors, the final determination of the line could not be specified "pending the conclusion of an armistice agreement with that third Party." At that time, the line would be drawn "in accordance with the intent" of the Security Council resolution of November 16, 1948, which called for "the withdrawal of the respective forces of the Parties" (Israel and Lebanon) to the points specified in the Lebanese-Israeli agreement. There was therefore, a connection between this unfinished third party business in execution of the Lebanese-Israeli agreements and an agreement between Syria and Israel. Both delegations then nominated their members for the Military and Drafting Committees, and the joint session of the delegations adjourned, agreeing to meet on July 5 and 6 to proceed with the drafting.

Drafting: Reconciling the Irreconcilable

Anyone who has participated in drafting a formal, contractual agreement involving issues regarded as important by the concerned parties appreciates the difficulties, even if only two people are empowered to determine the precise language and even if there has been general agreement that the substantive issues are understood. Such drafting exercises are not always simply a display by the lawyers, or principals, of their own hubris about literary style, semantics, or etymology. Language often conveys subtleties of substance, and reducing general agreement in principle to the meticulous precision of words, particularly where trust between the contracting parties is less than complete, is a crucial and potentially a hazardous business. Pity, therefore, the participants of the Drafting Committee, commissioned to write the definitive text of the Syrian-Israeli armistice agreement.

Two representatives of each party composed the committee. In the process of probing and pushing, suggestions and countersuggestions, for as long as human endurance and mental agility could sustain them, each side attempted to exploit every word, every clause, every ambiguity to support basic positions that had emerged early during the prolonged deliberations of the plenary meetings. Resolutions of the General Assembly and the Security Council had to be taken into consideration because both parties were concerned about world opinion, at least to the extent that neither wanted to be—or even appear to be—a barrier for a final peace.

The responsibility for reminding the two delegations of these obligations fell to Mr. Vigier and General Riley. Therefore, from time to time in the drafting process, as in the plenary sessions, the UN representatives felt obliged to enter the Tower of Babel to help find language that would, at the least, avoid glaring inconsistencies with the original intent of the UN resolutions.

Small wonder, therefore, that the *Main Volume* of Israeli documents concludes with fifty pages presumably reporting "for the record" every linguistic turn and twist of the Drafting Committee's efforts to finalize the texts for the matters that had been referred to the Military and Drafting Sub-Committees. It is virtually impossible to follow these linguistic debates, even with the basic, first draft prepared by Vigier in plain view. A few random examples, however, may illustrate some specifics.

In Article I, paragraph 4, the draft agreement declared that "establishment of an armistice agreement is accepted as an indispensable step toward liquidation of armed conflict and the restoration of peace in Palestine." Vigier interposed that he did not see what "indispensable" added to the text, or what advantage was to be gained by deleting it (*M.V.*, p. 639).

Rosenne continued the argument with a fairly lengthy speech. He suddenly expressed great concern for how the Syrians might look "to the rest of the world." He argued further that the word had been used in the Lebanese-Israeli agreement. Though Syria had not been a party to it and therefore "has no responsibility whatsoever for any of the previous agreements," Tarazi "cannot ignore the fact that previous agreements exist. . . . We cannot make changes simply because the text would be more aesthetic. If Mr. Tarazi suggests changes, he must be prepared to explain his point of view to the outside world" (*M. V.*, p. 639).

Tarazi replied that his amendments were not motivated by aesthetics. "We don't have to explain to the outside world the modifications brought to the text of the agreement. The outside world will know the text of the agreement itself." Rosenne persisted that it was "precisely because the convention [agreement] will speak for itself that the outside world will find peculiar differences between this [agreement] and previous ones" (*M. V.*, p. 640).

And then, with either short memory or total cynicism, considering the Israeli flouting of the partition boundaries and the December 11, 1948, General Assembly Resolution No. 194 (III), Rosenne added that "other agreements exist, we must build on them but not destroy them" (*M. V.*, pp. 639–40). Vigier ended this squabble by ruling that the word "indispensable" be kept in the text.

Most of the other disputes over language had to do with Articles V and II. The linkage of the two resulted from the substance of both. Article V concerned the demilitarized zone and regulations for governing and policing it and allowing for the return of civilians. There was no precedent for this problem in the Lebanese agreement, which was serving as the basis for the negotiations with Syria. Article II of the Lebanese agreement had addressed the obligations of the parties under the Security Council Resolution of November 16, 1948, calling for a truce. It prohibited both "military and political advantage" to be gained by either party and repeated the standard formula that declared that no provision of the armistice agreement "shall in any way prejudice the rights, claims and positions of either party in the ultimate peaceful settlement of the Palestine question, the provisions of this Agreement being dictated exclusively by military considerations" (*M. V.*, p. 643).

There cannot be much argument that some substantive inconsistency existed between the draft-texts of Article II in the prototype, Lebanese-Israeli agreement and Article V of the draft of the Syrian-Israeli agreement. The language of the original Article II stated that the final agreement pertained "exclusively" to military considerations and was difficult to reconcile with the conditions proposed for the demilitarized zone in the Syrian-Israeli agreement.

With hindsight, an analyst might speculate that the drafting might have gone more smoothly had the negotiators for this last armistice agreed to begin de novo. There is no explicit specification in the negotiations with Syria that the Israelis argued for using the agreement with Lebanon as the model. But throughout the discussions with the Syrians, it is clear that the Israelis preferred using the three previous agreements as a starting point, undoubtedly because those agreements favored the strategic objectives they had set for themselves in the armistice period. And while Rosenne, speaking most frequently as a trained lawyer, acknowledged that the Syrians had no responsibility for the previous agreements, such casual dismissals of the fact were no solace to Tarazi who performed legal acrobatics no less than Rosenne.

The difference was more than a petulant exhibition of the two adversaries' legal talents. For, although the Israelis were legally in a stronger position on questions of how future boundaries might be affected by the placing of the armistice demarcation line, the fact was that in the previous agreements Israeli claims—and military faits accomplis—had exceeded the partition-recommended boundaries. And the Israelis put great weight for establishing demarcation lines where fighting had been terminated. They did so despite the caveat in all of the agreements that stated the armistice agreements should not, in any way whatsoever, prejudice the "rights, claims or positions of either party."

In the negotiations with Syria, however, the situation was reversed. At the end of the fighting Syria was the occupier of territory that the UN resolutions had assigned to the Jewish state. It can only be speculation, therefore, why, in the drafting negotiations, the Syrians were stronger advocates for placing authority in the UN resolutions while the Israelis favored the previous armistice agreements in which, to their advantage, UN resolutions were frequently ignored.

A possible explanation is that a primary Syrian concern was western Galilee, which the Israelis had taken by force and refused to negotiate. It is also possible that having witnessed the general military and political defeats of their fraternal Arab belligerents, the Syrians felt some compulsion to retrieve something of Arab self-respect and honor. Thus, they insisted on principles for the ultimate peace negotiations, in which the Arabs might regain some of the territory the Israelis claimed to have a lien on by force of arms.

Such conjectures must remain no more than that until—and if—future researchers have access to Syrian intragovernmental records, comparable to the Israeli records now available. All that is clear at present is that neither of the parties to this last armistice negotiation came to court with clean hands. This may account for more loose ends in the Syrian-Israeli agreement than in the other armistices.

In another example of the unresolved confusions, on July 14, so close and yet so far from concluding the agreement, Bunche personally appealed to Sharett to receive General Riley and Vigier for a final, definitive decision on the outstanding issues. The tone of Bunche's letter reflects both his anxiety and, to some extent, his impatience. Several paragraphs are worth quoting:

> From the beginning of these negotiations, as you are well aware, our great problem has been to induce the Syrians to accept fundamental and unalterable Israeli conditions, namely, the withdrawal of Syrian military forces from positions now strongly held by them in Palestine. Our greatest efforts have had to be directed toward this end, since it was clear to us from the outset that an armistice agreement could not be otherwise obtained, and for this purpose Mr. Vigier and General Riley have spent most of their time in Damascus throughout these negotiations. The Syrians have now accepted the basic condition. It is proved also that your delegation has made concessions, and thus the present state of almost complete agreement has been reached. In this connection, I think you will agree that considering that this is an armistice agreement and not a final settlement, the concessions made by your delegation have not affected adversely any vital Israeli claim or position.
>
> You may recall that in our discussion in my office during your recent visit to Lake Success you indicated to me that the indispensable condition for the armistice was Syrian withdrawal, and that if this could be assured, the Israeli position could be adequately flexible on issues of detail. . . .
>
> I am requesting now only that you hear carefully the Syrian reservations which Mr. Vigier and General Riley will make in their conference with you and that you will go as far as you reasonably can toward meeting them, in order that this final agreement may

be speedily concluded. I am certain that what is involved in these reservations will in no way affect any vital Israeli interests.

I apologize for once again making a personal appeal to you, but I do so now as in the past only because of the crucial nature of the situation and the obviously imperative necessity of concluding this final armistice agreement . . . in order that the military phase of the Palestine conflict may be finally and fully liquidated.

With most cordial regards, I am, as always, your devoted servant in the cause of peace in Palestine.

Ralph J. Bunche
(*M.V.*, pp. 666–67)

The Bunche appeal was not unheeded. On June 14, Rosenne wrote to Mohn informing him of the specifics still at dispute and that the Israeli government was prepared to adopt a conciliatory posture with respect to some of them and to agree to Syrian proposals to place "troops" in certain areas in the disputed territory. Perhaps more important, Syrians "living in Syria" but owning land in the demilitarized zone are "in principle entitled to receive passes allowing them to enter the demilitarized zone in order to cultivate their land. Similarly, passes will be delivered to such persons who have fishing rights." So, while the proposals asserted Israeli sovereignty in principle, Syrians were not to be deprived of their property or source of livelihood. Rosenne added that this and several other paragraphs should not be in the "agreement itself," but "the Government of Israel will be prepared to confirm in writing the matters referred to . . . at the time of the signature of the agreement."[28]

Finally, Rosenne informed Mohn that the Israeli delegation would "be prepared to proceed to the armistice talks on Monday, July 19, 1949, and it is hoped that it will be possible then to initial the definitive text of the armistice agreement, which can be signed in the course of the week." He concluded, "It would be appreciated if we could be informed before Monday that the Syrian delegation will be in a position to complete the negotiations on the terms outlined above" (*M.V.*, pp. 667–68).

There were, however, some loose ends to be tied together on June 19 on "the use of aircraft in the defensive area," a discussion on the possibility of distinguishing between military and civilian aircraft and "naval forces." At one point, Rosenne, apparently weary of the protracted effort to dot every *i* and cross every *t*, offered that he believed that "this agreement is based on good faith, and anyway those present know that no written agreement can cover every eventuality." Tarazi noted that Rosenne had, at one point, said, "The use of civilian aircraft for military purposes would be an act of treachery" (*M.V.*, p. 673).

At this point, Colonel Selo rendered what amounted to a benediction. "Both parties are in good faith," he said, "and wish to assert their good faith." And on that note, after a brief intervention by Tarazi to explain that "it is understood" that in one of the annexed letters which both parties had agreed to sign pertaining to the stationing of troops in one area, the word "stationed . . . means the troops stationed there will not go beyond these [specified] points" (*M.V.*, p. 673). The plenary session set July 20, 1949, at 16:00 hours as the time for signing the agreement (*M.V.*, p. 672).

Lasting from April 5 to July 20, the negotiations with Syria were the longest and most bitterly debated of the four armistice negotiations. There had been thirteen plenary sessions of the two delegations. And yet, despite the protracted time, more issues were left unresolved than in any of the other arrangements.[29]

There are many reasons for the near failure or, if preferred, only partial success of the Syrian negotiations. First, Bunche, because of illness, was unable to be in the Middle East as he had been at Rhodes for the earlier negotiations. Vigier and Riley were both apparently dutiful representatives and had acted with integrity, but they lacked the commanding prestige that Bunche had patiently established for himself as successor to the slain Bernadotte. Bunche at the United Nations was available in New York, but his physical presence was missed at the scene of the negotiations. Problems of communication between the no-man's-land site of the negotiations and Lake Success compounded the complications.

Second, even the Israeli documents indicate that the Syrians were better equipped for tough, substantive bargaining than were the earlier Arab state negotiators. Furthermore, when the negotiations began, the facts on the ground favored them. They held territory that, according to UN resolutions, was to be part of the proposed Jewish state. This was a reversal of the earlier situations when Israeli forces occupied territories assigned to the proposed Arab state. This time the Syrians held what the Israelis wanted and were determined to use the chips for their greatest possible bargaining advantage.

Over and above this advantage, the diplomatic exchanges reflect that the Syrian negotiators were better prepared than any of the earlier Arab

delegations. They advanced more penetrating and relevant legal interventions supporting Arab states' claims or rights. Tarazi was a match for
the astute and agile Rosenne. And the Syrian military advisors appear to
have known the military value of the topography of the smallest piece
of disputed territory.

A principal disadvantage was that the Zaim government was living
a precarious existence, lacking the legitimation of full international
recognition. Several times during the plenary sessions, Rosenne led the
Israeli charge, needling the Syrians by questioning their credentials.
The Israeli tactic must have generated some psychological wear and tear
and weakened the self-confidence of the Syrians.

Last, an unimportant but contributing factor to the inconclusive
character of the Syrian-Israeli agreement was the shift of U.S. attention
from the armistice negotiations to the efforts of the Conciliation Commission to persuade the several parties to agree to a final peace, for
which the United Nations hoped the armistices would be the first step.
The 1949 volume of *Foreign Relations of the United States* provides
clear evidence of this shift of the American position.

Following Keeley's June 12 telegram to Acheson, reporting Zaim's
appeal for the United States to influence Israel "to respect its international engagements," there is no further cable traffic between Damascus
and Washington relevant to the negotiations until July 13 (*FRUS* 6 [1949],
p. 1119). Nor is there any between Washington and Lake Success, nor
any internal memoranda of conversations in the State Department with
Israeli or Syrian emissaries.

On July 13 Acheson sent in a brief telegram to the embassy in Israel
Bunche's July 14 letter of personal appeal to Sharett.[30] Acheson advised
McDonald, the U.S. ambassador, that he "might wish first to consult
with Riley and Vigier in order to obtain additional background of the
remaining points at issue." But McDonald was instructed by Acheson
to see Sharett as soon as possible and "give full support to the position
set out in the Bunche message, emphasizing the earnest hope of U.S.
Government that remaining obstacles to conclusion of the armistice
can be surmounted" (*FRUS* 6 [1949], p. 1225). There is no documentary
proof that Acheson's intervention had any direct influence on the almost simultaneous notification from Rosenne to Bunche of the Israeli
acquiescence, with only minor reservations.

On July 17, Keeley informed Acheson that he had discussed the Israeli
reply of the fifteenth with the Syrian foreign minister, who had re-

sponded that despite some misgivings, the Syrian government in "appreciation of the friendly advice of its friends [meaning the United States] would accept the Israeli compromise offer." On the sixteenth, in another session with the foreign minister, Keeley was told that "true to his promise" the foreign minister "yesterday had instructed the Syrian Delegation to accept the terms without further discussion" (*FRUS* 6 [1949], p. 1233).

And on July 18 Keeley sent his last telegram about the armistice negotiations to Acheson. Most of the message reported Zaim's apparent discouragement over what he regarded as continuing "Israeli intransigence." Keeley countered by urging the Syrians to "take the leadership in a constructive approach at Lausanne." Zaim answered, "Tell me what you want me to do." Keeley mentioned the problems of Jerusalem, territorial settlement, and the refugee question. He also persuaded Zaim not to diminish the stature of the delegation Syria would send to Lausanne, which Zaim had said he was inclined to do. According to Keeley, Zaim repeated an appeal made "months ago" reiterating a "hope that the UN under U.S. inspiration and leadership would speedily impose a Palestine settlement based on the partition plan of November 29, 1947 which the Arab states would in the present circumstances have to accept as a *force majeure*." All of which led Keeley to concur with an opinion General Riley had expressed, "that Syria now offers the best Arab leadership in reaching an overall peace settlement" (*FRUS* 6 [1949], pp. 1234–35).

But the right combination of American leadership and UN initiative never materialized. The Lausanne talks foundered on the three principal issues that had been evaded in the armistice talks: Jerusalem; determination of Israel's borders; and a free choice for the refugees between repatriation and compensation for those who elected not to return.

On July 21, Bunche reported to the Security Council that the truce had been "superseded by effective armistice agreements . . . in the transition from truce to permanent peace." However much in good faith the acting mediator believed this assessment, his conclusions were illusory. He recommended that the Security Council might "declare it unnecessary to prolong the truce" as mandated in its resolutions of July 15, 1948. It could also remind "the Governments and authorities concerned, pursuant to Article 40 of the Charter to desist from further military action and might also call upon the parties to the dispute to continue to observe an *unconditional* cease fire."[31] Bunche also recommended "the termination or the transfer to the United Nations Palestine Conciliation Commission . . . such functions as now remain to the position of Mediator under Security Council resolutions" (*FRUS* 6 [1949], pp. 1240–42).

chapter 10

ENTR'ACTE

Today, more than forty years after the events chronicled in this study, it seems fatuous to call this closing chapter "Conclusion." For the war in the Middle East is still going on, and most of the watching world probably no longer remembers that the UN Security Council resolutions of November 16, 1948, and August 11, 1949, described the armistice agreements as a "transition" from "truce to permanent peace in Palestine." But except for the "cold peace" between Egypt and Israel, this ultimate goal still eludes the world's diplomats as it eluded their predecessors in numerous "peace processes," while the belligerents have engaged in four (some observers count five) wars.

During each of these military engagements, an apprehensive world has feared escalation to a world conflict of unmanageable proportions. The battlefield confrontations have spawned assassinations of heads of governments, energy shortages, and crushing military budgets that have obstructed social, economic, and political progress desperately needed by most of the warring states. Many causes contribute to the persistent instability of most Middle East states. But there has been a persistent perception that the conflict over Palestine and the future of the Palestinians remains a major destabilizing factor. In short, it is still not possible to write "conclusion" to the war that the armistices were intended to terminate.

The record shows there is more than enough guilt to go around for all of the 1948–49 belligerents, with a good deal left over for some of the major powers. The increasing numbers of revisionist histories, such as those used in this study, suggest that it is risky to attempt any exact apportioning of responsibility for the persistent failures. But close scrutiny of the negotiations in the armistice talks—the first participation of the major belligerents in formal face-to-face political bargaining—may provide a rough guide to the mine fields that must still be traversed on the way to the goal of a just and enduring peace. This study claims no more than this modest hope.

One more word of caution is appropriate here. It is simple honesty to repeat the observation made in the preceding pages about the advantages of hindsight. There is too often only the thinnest line between pretensions to prophecy and the infallible wisdom acquired by watching history unfold. I confess that in the value judgments I made about some of the events recorded in these pages, I have occasionally crossed this thin line. The confession is not to be construed as an apology, for most recordings of history are to some degree selective, and it should suffice for the selector to be willing to defend any departures from pure objectivity in free and open debate with any responsible challenger. With these reservations, the following findings appear to be warranted by the study of the armistice negotiation documents.

The Palestinians: The People Who Weren't There

Probably the most striking fact about the four armistice negotiations is the complete absence of any direct, formal representations by the indigenous Palestinians. In the perspective of history, the omission was not an innocent oversight. The diplomatic history pertaining to Palestine, except for that beginning with UN resolutions from the early 1970s, set the precedent for such Palestinian anonymity. Many synonyms were employed. The first notable example is the phrase used in the Balfour Declaration—"existing non-Jewish communities." In the long, specific stipulations of the 1947 partition recommendation (G.A. Resolution No. 181), "inhabitants of the Arab State" is the substitute language. After the establishment of Israel, the majority of the Palestinians were identified simply as "refugees" in annually repeated UN resolutions calling for their right of repatriation or compensation for those electing not to return. The same terminology was consistently used in a number of international documents that asked for efforts to provide humanitarian assistance for or resettlement of "the Palestinian refugee problem."[1]

It was not that any of the major players believed the old Zionist misrepresentation that Palestine was "a land without people for a people without a land." On the contrary, at least as early as 1919 Balfour outlined the policy of "the four great powers" (Britain, France, Russia, and the United States). In a memorandum to his cabinet he discussed the Balfour Declaration in relation to the Covenant of the League of Nations, which stated that "the wishes of the communities of the former Turkish provinces must be the primary consideration in the selection of a Mandatory." With almost brutal candor Balfour told his colleagues, "I have never been able to understand how the commitment to Zionism can be harmonized with the Covenant. In short as far as Palestine is concerned, the Powers have made no statement of fact which is not admittedly wrong, and no declaration of policy which, at least in the letter, they have not always intended to violate."[2]

Even with the most honorable intentions, the British at the time might have been hard pressed to find a realistic and responsible representative for the Palestinians with whom the future political destiny of Palestine and its population might have been discussed. Even before the Paris Peace Conference—as early as 1916—too many backroom deals had been cut to fit the imperialist ambitions of the British and the French. The Arab world had been carved and recarved. Non-Palestinian Arabs inevitably had to be let in on the secrets that might have affected their particular area. Arab ambitions generally aspired to one Arab sovereignty, and Palestine was generally regarded to be a part of a greater Syria. The wishes of the country's indigenous people were therefore given little consideration. The British intention to separate Palestine from Syria was already fermenting in these pre–peace conference manipulations, for it was generally conceded that France would be the major power influence in Syria, and the British wished a southern buffer to keep the French at a safe distance from the Suez Canal. Palestine admirably served the purpose.

The Hashemite ruler in the Hedjaz continued to maintain an almost naive trust in the British, and Prince Faisal, his son, was to become the most influential Arab at the peace conference. It was not until General Allenby's conduct of the war in the East had advanced the Allied forces well into Palestine that the Palestinians were informed of the Balfour Declaration. Any apprehensions the knowledge may have aroused were dulled by promises to keep old promises, although the British had no intentions of keeping either the old or the new.

The cavalier disregard with which Balfour treated the Arabs of Palestine in his 1919 exposition to his cabinet was, therefore, no eccentricity; and with only the slightest and most grudgingly given moderation, the same depoliticization of the Palestinians has continued, in official American circles. Only recently, sparked by the Intifada, have the first indications of respect for the rights of the Palestinians emerged as a factor commanding serious attention in the search for peace.[3]

As Zionists moved into Palestine after the Balfour Declaration and the first Arab-Israeli war, the apparently endemic internecine quarrels of the Arabs and their distrust of one another did not escape notice by the astute and often opportunistic Zionist leaders. These soon became a working principle of their strategy and was reflected in the slogan "Zionism's secret weapon is Arab disunity."

Nor was this perception unfamiliar to the architects of the imperial ambitions of the great powers. The tenet was alive and well in the minds of the Israeli strategists during the negotiations for the armistices. One of its earliest applications is evident in the Israeli veto of Bunche's original idea to conduct the negotiations in a single conference at which all the belligerent states would be present. And the idea remained operative in the U.S.-Israeli preferred procedures for moving forward the Bush-Baker peace process as 1989–91 faded into history. It is also reflected in the effort to make the Camp David Egyptian-Israeli treaty the pattern to be emulated in the search for the still elusive, comprehensive peace. In plainer English, the strategy, lightly disguised, is an effort to reach separate peace agreements in one-at-a-time negotiations with divided Arab states, finessing the collective national rights of the Palestinians as a party to the negotiating process.

According to the Israeli account, only Egypt and Syria raised the refugee issue in the armistice negotiations. The Syrian prime minister offered to resettle as many as 300,000 in the context of a plan to liquidate the entire Arab-Israeli dispute over Palestine and in return for economic aid for Syria. The proposition was made privately to the Israelis, but the United States was kept informed. The other Arab states were not privy to the plan. The U.S. minister in Damascus was convinced that the offer was genuine. The Israelis were bobbing and weaving. Ben-Gurion rejected the idea of meeting Zaim for face-to-face negotiations. Moshe Sharett was at first intrigued by the plan but finally decided not to meet

Zaim on the grounds that the Syrian had neglected some diplomatic amenities. The United States clearly did less than it could have done even in response to some earnest entreaties from the Syrians. As Avi Shlaim put it after examining the relevant prime sources recently, the Zaim proposal withered on the vine because the Israeli "school of thought," led by Ben-Gurion, believed that "time was on Israel's side and that Israel could manage perfectly well without peace with the Arab states and without a solution to the Palestinian refugee problem" (see chap. 9, note 5).

It is now possible to say with considerable certainty that world consensus at last is that a peaceful resolution of the Palestine problem is impossible without a formula to satisfy the Palestinians' commitment to national self-determination. In November 1988, the Palestine Liberation Organization declared the establishment of the independent State of Palestine. Approximately one hundred nations granted some form of official recognition, and representatives of the PLO, led by Yassir Arafat, engaged in a campaign to add to the number. Finally, in December 1988, as one of his last acts as U.S. secretary of state, George Shultz authorized formal contacts with representatives of the PLO, and a series of meetings followed in Tunis.

Israel's prime minister, responding to some prodding by the United States, finally produced a plan for the Palestinians in the occupied West Bank and Gaza to elect representatives to meet with the Israelis to negotiate some form of autonomy. The proposal explicitly ruled out negotiations with the PLO and the option of an independent Palestinian state. At the end of a period of three to five years, discussions about a final determination of the West Bank and Gaza would be in order. The United States declared rather vaguely that the election proposal might serve as a place to begin moving the peace process forward, and the PLO agreed in principle to elections with certain reservations that, in its opinion, were essential to ensure free and fair choices.

The point of these still unrefined discussions about the possible elections is that at last the "wishes" of the Palestine "community," to use the language of the Covenant of the League of Nations, were approaching recognition in peace proposals that were on the table, so to speak, in 1988–89. Judith Kipper, a Middle East specialist with the Council on Foreign Relations, provided an updated summary.

Israel's problem with the Palestinians is not about individuals, but about a national community that demands political expression.

It may still take Israel some time to recognize the validity of Palestinian nationalism, a necessary step in the beginning to look at the most difficult issues. . . . The consequences of refusing could be extremely grave. At a minimum it would mean continued isolation for Israel and erosion of American and Jewish support.[4]

It is obvious that these conclusions to the failed objective of the armistice negotiations have crossed the line dividing wisdom, as of 1948–49, and hindsight provided over the next four decades. The trespassing may be excused if, as many now hope, the new crop of would-be peacemakers does everything possible (not only short-term politically expedient) to rectify the deliberate exclusion of the indigenous Palestinians from the earliest effort to initiate a peace process, beginning with the armistice negotiations.

The Arab States

Before summarizing conclusions about the conduct of the Arab states during the armistice negotiations, a caveat noted at the end of chapter 1 bears repetition. There is, as yet, no access in English to complete Arab state archives comparable to the Israeli situation. Consequently, we can only infer official Arab thinking through Israeli documents or rely on records of conversations between Arab emissaries and U.S. officials as reported in *FRUS*. The ultimate Arab motivations and political objectives, once the fighting does end, are not certain, and what we do see in these other-than-Arab sources may be deliberately or innocently inaccurate. Only in the early 1990s and on a noncoordinated basis have such scholarly and researched sources as the *Journal of Palestine Studies* and *Arab-American Affairs* offered competent scholars, including Palestinians, opportunities to publish previously inaccessible, official Arab documents.

Nevertheless, some reasonably entr'acte deductions may responsibly be made about Arab intentions, leaving it for future scholars to correct any erroneous, crucial errors. Flapan, also acknowledging this information gap, writes that "a review of the contributing Arab myths, misconceptions and fallacious policies must be done by an Arab—only then will it be credible, only then can it have some influence in shaping new Arab policies."[5] With these reservations, the following conclusions about Arab conduct seem justifiable, based on the sources used for this study.

It appears that at least tacitly—perhaps even tactically—the Arab governments reluctantly accepted the partition-recommended armistice lines. This acceptance called for no great Arab concessions because, for the most part, except for Syrian campaigns in the north and Transjordanian campaigns on the central front—principally in Jerusalem and its environs—it was Israel's troops that had occupied territory allocated to the proposed Arab state. Contrary to much widely believed conventional wisdom at the time, echoes of which still linger in uninformed media and in some pro-Israeli outlets, there is no credible evidence that before May 15, when the British effectively relinquished the mandate, any regular Arab state forces—with the exception of the Syrians—invaded territory that partition had assigned the Jewish state. Avi Shlaim, in a rather sparsely documented account, reports an Arab summit meeting in Amman on April 29, 1948, at which "it was secretly decided to send Syrian, Iraqi and Lebanese troops, in the guise of volunteers . . . crossing into Palestine on May 8 under instructions to avoid all contact with British and Jewish forces before May 15."[6]

Whether Palestine here is intended to include all of the mandated territory or only that part allocated to the proposed Arab state is not clear—a confusion generally true of most accounts of this turbulent period. The situation in Jerusalem, the context for the Israeli-Transjordanian fighting, in which both belligerents violated the partition resolution, was somewhat different. Again, Shlaim's accounts shed light on a complex of facts little known and understood until recently. Actual fighting on this front did not begin until a day after May 15. Shlaim postulates that it began then only because there had been no "agreement or understanding" between Israel and Abdallah covering Jerusalem in the secret talks between the two. It appears, however, that on this front also, Israel was the instigator, with Abdallah's Arab Legion acting essentially in a defensive role.[7]

In any event, after May 15 the Arab governments ended all their efforts to conceal their roles as belligerents. On May 15, the secretary-general of the Arab League sent a cable to the secretary-general of the United Nations informing him that "Palestine is a sacred trust" for the Arab states and fearing "a further deterioration of the prevailing conditions and to prevent the spread of lawlessness and disorder into the neighbouring Arab lands . . . and to fill the vacuum created by the termination of the Mandate and the failure to replace it by any legally constituted authority, the Arab governments find themselves compelled to intervene for the sole purpose of restoring peace and security and establishing law and order in Palestine." On May 16, Abdallah sent a separate but similarly worded cable to the UN secretary-general. Consistent with his ambitions revealed in the secret negotiations with the Israelis, the king added, as part of his motivation, the wish to protect "the unarmed Arabs against massacres similar to those of Deir Yasin [and of his] national duty towards Palestine in general and Jerusalem in particular, and also Nazareth and Bethlehem." The Transjordanian monarch also complained that "Zionism did not react to our offers made before the entry of Armed forces."[8]

Had the Arab states prevailed in the first Arab-Israeli war or in the following armistice negotiations, whether they would have set the Palestinians free to establish their own sovereign state must—at least for the present—remain moot. But this was certainly not Abdallah's intention. His collusion with the Israelis suggests that whatever priority he may have assigned Palestinian self-determination was measurably lower than his ambition to rule a greater Syria incorporating whatever part of Palestine he might obtain by bargaining with the Israelis. Had the conspiracy succeeded he might well have had to fight both Syria and Egypt.

A major factor contributing to Arab failure to curb the expansionist designs for which Israel manipulated the armistice negotiations was their appalling unpreparedness for meeting sophisticated, well-prepared Israeli negotiators on an even basis. Arab delegates to the negotiating meetings were often without maps of the contested territories. The Israelis usually came with clear instructions for both opening and fall-back positions. Arab negotiators often had to suspend sessions to return to their capitals for what appear to have been ad hoc adjustments to Israeli claims.

Inasmuch as many Israeli demands involved territory beyond the recommended partition boundaries, both parties frequently ignored Bunche's efforts to establish armistice lines where the opposing armies stood following various cease-fire orders. The Israelis, therefore, had little incentive to appeal to the United Nations. Bunche's rather frequent threats to take the negotiations back to the Security Council, together with accusations against one or another of the parties, were in a large sense his most effective ploy for curbing Israeli expansionist ambitions.

The Arabs, for their part, were no more enthusiastic about a return to the UN body, perhaps because they felt they could not come to a court of equity with clean hands inasmuch as they had resisted partition from the beginning. As a result, they may have lost opportunities for faring better in the substantive results of the negotiations, and, more certainly, they lost opportunities for winning popular opinion support throughout the world.

Finally, in assessing Arab failures, contrary to Israeli statistics on the relative military capabilities of the belligerents, the balance of both matériel and trained manpower was not nearly as favorable to the Arabs as generally reported. Beginning as late as the 1960s, detailed examinations of the facts and professional interpretations of their significance have demonstrated the reverse.[9]

The outstanding exception to this inventory of Arab state inadequacies and derelictions appears to have been Syria. How much of its stiffer resistance to Israel is attributable to the more careful preparation of its representatives and how much to the historic Syrian ambition to be the champion of pan-Arabism, including a greater Syria, is another question that can be answered with some certainty only when more historical Arab documents become available.

Speculating about motivations explaining the stubborn Syrian resistance for retaining territories their forces occupied when the 1948–49 fighting ended, it is important to remember that this contested territory embraced much of the water resources that the Zionist maps of 1919 held to be vital to the viability of the proposed Jewish state. The flow of water through Lake Huleh and the tributaries of the Jordan River and the importance of those lands to the riparian Arab states is apparent as well. Added to these international considerations, which Syria probably entertained, the Zaim offer to resettle what was then a high percentage of the displaced Palestinians included the confessed hope for much-needed economic assistance that, in turn, might have given the Zaim regime sufficient strength to challenge Egypt as the leader of the Arab world.

In reality, none of the professed Arab state aspirations for the outcome of the armistice talks or for the future of the Arab world that, to a large extent, depended on that outcome could transcend the divisiveness, corruption, and ineptness infecting them. With comparatively little competition, except for unpredictable British support for Abdallah, who was perceived differently at different times in service to Britain's national interest, the Israelis carried the day.

The Israelis

The Israelis' negotiating strategies cannot be understood without reckoning in the 1919 Zionist proposals to the Paris Peace Conference. Knowledge of that document makes it clear that the claims the Israelis made during the armistice negotiations to territory they had occupied in the war beyond the partition-recommended boundaries had long been part of their blueprint for a Jewish state that could survive economically by possessing the available water resources of the area. By the late 1940s this historic estimate of the territory needed for realizing their objective of self-contained, economic viability outweighed whatever commitment they may have felt to the UN recommendations for the territorial extent of their Jewish state and for the possibility of negotiating peace with the front-line Arab states.

This outlook boded almost certain failure for any hope that the armistices might prove to be stations on the road to peace. And it warrants more than this passing notice for any who attempt new peace processes to remember that since 1967 Israel has occupied much of these non-Palestinian lands in the Golan Heights and Palestine territory in the partition-proposed Arab state and since the 1980s a significant portion of Lebanon by maintaining mercenary forces in the south of that country. All of this expansion was previewed in the 1919 Zionist map (see Map 1 and accompanying text) and clarifies the following points.

(1) Israel was determined to retain Faluja and Beersheba and the hard bargaining before agreeing to the demarcation line in the Gaza area, because even while they were negotiating with Egypt they were planning the campaign to occupy the Negev. Gaza and Beersheba were not only included in their 1919 plan; they were also strategically important for the military campaign in the Negev.

(2) Similarly, on the northern front, Israel was reluctant to withdraw from southern Lebanon to the internationally recognized Palestine-Lebanese border and insisted on remaining in western Galilee (which partition had assigned to the Arab state), reflecting the 1919 map. Of contemporary significance, it is relevant to note that the so-called Israeli security zone in southern Lebanon, in which Israel exercises near-total control, is consistent with the 1919 claim to establish the border at the Litani River.

The Arabs of the 1940s should have been aware of the geopolitical history of these 1919 claims because Prince Faisal, son of Sherif Hussein of the Hedjaz, represented the Arabs at the Paris Peace Conference, and there had been discussions and even a negotiated agreement between Weizmann and Faisal. But whatever the reasons, Arab interventions in the armistice negotiations show little evidence that they were familiar with the historic, geopolitical designs of the Israelis and the critical importance of the water resources involved. The explanation for this failure may well be as Khouri puts it: "Most of them found themselves, at the end of World War I, lacking in political experience and ill prepared to compete with the political acumen of the Zionists. Even their leaders were insufficiently aware of the dynamic and subtleties of international diplomacy and ignorant of how to present their case effectively. . . . They failed to make adequately serious and determined efforts in the field of international propaganda to defend the Palestine Arab cause."[10]

(3) By 1947–48 and through the armistice negotiating period, the image of Israel as David in a modern reenactment of the biblical drama of David and Goliath served the Israelis well. The orchestrated picture of a weak, humanitarian-oriented Israel at the mercy of a powerful Arab world, unrelenting in its passion for revenge and vindication of its military losses in the war, reinforced a popular Western sense of guilt and sympathy for victims of Hitler's abominable crimes against the Jews. Giving the "Jewish people" some ill-defined national-political rights in Palestine appealed to the statesmen of the victorious Allied powers of World War II in what appeared to be for them a zero-cost move at the expense of the Arabs. Hannah Arendt, writing of the trial of Adolph Eichmann, the personification of the Holocaust perpetrators, characterized the general international mentality of the time as "the banality of evil."

(4) The Israelis bolstered their search for sympathy with arguments during the armistice talks that used claims for security to rationalize their claims for strategic territory assigned to the proposed Arab state. They buttressed these arguments with topographical maps that, by their interpretations, demonstrated the defensive, military necessity for such claims. These arguments were, indeed, plausible because of the patchwork borders of the map of the recommended partition. The division of the country had been determined largely by demography rather than by geographic logic. At several places, so-called borders were nothing more than nondimensional dots where borders intersected. Even with this crude demographic rule-of-thumb, significant pockets of Palestinians would have ended up in the Jewish state and somewhat less

significant numbers of Jews would be left in either the proposed Arab state or in Jerusalem, scheduled to become a *corpus separatum* supervised by the UN Trusteeship Council for ten years, after which the residents of the city were to be free to choose "possible modifications of the regime of the City."[11]

The partition plan allowed freedom of choice for Jews in the Arab state and Arabs in the Jewish state who elected to change their domicile to live with a majority population. Minorities in both states were to be assured of equality of rights and full citizenship.[12]

Under usual circumstances, such guarantees in a solemn, international document might have been enough to assure security had the document been the result of free negotiations between the involved parties. However, the partition recommendation was not such a document. Representatives of the Zionist movement and of the Arabs had participated in the UN debates preceding the adoption of the recommendation. But such general debate interventions were not the equivalent of face-to-face, systematic negotiations by the principal parties. Flapan argues that "Zionist acceptance of the Partition Resolution [represented] a far-reaching compromise." But, he continues, "acceptance of the resolution in no way diminished the belief of all Zionist parties in their *right* to the whole of the country" (emphasis supplied).[13]

Further, according to Flapan, Ben-Gurion's acceptance of the partition was selective. He welcomed those passages that "were all to the advantage of the Jewish state. [He] unhesitatingly rejected [those] less favorable to Zionist interests—beginning with the projected borders of the Jewish state and the transition period for the implementation of the various stages of partition . . . ending with the establishment of the proposed Arab state. . . . Ben-Gurion had always viewed partition as the first step toward a Jewish state in the whole of Palestine, *including Transjordan, the Golan Heights and southern Lebanon*" (emphasis supplied)[14]: the 1919 Zionist memorandum again—and much of the territory Israel occupied in the 1967 war. The resulting speculation that the territories Israel occupied in the 1948–49 fighting were strategic jumping-off points for planned, future expansion is not to be lightly dismissed.

Whether the Arabs knew of the 1919 map or not, the aggressiveness with which Israel fought the war and the tenacity with which it pursued the placement of the armistice lines to include these strategic points beyond the partition borders or the cease-fire lines provided the

Arabs no inducements for looking beyond the armistices to a peaceful solution of the conflict.

The Major Powers

The voting record of the major powers on the partition resolution is illuminating. France, the Soviet Union, and the United States supported it; Britain abstained. Until the last minute the French argued for some alternative to partition which, they felt, "could provoke a war." Despite its misgivings, however, France eventually supported partition, hoping to maintain a visible presence in the Middle East through an appointment as a member of the proposed "Administrative Authority" for the city of Jerusalem. Britain agreed to terminate the mandate "as soon as possible" but otherwise "played an inactive role and even abstained in all the votes taken on the various draft resolutions submitted."

The Soviets supported partition.[15] On its face, this was a surprising windfall for the Zionists. Consistent with Marxist ideology, the Soviets had been consistently anti-Zionist. With no accessibility to official Soviet documents, the explanations for this dramatic reversal of Soviet policy have been largely speculative, deduced from perceived Soviet global strategy under Stalin. Such speculations by both pro-Israeli and pro-Arab Kremlinologists place Soviet motivations squarely in the context of the cold war. The Arabs had hoped the Soviet Union would oppose both the Zionists and the United States. But on October 13, 1947, the Soviet delegate to the United Nations made a strong speech of support for the "concept of partition."[16] For public consumption the Russian is reported to have spoken "not without sympathy" about the "aspirations towards Palestine of a considerable part of the Jewish people, of the calamities and suffering they had undergone during the last war ('which defy description') and the grave conditions in which the masses of the Jewish population found themselves after the war."[17] But according to most of the speculators, the unpublicized motivations of the Soviets were somewhat less humanitarian and considerably more devious in terms of cold war geopolitics. They had

> apparently become convinced that they had more to gain than to lose from the partition of Palestine because it could (1) drive out British control and increase and influence anti-Western feeling generally in the Middle East, thus making it easier for the Russians

to make some headway there; (2) bring about a highly nationalistic, anti-British Jewish state containing many thousands of refugees from Soviet-dominated areas in Eastern Europe; (3) cause an increase in tension and unrest in the Middle East which would hurt the West and enable the Communists to exploit the situation; (4) compel the Security Council, where Russia had a veto, to deal with the Palestine dispute; and (5) require the UN to dispatch an international force, possibly including Russian troops, into Palestine.[18]

The Soviets had also provided the prestate Zionist forces with military hardware via Czechoslovakia.[19]

The United States

The role of the United States has been examined in previous pages of this study, using the official records from the *Foreign Relations of the United States* series. But in these summary pages a few editorial opinions not to be found in the official records may be in order.

President Truman was genuinely torn between compassion for the victims of Hitler, on the one hand, and the professional advice of the State Department's Middle East specialists (about which his several secretaries of state and their deputies generally agreed), on the other. Adding heavily to his general humanitarian considerations was the powerful Zionist lobby's extensive and consistent public relations efforts focusing on Nazism's Jewish victims, thousands of whom still languished in displaced persons camps. The reiterated central theme of the Zionist public information campaign was that the overwhelming majority wished to go to a "Jewish state in Palestine."[20]

A small number elected to return to the countries from which they had fled as the Nazi forces had moved through Europe. Some returned to Germany, some went to the United States and South American countries. Unflattering stories about Franklin Roosevelt's administration with respect to these helpless humans have multiplied in recent years. But their reception in other Western countries was also often less than cordial. Consequently, because of its history as a haven and the vigorously promoted visibility of Zionist achievements in mandated Palestine, it appeared to be the most practical and immediately available answer to the problem of liquidating the tragic condition of a large segment of the displaced persons.

Truman was not unmindful of Arab claims for the future of Palestine. He was also conscious of Roosevelt's commitment to King ibn Saud after the Yalta Conference to do nothing about Palestine without first consulting the Arabs. At one point, in response to a memorandum from the Egyptian prime minister to the State Department, the president responded that "the Arabs . . . would be consulted . . . as well as Jews . . . consistent with my position that the principle of self-determination required that Arabs as well as Jews be consulted." Similar assurances were sent to other Arab states. The State Department argued that the United States "should stay out of any activity that might offend the Arabs" (Truman, p. 365).

Truman, however, continued to press the British to lift some of their restrictions on immigration but also declined to accept responsibility for policing Palestine if larger-scale Jewish immigration incited the Arabs to violent protest. After the Potsdam Conference he had told an American press conference that, in private conversations in Britain, he had said, "The American view was to let as many of the Jews into Palestine as it is possible to let into that country. Then the matter will have to be worked out diplomatically with the British and the Arabs, so that if a state can be set up there they may be able to set it up on a peaceful basis. I have no desire to send 500,000 American soldiers there to make peace in Palestine."[21]

There is little reason to doubt the genuineness of the president's compassion for the victims of Hitler's savageries. But he was caught in a dilemma between these personal predilections and domestic Zionist political exploitation of them and his appreciation of the political complexities surrounding the problem of Palestine. This dichotomy probably accounted for the disagreement between the White House and the Departments of State and Defense.[22] In a candid confession in his memoirs, the president admitted that he knew at whom to point as a major contributor to his difficulties: "The Zionists . . . were impatiently making my immediate objective [of helping to resettle the displaced people] more difficult to obtain. They wanted more than just easier immigration practices. They wanted the American government to support their aim of a Jewish state in Palestine."[23] Some of this angst is reflected in the citations from the *FRUS* volumes analyzed in the preceding pages of this study.

But there is one significant element in this struggle that formulated American policy and to which there is only minimal reference in the archival documents. A reluctance to record in official documents that the persistent lobbying of the American Zionist organizations enjoyed considerable success is understandable. The in-house editors of the *FRUS* volumes are, after all, humans as well as bureaucrats. However, a more detailed account of this polarization in the American policy-making machinery is in a work authored by a staunch pro-Israeli advocate, Nadav Safran. In his opinion, the Arab proposal for a unitary, democratic Palestine state with minority guarantees for Jews would best have served U.S. interests. But, Safran quickly adds, without elaboration, this would have been "unfeasible."[24]

Truman was facing what promised to be a bitter election campaign, with Thomas Dewey his Republican opponent. The votes of states with large Jewish populations, such as New York, Illinois, and California, were considered critical. Dewey was a native New Yorker and a veteran practitioner of the state's political wisdom. Consequently, his campaign was unstinting in its support for partition. Truman's political aides in the White House, Clark Clifford and David Niles, advised him to outbid the Republican. And the advantage of being able to execute policy, of course, was the president's.

In a literal sense it can be argued this account of developments in Washington before 1947–48 does not belong in an analysis of the armistice negotiations. I would argue, though, that the inconsistencies of the American record during the talks cannot be fully understood without some awareness of the historic position of the Zionist precursors of the State of Israel with their territorial aspirations cartographed in the 1919 Zionist memorandum.

The United Nations

The last major player involved in the armistice negotiations was the United Nations. The collective intentions and motivations of the world body are clear from a careful reading of the relevant General Assembly and Security Council resolutions, cited at appropriate places in the preceding pages. But, as with many international agreements, the chasm between the language of the documents and their implementation is wide and sometimes unbridgeable. This certainly was true about the UN efforts to resolve the Palestine problem by political means rather than by force which, in any event, the United Nations does not possess except in the moral sense.

Ralph Bunche, in my opinion, is the most tragic figure in the rough-and-tumble politics of the armistice talks. He was the one who suffered the greatest torment as he attempted to turn the intentions of the United Nations into political and military realities. His most effective weapon as he tried to find some accommodation between Israeli and Arab demands appears to have been his threat to turn the dispute back to the Security Council.

Israel, in the process of petitioning for admission to the United Nations, was most susceptible to this pressure. Various Arab states had been UN members for some time. In addition, many of them had oil and markets for trade. The newborn Israeli sovereignty had no such assets, except for the often capricious support of the United States. Israel's greatest international asset at the time was the moral sympathy it commanded, which was still increasing because of unfolding accounts of the enormity of the human suffering brought on by the Nazis. In a similar but less tangible view, the Arabs enjoyed some support from Western Christians because of missionary activities and Christian contributions to educational institutions in the Arab world. At the time, there were no Moslem bodies capable of influencing policy in the important democracies whose UN votes were often decisive in determining UN decisions.

In the final analysis, the major powers were not above duplicity in their voting conduct. The British had abstained on all substantive UN proposals. At the same time, they were encouraging the conspirators in the Abdallah-Israeli secret talks, hoping to maintain a foothold in the Arab world by supporting the Hashemites in Iraq and Transjordan. The Soviets, early on, began to switch from supporting partition to pursuing a strategy of divisiveness that they hoped would weaken Western influence and provide leverage among the Arabs. The United States fell between a number of cracks, attempting to keep the Soviets out of the area, to protect American oil interests, and to cope with the domestic intimidation, real or imagined, of the Zionist lobby. In the end, Washington was unable, or unwilling, to back any of these with force. In the United Nations, it supported most resolutions for peace and for resolving the problem of the uprooted Palestinians. In quiet diplomacy, it condoned most Israeli flouting of UN efforts to legislate territorial limitations and to implement the Palestinians' rights to return. In a large sense, therefore, the armistice talks proceeded as if in a jungle of their own, with no clear road maps or protection against various predators.

EPILOGUE

A Personal Word

The suggestion to analyze the Israeli and American documents pertaining to the armistice negotiations originated with Dr. Anis F. Kassem, a Palestinian now practicing law in Kuwait. I met Kassem when he was a graduate student at the George Washington University Law Center in Washington, D.C. We have continued our friendship ever since.

When Kassem first asked if I would undertake the study, he contemplated using it as an essay in a future volume of the *Palestine Yearbook of International Law* series that he edits. I said that the subject interested me but that I was not a lawyer. (My smattering of knowledge in the field has been acquired through collaboration with Dr. W. T. Mallison, Jr., of the George Washington University Law Center faculty, now professor emeritus, who had been Anis Kassem's teacher.) Kassem replied that I was well informed on the history and political aspects of the Palestine problem and that he felt that if I would accept the assignment, it would qualify for inclusion in his yearbook series.

Soon after I began to examine the source material I concluded I would have difficulty doing the subject justice in even a long essay that Kassem had agreed the final product might be. When I informed him of my opinion, he urged me to proceed, adding when the work was completed we would discuss the format in which it might be published. The result of his patience and generosity is the present volume.[1]

The conception of this work evolved from the principal sources cited, plus other historical and political works with which I had become familiar in some forty years of specializing in the controversy over Palestine and the Palestinians. I had long entertained the theory that judgments of Israeli policies and U.S. reactions to them usually supported Israeli interests because they were predicated on the premise that much conventional wisdom about public affairs relies on short public memory—that is, without knowledge of the history of Zionism. As a contrary opinion, I had concluded that there was—and is—a continuum from Theodor Herzl up to and including the regimes of Menachem Begin and Yitzhak Shamir. The traditional policies of the Labor or left-of-center coalitions differed only tactically from those of Likud and the rightists. Behind the slightly different rhetoric and visible maneuverings, both Israeli main-line political movements shared ultimate national goals. Recent revisionist history, much of it authored by Israelis, confirms what had been for me a long-time working premise.

As I examined the archival material relevant to the armistice negotiations, I became increasingly convinced that in evaluating the evidence in isolation from what is known about prestate Zionism, Israeli negotiating strategy and tactics might be dismissed as defense against implacable Arab enmity. In that context, Arab diplomacy might be construed as determination, at almost any cost, to frustrate the expressed hope of the international community to have the armistices be the first necessary steps on the road to a lasting and comprehensive peace. But in the context of the prestate Zionist history, the more unguarded declarations of Herzl, the 1919 Zionist memorandum to the Paris Peace Conference, the terror campaigns of the Irgun and Stern militarists, the surreptitious Jewish Agency–World Zionist Organization support of those campaigns, the sophisticated selectivity by the Israeli armistice negotiating teams of the strategically important territorial points beyond the partition borders that had been occupied by Israeli forces in the 1948 fighting, neatly and—in my mind—irrefutably fitted into the historic Zionist continuum leading to a "greater Israel."

This reasoning accounts for my decision to begin this book with the 1919 Zionist memorandum. The same reasoning persuaded me, here and there in the notes, to observe the relationship of a development in the armistice talks to some more recent event. A few illustrations may be mentioned here: the ability of the contemporary pro-Israeli lobby to manipulate U.S. policy, although today the point of leverage is much more Congress than the White House, as it was in Truman's time; the tortured logic and disinformation used in recent years to bar the PLO from recent so-called peace processes, differing only tactically from the virtually complete suppression of earlier efforts to give public ventilation to UN and international consensus for coping with the original Palestinian refugee problem; the continuing Israeli occupation of southern Lebanon using the more palatable label of a "security zone," rather than calling public attention to the historic Zionist ambition to have the Zionist state's northern border established at the Litani River; the increasing support in Israel for "transfer" expulsion of the Palestinians in the occupied territories and the annexation of those territories by Israel.[2]

The origins of these and similar examples of Israeli conduct are clearly to be found in the official records of debates and adopted resolutions of the various Zionist congresses and, in somewhat muted tones and garnished with plausible rationales, in the continuing public information programs of the Zionist movement. There has been little or no conspiracy in this history. The concealment of motives and of political-territorial ambitions has been essentially that of the great powers, in their manipulation of the League of Nations and more recently in the United Nations and in their exploitation of the problems and resources of their various client states in the area while they protest deep concern for the welfare of the native populations. Thus, a Zionist idea advertised as a haven for Jews who have suffered various forms of inequality and discrimination has been allowed—often encouraged—to become the hegemonic power over the Arab states, perpetuating policies of theological and ethnic exclusivism against native Palestinians, both those displaced and those still within generally recognized Israel.

I am not saying that the Arabs have been without fault. Their governments have been derelict in assuming responsibility for their own people. Even today as Arab-state economic power and strategic importance has increased, a mere pittance of resources is devoted to the kinds of sophisticated cultivation of world public opinion that is essential to any efficacious implementation of policy. Instead of such effective informational weapons of international conflicts, there is more than a little suspicion that Syria is a headquarters for terrorism that is condoned and probably financed by Saudi Arabia and perhaps Libya. And although Arafat and the mainstream constituents of the PLO, since their November 1988 meeting in Algeria, have renounced terrorism and explicitly recognized Israel as a part of the Middle East, only Egypt and Jordan have, with some consistency, provided public support for these declarations as contributions to a possible peace.

But these efforts and the now-active diplomacy of the PLO are eclipsed by the rhetoric and media visibility given to the Israeli disparagement of the PLO's declared positions and by the wearying repetition of U.S. demands for proof of sincerity. Neither Israel nor its powerful ally had the courage to invite responsible representatives of the PLO to a negotiating table to put both Israel and Arafat to the test to determine which, if either, is a good-faith party to an honest search for a genuine peace. This kind of vicarious negotiating with legitimate Palestinians had characterized the entire history of the Palestine controversy.

In the four decades between the armistice signings and the late 1980s, Middle East history has been characterized by charges, countercharges, wars, and interruptions of wars, a syndrome inspired and perpetuated by ambiguously worded UN resolutions. Over the years, Israel encroached more and more on Arab-Palestinian territory and on Palestinian rights, while the United States vacillated between mild rebukes and shame-faced support for Israel's actions on the grounds that Israel was helping to check Soviet expansion in the Middle East. Meanwhile, because the United States provided funds and increasingly sophisticated American arms to its "Middle East ally," the Israelis were encouraged to believe that their aggressiveness and constant threat to the Arabs were indispensable to the United States in the area. As a result, Israel and the Zionists gained a confidence which often bordered on arrogance along with their political clout in Washington. The single exception to this pattern was the cold peace produced by the Israeli-Egyptian accord.

Although it was not perceived widely at the time, in December 1987, young frustrated Palestinian activists in Gaza launched the Intifada in an open attack upon a small group of occupying Israelis. To use an overworked phrase, it was "the shot heard around the Arab world"—and beyond. In Algiers less than a year later, after full consultation with the Palestine National Council, which had emerged as authoritative representative of the Palestinians, Arafat publicly declared that the PLO recognized the existence of two states in Palestine—thus recognizing Israel in November 1988. He called also for the recognition of the "State of Palestine," the withdrawal of Israeli forces from the occupied territories, the placement of "the territories" under UN supervision for "a limited time," a solution to the problem of "Arab refugees," a Security Council plan for assuring "the security of the parties to the conflict," and an international conference to produce a formula for a comprehensive peace. On December 6, 1988, the Swedish Foreign Ministry announced that Arafat and a delegation of Palestinians had met in Stockholm with a group of influential American Jews, the Swedish prime minister, and members of the Swedish government. With hindsight these meetings appear to have been undeclared explorations of the idea of formally inviting the chairman to the General Assembly to announce the substance of his November declaration. But the United States, defying the near-universal recognition of the existence of the PLO and so of a Palestinian national entity, and insisting that Arafat had no mandate to speak for what the United States called "the Arab refugees," refused the chairman a visa to come to New York to make a formal presentation of his proposals to the United Nations. The anachronistic American policy, dictated more by traditional American subservience to Zionist pressures than by rational appraisal of the current international landscape, was out of step with world opinion. Underlining that fact, the General Assembly moved a session to Geneva where Arafat did appear to state the Palestinian case formally. At this assembly, the PLO declared its acceptance of the conditions the United States had stipulated for it in order to participate in formal negotiations for settlement of the Israeli-Palestinian confrontation.[3]

With the winding down of the cold war as the principal focus of U.S. policy and the growing concentration of the expiring Soviet Union on its internal problems, the United States clearly emerged as the world's only superpower. High on the international agenda was ending the historic instability of the strategically important Middle East. The Iran-Iraq war had to be ended. That accomplished, it left the Arab Gulf states and their vast reservoirs of oil vulnerable to Iraqi military power on one side of the Gulf and to the potential threat from the eastern side in Iran's population advantages and still considerable petroleum reserve. Saddam Hussein's wholesale slaughter of the Kurds in the north of Iraq, his repressive policies throughout his country, the massing of his elite troops in the south, and his eventual invasion of Kuwait made him the most visible and vulnerable target as a starting point for George Bush's determination to re-establish Western hegemony over Gulf oil and particularly to shield Saudi Arabia. To do this and to attempt to give the maneuver the appearance of an Arab effort, Bush cobbled together the loose coalition of traditionally fractious Arab states. The coalition excluded only hapless King Hussein, who faced ostracism from his Arab confreres, feared Israeli power in the west, and dreaded a potential attack from Saddam. With a base of half a million American troops, superior military equipment, and the orchestrated international support of most of the industrial world that depended upon Arab oil, Bush emerged with a predictable military achievement as leader of what he christened the "New World Order." The flattering designation became tarnished as Saddam Hussein regrouped in Iraq and by 1992 was again projecting a threat to Middle East stability.

Nevertheless, in the momentum of the apparent victory over Baghdad, the Bush-Baker team organized the international conference in Madrid in October 1991. The Israelis and the Arab-Palestinians sat at the same table. By September 1992, six more international conferences had been convened to try to settle the long-standing Palestine problem. Satellite conferences presumably addressed threats to peace from instability in Lebanon and Hafez Assad's irreconcilability to the U.S. half-way measures for resolving the problem of Palestinian and Arab rights in the territory, as stated in the historic UN resolutions 242 and 338. By October 1992, despite much diplomatic verbiage and numerous international conferences, no substantial progress had been achieved.

It is, therefore, not surprising that many veteran Middle East observers look on the existing situation with less than robust hope. The one nearly universally acknowledged light in the pervasive darkness is the Intifada's insistence that the Palestinians help determine their future and the future of at least a remnant of their native land. Significantly, a growing number of Israelis agree with this general principle. Their activity within Israel threatens to polarize Israeli politics as they advocate recognition of the PLO—however structurally reorganized—as the legitimate representative of the growing national consciousness of Palestinians.

It is still too early to predict whether the stones hurled by Palestinian youths will ignite the flames that will burn away the contrived confusions and derelictions of great powers; Arab disunity, mutual suspicions, and tribal jealousies; the pall of public indifference; the limitations of cold war diplomacy; and the arrogance of Israeli super-power mentality—all of which at times have obstructed rational progress toward peace. This detailed analysis of the 1948–49 armistice talks does not presume to be a panacea. But insofar as it highlights the causes for the failure of those talks—in fact, insofar as it discloses that glossing over the basic issues assured a continuation of war—it may identify those basic issues. In turn, this might allow newer, more imaginative, less parochial peace seekers to avoid previous errors. Responding to the aspirations of the average inhabitants of the area, new diplomats may be able to devise a formula for authentic justice and equity, one that respects the humanity of the still-suffering victims of cynical and half-measure negotiations by providing a solid foundation for genuine peace.

Santayana warned that those who cannot remember the past are condemned to repeat it. Beyond this entr'acte there may be no more fitting next chapter to this drama of Palestine than the earnest hope that the insights of the preceding pages may help guide the peacemakers to the goal for which all people of good will never cease to aspire.

NOTES

Preface

1. Yemina Rosenthal, ed., *Documents on Foreign Policy of Israel.* The Foreword to *Companion Volume* 3 refers to this principal collection of documents as the *Main Volume* (cited hereafter in the text as *M. V.*). The *Companion Volume* will be cited in the text as *C. V.*

2. It is of some significance that standard histories of Zionism and Israel, written by such scholars as Nadav Safran, Walter Laqueur, and J. C. Hurewitz, often contain no detailed account of the armistice negotiations or the substance of the final agreements. In two such standard works the armistices are not even mentioned in otherwise extensive indexes. See Nadav Safran, *Israel the Embattled Ally*; Walter Laqueur, *A History of Zionism*; and J. C. Hurewitz, *The Struggle for Palestine.*

1. Original Sins and Present Motives

1. *The Pentagon Papers*, ix, x.

2. For a detailed analysis of seven popular myths by an Israeli, see Simha Flapan, *The Birth of Israel: Myths and Realities.* The author deals with the following points: Israel had reservations in accepting partition; the Arabs did not categorically reject partition; the original Palestinian refugees in 1947 were not called on to flee by the Arab states; the Arab states did not invade Palestine on May 15, 1948, with the intention of expelling Jews; the 1948 war was not inevitable; the newborn state of Israel was not David facing Goliath; and Israel has not been the lonely seeker of peace.

3. David Hirst, *The Gun and the Olive Branch*, responsibly combines a good overview with close analyses of crucial, specific events. Hirst used a wider variety of sources than I have found in any other one-volume historical survey. He provides an insightful understanding of the state of mind with which the Israeli negotiators came to the armistice negotiations.

2. History, Sources, Law

1. General Assembly Resolution 181 (II), "Plan of Partition with Economic Union." For a convenient source of the complete text of this and all other UN resolutions cited passim, see *United Nations Resolutions on Palestine*, ed. George J. Tomeh, 11–14 (henceforth cited in the text as *UN Res.*). The recommended "Boundaries of the City of Jerusalem" are in part III, B.

2. Fred J. Khouri, *The Arab/Israeli Dilemma*, 60.

3. Ibid., 59.

4. Joseph Badi, ed., *Fundamental Laws of the State of Israel*, 8, complete text of the "Declaration of Establishment." For historical—and legal—reasons, the declaration is *not* called a declaration of independence. The Zionist movement was a party to the establishment of the state. The two facts are connected. The state was conceived as the "sovereign state of the Jewish people," not only of Jews who lived in Palestine, or who might come there, and certainly not a state in which non-Jewish inhabitants were regarded as establishers. The Zionist movement, an extraterritorial national instrumentality of the new state, would, in 1952, be recognized in Israeli law as a part of the conventionally recognized government, representing the interests of the "Jewish people." For a more detailed exposition of the continuing legal and political significance of these later developments, see W. Thomas Mallison and Sally V. Mallison, *The Palestine Problem in International Law and World Order*, particularly chap. 2 and passim.

5. According to Hirst, *Gun and Olive Branch*, 134, an Arab Liberation Army of 3,830 volunteers, of which only 1,000 were Palestinians, under the command of an army officer of Lebanese origin, Fawzi al-Kawekji, crossed into Palestinian territory in January 1948. Kawekji had become a guerrilla leader in Palestine in 1936. On the Zionist side, the Irgun Zvai Leumi, led by Menachem Begin, had been operating for some years. Their principal target had been the British. They hoped to end mandate rule and establish a "Jewish Government . . . chosen from representatives of all the Jewish [Zionist] parties." See Menachem Begin, *The Revolt*, 178. In January 1948, the Irgun adopted a strategic plan to attack heavily populated Arab sectors and cities that—except for Jerusalem—had been designated for the Arab state in the partition proposal: Jerusalem, Jaffa, the Lydda-Ramleh plain, and the Triangle (an area of central Palestine including "the towns of Nablus, Jenin, Tulkarm, the bulk of the non-desert area west of the Jordan") (348 and note). Targeted in the January 1948 Irgun

plan, these sites play an important role in the 1948–49 military campaigns and the armistice negotiations. The Jewish Agency and the Haganah, its police force, frequently distanced themselves from the Irgun before 1948. But the Israeli negotiators at the armistice talks included these territories in their claims, although they had been excluded from the proposed Jewish state in the partition recommendation.

6. Khouri, *Arab/Israeli Dilemma*, 62. During the prolonged debate on this American working paper, the Israeli Declaration of Establishment was published—followed within hours by de facto recognition of the new state by both the United States and the Soviet Union.

7. Ibid., 80.

8. Count Folke Bernadotte, *To Jerusalem*, 237. Bernadotte's letter of transmittal of his report to the secretary-general of the United Nations, dated September 16, 1948, from Rhodes, explained the reasoning for his recommendations and expressed hope for an imminent convening of the regular session of the General Assembly.

9. Ibid., 240.

10. Ibid., 238–39.

11. Ibid., 237.

12. Ibid., 241.

13. Ibid., 235ff., esp. 237–42.

14. Mallison and Mallison, *Palestine Problem*, 150.

3. The Starting Point—Paris, 1919

1. Hurewitz, *Diplomacy in the Near and Middle East*, 46. These claims have never been renounced by Israel, which has never voluntarily, even for bargaining purposes, declared what its boundaries should be.

2. Ibid. The complete text of the Zionist "Memorandum," with a prefatory comment by Hurewitz, is on 46–50, the section on boundaries on 47–48.

3. Ibid. The text of the Biltmore program is on 234–35. The text of the Balfour Declaration, a condensed record of its negotiating history, and the British government's agreement in principle are in Hurewitz, 26, sec. 2 and 3.

4. For an excellent account of the intragovernmental debate on partition in Washington, see Michael J. Cohen, *Truman and Israel*, particularly chap. 9, "The UN Partition Resolution," 149ff.

5. Robert John and Sami Hadawi, *The Palestine Diary*, 93.

6. William Roger Louis, "British Imperialism and the End of the Palestine Mandate," in *The End of the Palestine Mandate*, ed. William Roger Louis and Robert W. Stookey, 5–6, 9, 13.

7. See *Foreign Relations of the United States* 5, part 1 (1947); 5, part 2 (1948); 6 (1949) (Washington, DC: Government Printing Office, 1971–77) (hereafter

cited in the text as *FRUS* with volume number and year). For references and interpretations of the 1947 volume, see Elmer Berger, "Pentagon Papers—1947."

8. Hurewitz, *Struggle for Palestine*, 260.

9. Hurewitz, *Diplomacy*, 264–65.

10. Hurewitz, *Struggle for Palestine*, 71.

11. Ibid., 94ff.

12. Flapan, *Birth of Israel*, 13ff.

13. Quoted in Hirst, *Gun and Olive Branch*, 194. Ben-Gurion reiterated the statement in his introductory article to the official *Israeli Government Year-book* (1952), 15: "It must now be said that the State of Israel has been established in only a portion of the land of Israel." It is evident therefore, that Begin's vision of "Greater Israel," and that of Arens, Sharon, and other maximalists, including the Likud party, is no eccentricity. The moderates of Labor, under Peres, still refuse to declare the borders that they are willing to accept.

14. John and Hadawi, *The Palestine Diary*, 377, n.

4. Partition—Less than Half the Loaf

1. The resolution was supported by the Soviet Union as well (which remained friendly to Israel into the early 1950s). Moscow wanted a speedy end to British imperialism and hoped to gain influence in a "progressive" Middle East that would include a socialist Jewish state. On May 14, 1947, Andrei Gromyko announced that, though his government preferred a binational state, it would support partition as the next best alternative. Citing Jewish history and suffering, Gromyko further rejected "any unilateral Arab solutions to the Palestine problem." Zionist leaders were elated, and a Jewish Agency spokesman saw Gromyko's speech as "paving the way for the establishment of the state," according to Arnold Kramer, *The Forgotten Friendship: Israel and the Soviet Bloc, 1947–1953*, 16–17.

2. Hirst, *Gun and Olive Branch*, 108.

3. Ibid., 121.

4. This committee was created by the General Assembly and subsequently, in a majority report, recommended partition.

5. Chaim Weizman, *Trial and Error*, 556.

6. Quoted from the British Laborite and strong supporter of Zionism Richard Crossman, in Begin, *The Revolt*, 184.

7. Quoted in Ian Lustick, *Arabs in the Jewish State*, 28.

8. Begin, *The Revolt*, 226.

9. Palmach was composed of units selected from the Haganah and served as special forces or a commando unit. Theoretically it was under Haganah control.

10. John and Hadawi, *Palestine Diary*, 83.

11. For a vivid account of the Haganah activities in Europe, in organizing

illegal immigration and buying and importing illegal arms to Palestine, see Monya M. Mardour, *Haganah.*

12. Tomeh, *United Nations Resolutions on Palestine and the Arab-Israeli Conflict, 1947–1974,* 5.

13. Khouri, *Arab/Israeli Dilemma,* 59–60.

14. John and Hadawi, *Palestine Diary,* 303.

15. Khouri, *Arab/Israeli Dilemma,* 59.

16. Larry Collins and Dominique Lapierre, *O Jerusalem,* 273, 279.

17. Hirst, *Gun and Olive Branch,* 124.

18. John and Hadawi, *Palestine Diary,* 329.

19. David Ben-Gurion, *Rebirth and Destiny of Israel,* 296.

20. Sami Hadawi, *Bitter Harvest: Palestine, 1914–1979,* 86.

21. Ibid.

22. Ibid., 87.

23. Flapan, *Birth of Israel,* 150–51. For details of the Israeli-Jordanian agreement, see chap. 9, "Transjordan."

5. Warring Their Way to "Peace"

1. Walid Khalidi, ed., *From Haven to Conquest,* lxv. Khalidi's Introduction is a superb overview of the history of Zionist aggression—and Arab resistance—from 1897, the date of the First World Zionist Congress, up to the UN partition recommendation.

2. Hirst, *Gun and Olive Branch,* 133.

3. The Israeli withdrawal from and restoration of the Sinai as part of the Egyptian-Israeli Peace Treaty of 1979 should not be construed as a negation of this assertion. The Sinai was never regarded as part of Palestine and was not included in the 1919 Zionist territorial proposals. Political conditions had changed in the years between 1948–49, the armistice negotiations, and the post-1967 war years. The United States made generous financial contributions to Israel to build new military airfields to compensate for those that Israel had to abandon along with the Sinai. The United States also made guarantees to supply Israel with oil to compensate for the Sinai fields Israel had been exploiting. Egyptian forces had broken the Israeli defenses along the east bank of the Suez Canal, and the Egyptians could claim a measure of military victory while the image of Israeli military invincibility was, at least, challenged. Israeli losses shook the confidence of the Israeli population. Israeli illegal settlements in the Sinai had to be dismantled, and there was visible opposition to the Begin government's decision to return the Sinai. Israel did succeed, however, in militarily neutralizing the largest Arab power. The return of the Sinai, therefore, cannot be said, in any strict sense, to have been a trade-off of "territory for peace." On the contrary, the separate Israeli-Egyptian deal invited the subse-

quent Israeli invasion and war in Lebanon and contributed substantially to the possibility of indefinite Israeli rule of the West Bank.

4. Khouri, *Arab/Israeli Dilemma*, 86, 87.

5. On October 14, the American special representative in Israel, James Mc-Donald, reported in a telegram to the acting secretary of state that he had been informed, from Israeli sources, that "for the last 10 days Egypt forces have been moving reinforcements and deploying troops toward Israeli positions" (*FRUS* 5, part 2 [1948], 1476). There were some Israeli settlements in the south, and Bunche had agreed that Israel might supply them during the truce with "non-military supplies," under UN supervision. He had reported, however, that Israel had "refused to allow the UN supervision." Khouri, *Arab/Israeli Dilemma*, 87.

6. Harry S. Truman, *Memoirs by Harry S. Truman*, vol. 2, *Years of Trial and Hope*, 153, 158.

6. First Try for Peace—With Egypt

1. Khouri, *Arab/Israeli Dilemma*, 95.

2. For a thorough, detailed, and documented negotiating history of the declaration and a legal analysis, phrase-by-phrase, of the final text, as well as authoritative statements of Zionist disappointments, see Mallison and Mallison, *Palestine Problem*, 25–62. For international law interpretations of the declaration and of the Jewish people concept, see ibid., 62–102.

3. For an account of British-Zionist diplomacy leading to the declaration and a survey of the League of Nations supervision of the mandate, see Allan R. Taylor, *Prelude to Israel*, particularly chaps. 2 and 3, pp. 10–39.

4. The November 4 resolution (No. 61) called for the withdrawal of all military forces "which have advanced beyond the positions held on October 14." It also provided for the acting mediator to establish "provisional lines beyond which no movement by troops shall take place."

5. Security Council Resolution No. 61 called on "the interested Governments . . . to withdraw those of their forces which have advanced beyond the position held on October 14" and authorized the acting mediator "to establish provisional demarcation lines." But the latest Israeli aggression had occurred on December 22. It continued until January 7 when both the Israelis and Egyptians agreed to a cease-fire and to begin negotiations to replace the violated truce with an armistice.

6. The implementation did not begin until February 26. See also Eytan to Bunche, *M.V.*, 71.

7. This opinion is supported abundantly in *FRUS* 5, part 2 (1948), and 6 (1949).

8. See the same 1948 and 1949 volumes of *FRUS*. For a detailed exposition of the position of anti-Zionist American Jews that had been presented to President Woodrow Wilson thirty years earlier in opposition to the Balfour Declara-

tion, see Morris Jastrow, *Zionism and the Future of Palestine*, esp. 151–59, and the more public record of the American Council for Judaism, ably summarized in Thomas A. Kolsky, *Jews Against Zionism*.

9. The following biographical notes and those used throughout this volume are from the *C. V.* index: Walter Eytan, director-general, Israeli Ministry of Foreign Affairs, head of Israeli delegation to armistice negotiations with Egypt.

10. Advisor on Special Affairs, Ministry for Foreign Affairs, and member of the Israeli delegation to Rhodes. Also headed delegation to armistice negotiations with Jordan.

11. Constantine Stavropoulos, legal counsel, Legal Affairs Department, UN Secretariat, member of Bunche's staff.

12. The following section deals with U.S. decision making and policy determination at this period. It is based on material in *FRUS* 6 (1949), 702 and passim, beginning with a memorandum from Secretary of State Acheson to President Truman, "*De jure* recognition of the Governments of Israel and Transjordan." The first duly elected Israeli government was selected by popular vote on October 1, 1948.

13. In March 1948, Clifford had advised Truman that U.S. support of partition "offers the best hope of a permanent solution of the Palestine problem *that may avoid war.*" Clifford also argued that the Arabs would be compelled "to sell their oil to the United States" (*FRUS* 5, part 2 [1948], 691, 695).

14. Born Epstein, he changed his name to the Hebrew Elath after appointment as full ambassador, following U.S. de jure recognition on January 31.

15. Until Jordan annexed the West Bank, it was known as Transjordan. The usage of the two names in the Israeli documents does not always reflect the chronology.

16. It is significant that following the 1967 Israeli occupation of Arab East Jerusalem, Abba Eban used the same semantic legerdemain with the terms "annexation" and "administrative" to interpret the Israeli action to the United Nations.

17. Ethridge was a U.S. member of the Palestine Conciliation Commission (PCC). The working of the PCC and of the Truce Commission overlap. Both were established by UN resolutions at different times to address different phases of what was generally hoped would be a process of negotiation leading to a final, comprehensive peace. The Truce Commission was established by Security Council Resolution No. 48 on April 23, 1948. Its function was "to assist the Security Council" in supervising and implementing a truce that had been called for by Security Council Resolution No. 46, April 17, 1948. On May 14, 1948, the General Assembly created the "Mediator in Palestine" by enacting Resolution No. 186 (S-2). Other functions detailed by the resolution: the mediator was to "promote a peaceful adjustment of the future situation of Palestine" (para. 2, a, III) and was "to cooperate with the Truce Commission" to implement Security

Council Resolution No. 48. The PCC was established by General Assembly Resolution No. 194 (para. 2). The commission was "to assume, insofar as it considers necessary in the existing circumstances, the functions given" to the mediator (para. 2, a).

In December 1948, when the PCC was authorized, the UN consensus was that the belligerents would abide by the truce and they could—under UN auspices—negotiate a final and comprehensive peace. That estimate proved to be overly optimistic, but the mediator was still left to work for the desired truce. The truce failed to materialize, and the UN legislation called for more specific terms in negotiated armistice agreements. At the same time, the PCC was charged with exploring the possibilities for a final, comprehensive peace. Consequently, while the PCC's work and the continuing efforts of the mediator and the Truce Commission to effectuate armistices were proceeding simultaneously, in a legal and technical sense the two were separate. Many ultimate Israeli territorial and demographic objectives, which they stated rather candidly to the PCC, dictated Israeli tactics in the armistice negotiations. The reference to Shertok just quoted and reports of his responses to the PCC that follow are typical. Their substance will appear again as the armistice discussions progress, usually in the form of Israeli rejections of compromise proposals offered by one or another of the Arab states or by Bunche.

18. United Nations, *The Origins and Evolution of the Palestine Problem*, 50.

19. Hurewitz, *Struggle for Palestine*, 323.

20. Niles was an Israeli supporter on Truman's staff; Clifford was an associate of Truman's from the president's Kansas City days. During the UN partition debate when the State Department was urging the president *not* to support partition, Clifford unburdened himself of the profound observation, "What will the Arabs do with their oil? Eat it!"

21. Abe Feinberg, wealthy Zionist, and later head of Israeli bond sales in the United States.

22. This account was sent to Acheson by the U.S. ambassador to the United Nations on February 18. See also *M.V.*, 228.

23. The importance Israel attached to the Negev is apparent in an anecdote Eytan reported to Sharett in a letter dated February 17. "Incidentally, one of us asked Bunche yesterday evening, 'The Egyptians seem to be getting all the benefits from this agreement. What are *we* getting out of it?' Bunche replied without hesitation: 'The Negev!' I hope he is right. It will have made all these six weeks of trouble and endless discussion at Rhodes worthwhile" (*M.V.*, 255).

24. The burden of pressing for a positive American position on the refugee problem was left to Mark Ethridge, the American representative on the Conciliation Commission. This strategy satisfied the Israeli position as put by Sha-

rett on February 8, to leave the refugee question to be resolved in a "final peace." Ethridge, however, believed if the refugee problem were not resolved there could not be a peace. Furthermore, a continuation of their displacement would destabilize the area. He found himself imploring Washington for support in carrying out his task. He never obtained such support and after a stint on the commission he resigned in a gesture of futility and despair (see *FRUS* 6 [1949], pp. 782–83).

25. In a footnote appended to the Patterson telegram, *FRUS* reported that on February 26 the censorship had been relaxed to some extent, permitting the publication of seven brief points that were attributed to sources outside Egypt. The local press of February 25 published them in this form: (1) the coastal strip from the Egyptian frontier on a point fifteen kilometers north of Gaza will remain under the control of the Egyptian forces; (2) the Egyptian forces in Faluja will start evacuating the town today; (3) El Auja becomes a headquarters of the UN observers enforcing the armistice; (4) prisoners of war will be exchanged within the next ten days; (5) both parties will not undertake any military operations or bring in reinforcements in arms and equipment; (6) both parties will not build new airfields in Palestine; and (7) both parties are to reduce their main forces within four weeks in compliance with the armistice.

26. The word *plot* is a reference to the secret negotiations between Abdallah and the Israelis. It involved an agreement by Abdallah for a separate peace and not just an armistice. The king would claim most of the territory that partition had contemplated for the Arab state. In addition, Israel would acquiesce to an Abdallah invasion of Syria with the objective of establishing his old dream of Greater Syria. The details of these bilateral discussions will be discussed and analyzed below as part of the Israeli-Transjordanian negotiations.

27. Neither Israeli nor U.S. documents support this opinion. Israel had ignored or broken one truce after another ordered by the Security Council in order to extend its military occupation beyond the partition borders. The United States, often feebly, tried to influence Israel to cease and desist. The ostensible intent was to bring the military phase of the confrontation to an end. But when negotiations addressed political-territorial issues, the evidence is preponderant that American arm-twisting was directed almost exclusively at the Egyptians. This is supported by the *FRUS* record in Washington's affirmative responses to Israeli importuning and by an absence of complaints in the Israeli documents, together with several restrained objections from the Egyptian side.

28. *M.V.*, p. 277. Author's note: To those familiar with the politicking at Lake Success in those days, this partisanship on the part of Trygve Lie would come as no surprise. The secretary-general's pro-Israeli feelings were common knowledge in the Delegates' Lounge and the dining room. When he completed his term of office he was formally hailed and treated as a hero in Israel.

29. Kenneth Bilby was special foreign correspondent for the *New York Her-*

ald-Tribune for Europe and the Middle East. Sam Brewer was the *New York Times* correspondent in Palestine.

30. Flapan, *Birth of Israel*. Simha Flapan, an Israeli liberal writer and political essayist, demolished the "seven myths" of Zionist-Israeli history. He says these myths "are located at the core of the nation's self-perception." In a search of documents declassified from official archives, Flapan found that they "not only failed to substantiate these seven popularly believed myths, they openly contradicted them" (p. 8).

The first of these myths is that the Zionists accepted the partition resolution and "abandoned the concept of a Jewish state in the whole of Palestine and recognized the right of the Palestinians to their own state." Not so, says Flapan, quoting Ben-Gurion in December 1947 as an example of the attitude of *all* Zionist parties: "Every school child knows that there is no such thing in history as a final agreement—not with regard to the regime, not with regard to borders, and not with regard to internal agreements" (p. 13).

Flapan describes Zionist-Israeli diplomacy as a "tactical move in an over-all strategy" (p. 8) consistent with the 1919 Zionist memorandum to the Paris Peace Conference—a Jewish state in the whole of Palestine, including Transjordan, the Golan Heights and southern Lebanon (p. 31). See also 9, 119ff.

7. Lebanon

1. At the end of this summary of his report, Rosenne suggests, "Only direct negotiations will lead to a successful conclusion of the talks. This conclusion should be borne in mind at the forthcoming peace talks on the final settlement of the Palestine question."

Throughout the years and after many proposals to resolve the Palestine problem, Israel has consistently favored direct negotiations with one Arab party at a time. This strategy implemented a Zionist negotiating principle: "Zionism's secret weapon is Arab disunity."

2. Flapan, *Birth of Israel*, 118–52. Emphasis on the word *apparent* is deliberate. These pages from Flapan's book are a sensational revelation. Reference has already been made to the secret Israeli-Transjordanian negotiations. The Israeli volumes reviewed here do not disclose the full Israeli and Transjordanian motivations. Flapan carefully knits together documentation demonstrating that Abdallah and Ben-Gurion (together with a small contingent of advisors from both parties) were conspiring to partition Palestine between them, shutting out Egypt and Syria and contemplating "politicide" (liquidation) of the Palestinians (150). The conspiracy consisted of Transjordanian acceptance of a Jewish state, essentially in the partition-recommended boundaries, and the annexation, by Abdallah, of the territories assigned to the Arab state. This part of Palestine was then to be joined with Lebanon and, after the defeat of Syria, it would be taken over by Transjordan, to realize Abdallah's lifelong dream of

Greater Syria, with the Transjordanian throne as sovereign. The British, according to Flapan, were prime background movers in this scheme. The United States was less than a vigorous opponent. The plan failed for complex reasons, not the least the Israelis' reluctance to grant some concessions that Abdallah was demanding in the territory assigned the Jewish state. Also many Palestinians, already displaced by the activities of the Irgun and Stern campaigns, were violently opposed, and, further, once the armistice with Egypt was concluded, the Israelis saw their way to take all of the Negev.

The conspiracy also contemplated maintaining substantial British (and some American) control of the political future of the Arabs. At the time, the continuing influence of a Western alliance presented no problem to the Zionists with their already established history of dependency on British (and incipient American) colonialism. Egypt and Syria remained the staunch protagonists of Arab nationalism and freedom from domination by any power outside the region. Flapan argues that Egyptians' entrance into the war—with their forces advancing no farther than the boundaries that had been projected for the Arab state—was motivated by their ambition to frustrate the Israeli-Transjordanian conspiracy and not by any policy designed to destroy the Jewish state.

None of this is clearly visible in the published Israeli or American records. But in 1948–49—as now—American policy with respect to Israel/Arabs/Palestinians is, more often than not, "not what you are permitted to see." Then, as now, there was plausible rhetoric to camouflage the unspoken ambition to maintain American hegemony in the area.

8. Transjordan

1. See General Assembly Resolution No. 194 (III), December 11, 1948, para. 2. This resolution incorporated a number of the recommendations Bernadotte had made in the report submitted to the General Assembly prior to his assassination on September 17.

2. This conflicted with Jordan's proposal to divide the Negev and with the contemplated Operation Uvda already on the Israeli drawing board.

3. The story of the Negev Bedouin is one of the least-known episodes in the generally little-known record of Israeli elimination of Arabs from territory that came under their control. For fragmentary reports in English, see Major-General Carl van Horn, *Soldiering for Peace*, 124. Van Horn, a Swede, was commander of the UN Truce Supervisory Organization from 1958 to 60. A detailed account of the harassing and expulsion of one Bedouin tribe is given in E. H. Hutchison, *Violent Truce*, 30ff. Hutchison, a commander in the U.S. Navy, was assigned to the UNTSO in 1951 and served until 1954. He was head of the Israel-Jordan Mixed Armistice Commission. For some population and demographic statistics on the Bedouin, see Khalidi, *From Haven to Conquest*, 698–99.

4. Preliminaries for the Egyptian-Israeli negotiations at Rhodes had begun

only on January 5. The first meeting was scheduled for the twelfth. It was widely accepted that disposition of the Egyptian-occupied Gaza Strip would be resolved not only to establish an armistice but also for any final peace.

5. The Israeli documents use *Transjordan* and *Jordan* (*Transjordanian* and *Jordanian*) interchangeably. In this analysis, usage generally follows the texts of the cited documents. The two terms refer to the same people and political entity. *Transjordan* and *Transjordanian* were the accepted nomenclature from 1922, when Great Britain divided the land east of the Jordan from Palestine and governed the territory under a League of Nations mandate with a member of the Hashemite family as the titular ruler. After the 1947 UN recommendation to partition Palestine west of the Jordan and in the Zionist (Israeli)-Arab conflict that followed, a considerable area of central Palestine was not occupied by Israel and had been allocated to the projected Arab state. After the failure to establish the proposed Arab state, and in the confused political and military confrontations that took place, Abdallah persuaded his parliament on April 24, 1950, to annex this area of western-central Palestine and to change the names of the combined territories from Transjordan to the Hashemite Kingdom of Jordan. The portions of eastern-central Palestine that were annexed formally in 1950 comprise, essentially, what has come to be known as the West Bank.

6. Operation Yitzuv involved Israeli occupation of the southern half of the western shore of the Dead Sea from Ein Gedi to Edom. There was a valuable potash works at Edom. The Israelis demanded the right to transport potash in Israeli vehicles from the northern end of the Dead Sea to Jerusalem (*C. V.*, 64).

Operation Yitzuv was consistent with the partition-recommended boundaries that had awarded the Negev to Israel. It was, however, contrary to the Bernadotte proposals that had recommended the Negev be included in the Arab state. Whichever criteria are chosen, however, these Israeli military campaigns were all in violation of the UN cease-fire and truce resolutions. See also *M. V.*, map opposite 458.

7. Commander, Arab Legion, head of the Jordanian delegation to the armistice negotiations.

8. For a contrary assessment of Abdallah's motivations and goals—that he was profoundly concerned with preserving pan-Arab interests and rights—see King Abdallah of Jordan, *My Memoirs Completed.* There is a Foreword by King Hussein, Abdallah's grandson. Pages 9–25 deal specifically with the cause of Palestine and what Abdallah considered "the verbal blustering of Arab policy, defence by word instead of by deed" (9). Egypt was the particular object of his anger, and he suspected that Egypt was manipulating the Arab League. He believed strongly that the league's decision "refraining from advancing into Palestine" was wrong. And he speculated that this strategy might have been dictated by "some distrust of me!" (21). The volume is persuasive, and the reader must keep in mind that the condensed record of the secret negotiations be-

tween Abdallah and Israel and Abdallah's *Memoir* both reflect the views of interested partisans.

In 1988 the appearance of a highly readable, massively researched, and well-documented volume, Avi Shlaim, *Collusion Across the Jordan*, may have provided *the* definitive history of this seemingly improbable "adversary partnership" or "tacit alliance," as Shlaim describes it. Only a teasing sampling of findings in his 600-page work is possible here. He has used British, American, Arab, and Israeli sources together with numerous private papers. The Israeli and American records of the armistice negotiations used in this study make many references to the off-stage Israeli-Abdallah talks. They influenced the formal negotiations, and some knowledge of them is "essential for the light [they shed] on one of the most complex and protracted international conflicts of modern times" (2).

Among Shlaim's findings: the origins of the "collusion" date to the 1930s. Abdallah had agreed to "lease" some of "his lands" to Zionism's Jewish Agency (the World Zionist Organization) (616). The deal "was aborted by British and Palestinian opposition." By 1947 the more or less continuing covert negotiations had proceeded to "an explicit agreement . . . on the carving up of Palestine following termination of the British mandate." Freely acknowledging it as a thesis—but based on his exhaustive and comprehensive research—Shlaim writes, "Britain became an accomplice in the Hashemite-Zionist collusion to frustrate the United Nations partition resolution of November 1947 and to prevent the establishment of a Palestinian Arab state" (1).

Shlaim probes much of the intragovernmental intrigue and debate on both sides, which preceded the negotiating positions reported in the documents used in my study. The horse trading in the Israeli-Abdallah talks is not, strictly speaking, a part of the armistice negotiations. In fact, the negotiators for the highly secret talks were under strict orders *not* to inform any but the need-to-know members of their own governments.

The arrangement, therefore, was of dubious longevity from its inception. Both parties knowingly and secretly planned to flout UN consensus (359). Both parties harbored territorial aspirations that were largely in conflict: Abdallah dreamed of some form of sovereignty over all of Palestine, leading eventually to diminishing Syrian influence; the Israelis secretly aspired to the 1919 proposed boundaries of the Jewish state. Neither party could afford for their negotiators at Rhodes—or Bunche, attempting to implement UN resolutions—to know the agenda for the collusion talks. Because neither party was yet admitted to membership in the world body as a "peace-loving state," neither could politically afford to be seen thumbing its nose at world public opinion, reflected in those same UN resolutions. Both parties also had a major power, which was a permanent member of the Security Council, as a sponsor and benefactor. Israel had made progress in solidifying U.S. support, and Transjordan remained Britain's last best hope for retaining some vestige of its former dominant position in the Middle East. Both parties, for different reasons, shared the enmity of a majority of Arabs. Ben-Gurion saw this sharing-by-convenience as a reason to support Abdallah. Abdallah saw the emergent Israeli military prowess as an obstacle to his "Arab brothers" who opposed his design to move his Arab Legion to control the UN-designated territory for the proposed Arab state (536, 595). Despite these never-quite-intersecting circles of national interest, in several low-key inserted asides Shlaim offers testimony by Israelis who were involved in the collusion, admitting "that Israel was to blame for the failure to attain peace because she had no constructive Arab policy" (603).

Personal opinion commentary by author: It may perhaps be judged as unfair for me, using only these scattered references to Shlaim's evidence, to offer a value judgment on major responsibility for the repeated failures of peace efforts between the two parties to the collusion. But there may also be some who find it equally unfair to take without reservations the too prevalently used vocabulary of contemporary statesmen who begin some new search for peace by equating the legitimacy of claims and credentials of "two nationalisms with competing rights for the same territory." However slight the nuance of difference between justice for the Palestinians and legitimate security for Israel may appear to partisans of either side, the overall record of the armistice agreements tips the scales of justice perceptibly in favor of priority for the *fundamental* legitimacy of the Palestinians' case.

The Intifada's apparent determination in this round of Arab resistance to "stay the course," and mounting world opinion in support of their effort, is in striking contrast to previous chapters in this near century-long struggle of Palestine's indigenous people for their own national identity and its concomitant rights. The combination this time may offer genuine statesmen what may be one last opportunity to even the balance by requiring Israel to respond affirmatively to the claims of the Palestinians, greatly reduced from the original, to "a passport and a flag of their own," as one of their occasional spokesmen has defined their aspirations. Such statesmanship, gently but firmly applied, together with equally firm assurances of Israel's carefully negotiated legitimacy, may finally make a major contribution to Middle East stability.

9. The Israelis had, on January 18, authorized their ambassador in Washington to inform the U.S. State Department about the secret negotiations, but they may not have been certain at the time that the British knew.

10. The PCC was established by paragraph 2 of the December 11, 1948, General Assembly resolution. It consisted of three member-states. Its functions were essentially to take over "at the request of the Security Council" the "functions" of the mediator as they were specified in Security Council resolutions. The existence and jurisdiction of the PCC, while the acting mediator was pre-

siding over the negotiations for armistices, complicated Bunche's work. The complications derived basically from the fact that the armistice negotiations were *intended* to confront only military matters. But the Israeli practice—in which the United States often acquiesced—of attempting to establish bases for political-geographical or even future military advantages by positioning the armistice lines contributed to vitiating the authority of the PCC and the mediator. The responsibilities of the two often were, or appeared to be, overlapping. The confusion was compounded in the effort to obtain a separation of forces and to establish armistice lines in Jerusalem.

11. Henry Cattan, *The Palestine Question*, 82-83. Elsewhere (244) Cattan observes that as accommodating as President Truman was to Zionism, he did try to correct some of Israel's excesses, criticizing its attitude at the Lausanne Conference. In a May 29, 1949, note to Israel, Truman expressed disappointment about its intransigence on the problems of the boundaries and called for a change in these policies. But no concrete action followed. More PCC findings relevant to some of the armistice negotiations' agenda are found in Cattan's study on 201 (n. 151), 203-4, 220, 230, 265, and 278. For the text of the Lausanne Protocol, see the Appendix.

12. Khouri, *Arab/Israeli Dilemma*, 76.

13. Begin, *The Revolt*, 155.

14. Safran, *Embattled Ally*, 248.

15. The summary of the agreement in the Israeli documents (*M.V.*, p. 496), dated March 31, simply notes that among several amendments to which both parties agreed, Article 12 "is hereby deleted." No explanation for the deletion is offered in the Israeli records. But there are several significant entries in *FRUS 6* (1949) that shed some significant light on Abdallah's distaste for the agreement and his resentment over the Israeli blackmail. The first entry conveys something of Abdallah's frame of mind. "On the afternoon of March 25, King Abdallah Ibn el-Hussein handed the Chargé in Transjordan, Wells Stabler, a message which he requested be urgently transmitted to President Truman. The message dealt with the subject of territory occupied by Iraqi forces and with the request of Israel for a modification of the present front between Iraqi and Israeli forces. The message was transmitted to the Department by Amman in telegram 132, March 25, 8:00 P.M."

The import of this message was amplified in an urgent telegram from Stabler to Acheson on March 26; the following quotes are all taken from Stabler's message, *FRUS* 872-73. Stabler reported, inter alia, that the prime minister had "raised objections both as to form and substance of negotiations" and that "it is possible the Prime Minister may resign." The king and all Transjordanians "participating in current negotiations . . . are convinced" that if the agreement is not ratified Israel will use force to dislodge the Iraqis and "make territorial adjustments which would probably far exceed what they are endeavoring to extort from Abdallah through negotiation." Abdallah believes neither the United Nations, the United States, nor Britain will take "any effective action . . . to stop them." Stabler's next paragraph merits verbatim reproduction, for it reveals Abdallah's sense of abandonment and despair: "He approved postponement final action on agreement in hopes some way could be urgently devised to prevent Israel from forcing him into this agreement which he also knows will not improve his position, not only re other Arab States but also re his own people and Palestine Arabs. Hence his message to the President March 25."

Stabler then reminded Washington that Sharett had given "formal assurances to President . . . that Israel has no intentions whatsoever commencing hostilities on Iraqi frontier." But "now," Stabler chided Acheson, the U.S. government "seem[s] prepared permit Israel to force Transjordan into paying excessive price without compensation for privilege of taking over Iraqi areas, while at same time threatening that if price not paid, Israel will exact it anyway" (872).

At 5:00 P.M. on March 25, Acheson told Stabler to tell the king that the United States would regard any attempt to breach the "provisions of secret agreement as serious obstacle to progress being made toward peace . . . and would be prepared to give strong advice against any such action to any party attempting major breach" (871). But on the twenty-sixth, Stabler, in his report, told Acheson "Israel has so many times been able to violate truce without consequences" this American "assurance" would give the king "little comfort or support" (873).

And in what has proven to be a prophetic prediction, Stabler concluded his March 26 telegram, saying, "If USG does not take strong line now to stop Israel's constant, defiant and threatening attitude, I venture to suggest that before Palestine peace is concluded, Israel may well have its frontiers on the Jordan. If this does occur, I submit that it will be only because Israel found apathy and appeasement toward its defiant policy" (873).

16. The practice of ignoring intelligence reports and recommendations from American Foreign Service personnel in the field in the Middle East was not new to the Truman-Acheson administration in 1949. For the earliest examples of this practice see the volumes of *FRUS* for 1947 and 1948. For an abridged version of the references to the Palestine problem in the 1947 volume, plus some historical-editorial comments, see Berger, "The Pentagon Papers—1947."

17. In February 1989, Eduard Shevardnadze made an extended trip to the Middle East visiting Syria, Jordan, Egypt, and Iraq among the Arab states. On February 28, the *New York Times* said, in a subheadline, the trip "looks successful" (7). In Cairo, in "back-to-back meetings, the Soviet foreign minister held talks with Moshe Arens, Israel's foreign minister, and with Yassir Arafat." Alan Cowell, the *Times*'s regular Cairo correspondent, wrote, "Western diplomats said [Shevardnadze] had staked out a Soviet position . . . by fostering

Arab unity in areas where the influence of Washington is offset by its allegiance to Israel and its reluctance to offer the P.L.O. more than a tentative hearing."

President Bush, at a news conference on February 21, was asked for his comments on the "perception . . . that the Russians moved into the vacuum." Bush replied he had "never heard such outrageous hypothesis." Middle East policy, he added, "is to encourage discussions between King Hussein and the Israelis." He offered no evidence that he knew of Hussein's surrender of responsibility for negotiating the future of the West Bank and the Palestinians. In more general terms he said he would not be stampeded into hasty action simply because of Shevardnadze's trip. And he concluded a Soviet role in the area would be all right if it were "limited." On February 23, the Associated Press reported from Cairo that Radio Moscow "criticized President Bush for his statement on Tuesday [the twenty-first] that Moscow's role in the Middle East peace talks should be limited" (*Sarasota Herald-Tribune*, February 23, 1989, 4A).

18. This position was outlined in a top secret telegram to General George C. Marshall, then secretary of state. It had been formulated after consultation with the president. Its essential point was approval of the Israeli claim to boundaries as set forth in the partition resolution. Any modifications must be "fully acceptable to the State of Israel." This meant the United States would *not* support an Israeli claim to Jaffa and western Galilee. But Bernadotte recommended that Israel relinquish part of the Negev to the Arab state "as *quid pro quo* for retaining Jaffa and western Galilee." There was also a strong suggestion the United States believed "the Arabs [Transjordan] should have a port on the Mediterranean" (*FRUS* [1948], p. 1567).

The following verbatim paragraph from the November 10, 1948, position paper provides a summary of the *principle* that the United States recommended for resolving territorial disputes. Marshall was told:

> In plain language, the President's position is that if Israel wishes to retain that part of the Negev granted it under Nov 29 resolution, it will have to take the rest of Nov 29 settlement which means giving up western Galilee and Jaffa. We feel that there is room for a mutually advantageous arrangement—Israel to retain western Galilee and Jaffa in return for relinquishing part of the Negev to Arab states, presumably Transjordan and Egypt.
>
> We feel that it would be contrary to the President's wishes if US De[legation] came up with a plan of its own at this stage. He feels that our efforts should be directed toward having two parties settle the matter or stick to the Nov 29 boundaries. (*FRUS* 6 [1949], pp. 1566–67)

19. In an interesting note to Sharett, dated April 3, Eytan reviewed for the foreign minister, who was in New York, the scenario that produced the secret deal. In an unusual—and subjective—paragraph, the skilled Israeli diplomat

revealed to his superior that he and Yadin experienced moral qualms about some aspects of the official Israeli line they had been required to advocate. The following, therefore, provides a refreshing human touch to the more consistent Israeli hard-line exploitation of the obvious Jordanian military and political weaknesses. And, more important in the history of the Palestine problem, Eytan's personal confession sheds some light on Israeli responsibility for causing the massive Arab refugee problem.

> I should like here to add a little piece by way of personal reaction, which as far as I am concerned qualifies somewhat the "tremendous diplomatic victory" you speak of in your cable of April 1st. I do not know how Shiloah and Dayan felt about this, but certainly Yadin and I had qualms, and if you like, moral scruples, about what we were doing. Although the Transjordanians had agreed that there would be no further discussion of the new line, we discovered soon after we got to Shuneh that they in fact wanted to change the line to the extent of leaving on their side of it the largest villages in the area to be evacuated by the Iraqis—for example, Umm el-Fahm, Baqa Gharbiya, and Taibiya. We resisted this claim for all we were worth, and resisted it successfully. But both Yadin and I were acutely conscious of the Transjordanians' right to take up the position they did. We were, after all, discussing the future villages which were wholly Arab in population and situated in territory under Arab control. They were not villages we possessed, but villages we would possess if the deal between us and the Transjordanians went through. In spite of all guarantees and fine phrases, it was clear to the Transjordanians, as to us, that the people of these villages were likely to become refugees as soon as the Iraqis withdrew, and possibly even before. (It was reported yesterday evening that Mr. Ethridge had stated in Beirut that the mere rumour of impending changes had already made 32,000 Arabs leave their homes on the rim of the Triangle. I do not think this is true, but it is an indication of things to come.) The people who are letting these Arab villagers down are of course the Transjordanians, but that does not make it any more agreeable for us. We are partners to this deal, and it is we and not the Transjordanians who will be blamed for its results. (*M.V.,* 498–500)

20. René Neuville, French consul-general in Jerusalem.

21. Thirty years later, Israel could—and did—defy UN law. It deplored the division of Jerusalem and declared it would be a united city and the permanent capital of the State of Israel and of the "Jewish people."

22. My speculation about Abdallah's and the Israelis' real intent and objectives is substantiated in *C.V.,* 83–85, as well as in the earlier references to the secret negotiations.

23. "Efrat" refers to Yitzhak Efrat, who was "in charge of telegraph office, Ministry for Foreign Affairs" (*C.V.*, p. 177).

24. This shift of U.S. policy on the refugee question is fully explained in a State Department policy paper, dated March 15. For the distribution of the refugees who had fled to the Arab states, see *FRUS* 6 [1949], p. 829. The Conciliation Commission's estimate on April 22, 1949, was a total of 950,000 (935). Washington believed that 600,000 of the refugees would have to be "permanently resettled in the Arab states" (831).

25. Some recent failures to comply with the General Assembly's resolution to incorporate rights and equity for the Arabs through partition are as follows.

(1) The Camp David Frameworks (1978) and the Egyptian-Israeli Treaty (1979). Neither of these related agreements required of either party any strict observance of the General Assembly's partition resolution. Nor did the United States, as the principal proponent of the Camp David negotiations and the official host of the negotiating delegations representing Egypt and Israel, display much diplomatic vigor in support of those principles. The result was that though Egypt regained virtually all of the territory that it had lost in the 1967 war, Israel was not required to return to the proposed Arab state the territories it had occupied between the recommended partition borders. And although Gaza had been under Egyptian control as the UN negotiations to implement partition began, it was not ceded back to Egypt at Camp David as much of Egypt's territory was. The reality was that the much-heralded Camp David sessions and the following treaty isolated Egypt from the Arab world and neutralized it as a potential obstacle to the Israeli strategy of "creeping occupation" (Alfred Lilienthal, *The Zionist Connection*, 694–713). For the full text of the Egyptian-Israeli treaty and related agreements, see *The Egyptian-Israeli Treaty, Text and Selected Documents* (Beirut: Institute for Palestine Studies, 1979), particularly 29, 78, and 87. See also Seth P. Tillman, *The United States in the Middle East*, 24–34.

(2) In February 1986, Arafat and King Hussein agreed on the broad principles for a common Palestinian-Jordanian position for possible negotiations with Israel. This was no small accomplishment after the bitter conflict between the two representatives of Arab entities whose importance for any comprehensive peace was indispensable. The Palestinians modified their historic claim for an independent, sovereign state of their own and agreed to a less definitive formula of self-determination and a confederation with Jordan. Hussein undertook to win U.S. support for this agreement but was unceremoniously turned down by Washington. Yet there was nothing in this initiative that was in irreconcilable contradiction or violation of the UN's partition recommendation, which the United States originally had not only supported but had actively lobbied for. The almost inescapable conclusion is that there was at least a tacit

understanding between the United States and Israel to obstruct any political maneuver that might lead to negotiations for the partition recommendation's Arab State or to acceptance of the Palestinians as a recognized party.

26. Ethridge urged Acheson to call in Sharett (Shertok) and to "pressure" Israel to abide by the December 11, 1948, General Assembly resolution "as to refugees," to inform Israel "it is not entitled to keep both the areas" allotted to it by the partition recommendation "and areas allotted to the Arabs," and that "Israel should make appropriate territorial compensation for any territory it seeks to retain beyond that allotted to the Jewish state by the November 29 resolution." Acheson was also urged to tell Sharett the United States considered it "essential that Jerusalem be placed under the overall supervision of some representation of the United Nations" with perhaps trusteeships administered by Israel in "Jewish Jerusalem" and Transjordan playing a similar role in "Arab Jerusalem." Acheson was also urged to advise Sharett that Israel was expected "to play a major role in the solution" of the refugee problem by "offering financial assistance" for resettlement of those who elected not to return, "also in the repatriation to Israel of a substantial number of the refugees." Acheson reviewed these matters with President Truman and saw Sharett in New York on April 5. The Israeli-Transjordan Armistice Agreement had been signed at Rhodes on the third. Detailed accounts of the Acheson-Sharett exchanges are recorded in *FRUS* 6 [1949], pp. 890ff. Failure of the Conciliation Commission warrants a separate review and analysis. A solid basis is established for judgments about responsibility for the continuing confrontations between Israel, the Arab states, and the Palestinians. Truman agreed "to go over the same points" with Chaim Weizmann, newly elected president of Israel, on a scheduled visit with Truman. The only available record of the conversation between the two presidents is a "Memorandum of Conversation" written by Acheson, dated April 25, 1949 (*FRUS* 6 [1949], p. 943).

Weizmann apparently took "a helpful attitude" on the "internationalization of Jerusalem, on boundary settlement, the refugee question and Israeli membership in the United Nations." But his offer of a helpful attitude was contrary to Sharett's responses to Acheson at their April 5 meeting when he had rejected any Israeli offer of "territorial compensation" for any Arab territory occupied beyond the partition recommendations. He mentioned western Galilee particularly as "an area Israel had no intention of giving up." On the refugee problem he repeated the Israeli position that "basically resettlement is the proper solution." Allowing their return, Sharett stated, would "disturb the homogeneity of Israeli areas" (*FRUS* 6 [1949], pp. 892–93).

27. For a detailed, authoritative exposition of the weight of UN resolutions in international law and the obligations of member-states to enforce UN legislation, see Mallison and Mallison, *Palestine Problem*, 1, 145, and other indexed references.

Significantly, the most popular Zionist historians make almost no references to the refugees or Palestinians in their accounts of the so-called War of Independence and the critical negotiations under UN supervision, which were charged with the responsibility of finding a formula for a lasting peace. One example of many: in Safran, *Embattled Ally,* there are only three grudging references to refugees in the author's treatment of the 1948–49 period (62, 224, 225).

28. For a more detailed and closely documented confirmation of this conclusion by an Israeli, see Flapan, *Birth of Israel,* 8–10. In his summaries of research into two of the myths circulated by Zionists, he asserts that Israel "sought to increase the territory assigned by the UN to the Jewish state." About refugees, Flapan says, "The refugee problem was created by Israel's political and military leaders who believed that Zionist colonization and statehood necessitated the 'transfer' of Palestinian Arabs to Arab countries," and, on territory, "My research indicated that the Arab states aimed not at liquidating the new state, but rather at preventing the implementation of the agreement between the Jewish provisional government and Abdallah for his Greater Syria scheme" (9). And, Flapan again, on Israeli rejection of compromises: "From the end of World War II to 1952, Israel turned down successive proposals made by Arab states and by neutral mediators that might have brought about an accommodation" (10).

9. Scorning Syria

1. Different sources transliterated this man's name as both Za'im and Zaim. We have retained the various spellings of the original sources.

2. For a concise review of the Lausanne Conference and the Lausanne Protocols that it produced and that were signed on May 12, see Khouri, *Arab/Israeli Dilemma,* 293–94.

3. The demilitarized zone, which included Arab villages, was established by the armistice agreement. In 1953, the Israelis began a creeping occupation of it. From the Golan Heights, the Syrians shot down on settlers, creating a crisis.

4. Niles described himself as a Zionist. Clifford and Daniels were concerned about Thomas Dewey's bid for the presidency and particularly Jewish votes in New York, Chicago, Los Angeles, and other population centers. For an official record of the interplay between the White House and State Department, see *FRUS* 5, part 1 (1947), under "Palestine" and *FRUS* 5, part 2 (1948), which is devoted entirely to "Israel." For a summary of the *FRUS* record see, Berger, "Pentagon Papers—1947." See also Cheryl Rubenberg, *Israel and the American National Interest,* 23–51, and Evan M. Wilson, *Decision on Palestine.*

5. For reinforcement of this opinion, see *FRUS* 5, part 1 (1947), under "Palestine."

6. There is abundant confirmation of this analysis, from both pro-Arab (Palestinian) and Zionist (pro-Israeli) sources. See Sabri Jiryis, *The Arabs in Israel,*

235–39, and Jiryis, an earlier version of the same title (published in Beirut by the Institute for Palestine Studies in 1969, 178–80). Zionist views often offer extenuating circumstances, such as the difficulties facing the early Zionist pioneers, including Arab hostility to the establishment of a Zionist state. For candid Zionist analyses, see Nahum Goldmann, *The Autobiography of Nahum Goldmann: Sixty Years of Jewish Life*, 185, 186, 289, and Lustick, *Arabs in the Jewish State*, 53, 98, 106, 270–71; for an exposition of the institutionalization of such discrimination, see Roselle Tekiner, "Jewish Nationality Status as the Basis for Institutionalized Racial Discrimination in Israel."

7. Because of Syria's internal political chaos at the time, the authenticity and seriousness of Za'im's offer has been questioned. He headed the Syrian government for only four and a half months. One of his "top priorities was to make peace with Israel." He offered to resettle 300,000 of "the Palestinian refugees . . . if enough outside economic assistance could be provided." His primary consideration was "to generate nationwide economic development, rather than purely humanitarian concern to alleviate the suffering of the refugees." He was "deposed and executed" however, on August 14, 1949. See Avi Shlaim, "Hosni Za'im and the Plan to Resettle Palestine Refugees in Syria." Shlaim's conclusion about Za'im is that "during his brief tenure he gave Israel every opportunity to bury the hatchet and lay the foundations for peaceful coexistence in the long term. If his overtures were spurned . . . the fault must be sought not with Za'im but with the Israeli side. And the fault can be traced directly to that whole school of thought of which Ben-Gurion was the most powerful and short-sighted proponent, which maintained that time was on Israel's side and that Israel could manage perfectly well without peace with the Arab states and without a solution to the Palestinian refugee problem" (79). This conclusion is confirmed by Israeli historian Benny Morris, who is also diplomatic correspondent for the *Jerusalem Post*. In the *Post's* International Edition of February 21, 1987, he wrote, "The [Za'im] offer, whether serious or not, was tardily considered in Jerusalem and never seriously responded to."

8. Flapan, *Birth of Israel*, 8, 15–53, "Myth One." Flapan describes the Zionist acceptance of partition as "a tactical move" to thwart "the creation of a Palestinian Arab state" and "to increase the territory assigned by the UN to the Jewish state."

9. Begin, *The Revolt*, passim, esp. 348ff.; Netanel Lorch, "Plan Dalet," in *From Haven to Conquest*, ed. Walid Khalidi, 755 ff.: "The main objective was to seize as much territory as possible both within and outside the areas 'allotted' to the Jews by the UN partition resolution, preliminary to the declaration of the Jewish state on the 15th of May, the date of the formal termination of the British mandate over Palestine" (756, note).

10. Khouri, *Arab/Israeli Dilemma*, 80.

11. For details of Sykes-Picot Agreement, see Hurewitz, *Diplomacy*, 18ff.

The agreement consisted of eleven letters exchanged among Britain, France, and Russia between April 26 and October 23, 1916. The three nations agreed to divide the Asiatic Ottoman lands among themselves.

12. Rosenne appears to have been a competent and scholarly researcher in international law, rarely matched by any Arab contemporaries.

13. *Encyclopedia of Zionism and Israel*, 1:620, 2:869.

14. Identified as Nasser in the text of the Israeli record but as Naser in the index.

15. See Khouri's excellent summary in *Arab/Israeli Dilemma*, 68–101.

16. For documented evidence, see Paul Findley, *They Dare to Speak Out*, and Edward Tivnan, *The Lobby: Jewish Power and American Foreign Policy*. For a pro-Israel version, see Stephen D. Isaacs, *Jews and American Politics*.

17. This speculation about the stiffening of U.S. attitudes toward Israel is confirmed in the record of exchanges between the State Department and Mark Ethridge. Instructions to Ethridge may be found in the index of *FRUS* 6 (1949), s.v. "Palestine Conciliation Commission."

18. It is not not precisely clear to what territory "outside Palestine" refers; perhaps it is to sectors east of the Jordan River and the Sea of Galilee, to be designated in the proposed armistice agreement demilitarized zones between the international border of Palestine and Syria. See *M.V.*, map facing 522.

19. On March 29, the U.S. consul general in Jerusalem had informed Acheson that the Israeli government had announced it was moving its "Ministries of Health, Education, Religion and Social Welfare and War Sufferers to Jerusalem together with departments of additional ministries." The move was regarded by both the Conciliation Commission and the United States as a fait accompli amounting to virtual annexation (*FRUS* 6 [1949], p. 883). See also many references to authoritative Israeli government declarations to this effect in *FRUS* 6 (1949) index, s.v. "Jerusalem, Israeli Position."

20. On June 24, Acheson sent the Israelis a reply to their reply. Inter alia, he observed the inconsistency with which the Israelis regarded the partition recommendation.

> The Government of the United States notes that the Government of Israel maintains that it cannot accept the principle of territorial compensation, related to the 1947 partition award, since that award was based on a series of assumptions which failed to materialize. It is observed, however, that the Government of Israel places considerable emphasis upon the continuing validity of the 1947 award where such emphasis supports its own military occupation by Israel of the southern part of the Negev during a period of truce and in connection with the presence of Syrian troops in a portion of Palestine alloted in 1947 to Israel. In any event, the partition of 1947 is the only authoritative expression of the views of the United Nations with

respect to a just territorial division of Palestine between Arabs and Jews. The General Assembly has not indicated in which respects, if any, it believes the territorial basis of that award should be modified in the light of any changes in the assumptions on which that partition was based. (*FRUS* 6 [1949], p. 1175)

21. The Israelis admit nothing of the Zionist terror, which began before the mandate was terminated. For details—and the involvement of the Jewish Agency's Haganah in the terrorist attacks—see Begin, *The Revolt*.

22. See Jacques de Reynier, "Deir Yasin," in *From Haven to Conquest*, ed. Khalidi, 761; Jon Kimche, "Deir Yasin and Jaffa," ibid., 775–78; Erskine Childers, "The Other Exodus," ibid., 795–803; and Flapan, *Birth of Israel*, chap. 3. Yitzhak Rabin, in his *Rabin Memoirs*, does not deal with this matter. This is hardly surprising since that year five Israeli cabinet members, acting as a censorship board, "prohibited former Prime Minister Yitzhak Rabin from including in his memoirs a first-person account of the expulsion of 50,000 Palestinian civilians from their homes near Tel Aviv during the 1948 Arab-Israeli war" (David K. Shipler, *New York Times*, October 23, 1979). And Nadav Safran observes, in *From War to War*, "On the basis of first-hand observation it can be said that until about the end of May–early June 1948 the refugees from areas under Jewish control left, and left in the face of Jewish efforts to persuade them to stay. From that point on they were *expelled* from almost all new territories that came under Israeli control." Naturally, the Zionists "thought it advantageous to have in it a homogeneous population and proceeded to push the Arabs out" (34–35).

The single most comprehensive, detailed, and thoroughly documented account of Israeli diplomatic strategy for dealing with the refugee problem is Benny Morris, *The Birth of the Palestinian Refugee Problem, 1947-49*. The example Morris describes in greatest detail concerned the Gaza Strip (266–75). All parties to the Gaza negotiations were concerned with whittling down the rights of the refugees as stipulated in paragraph 11 of General Assembly Resolution No. 194, of December 11, 1948.

23. A consistent Israeli propaganda line was to turn back "the wheel of history" 4,000 years to the biblical patriarch Abraham to legitimate the claim to Palestine as the homeland of the "Jewish people."

24. For numerous other references, see *FRUS* 6 (1949), index, s.v. (Raymond) Kane, (Wells) Stabler, (William) Burdett, et al.

25. It may be in order to ask now if the United Nations was too optimistic or precipitate in mandating the creation of the Conciliation Commission to establish a lasting peace *before* the armistice negotiations were completed. The existence of the commission made it easier for the parties with conflicting and still unresolved issues and interests to play diplomatic ball between the two

UN-sponsored bodies. The armistice agreements all contained an escape clause stating the armistices were "without prejudice" to the ultimate claims or interests of the parties. Consequently, fundamental interests and relevant law were left dangling and the *basic* causes of the first Arab-Israeli war remained. To the present time, most of the peace formulas have also skirted the basic issues of both human rights and national interests that had brought on the war.

26. For amplification of this point, see a lecture by Berger, "The United States/Israeli Axis: Peace-Seekers or Rejectionists?" (November 1986, AJAZ office, 347 Fifth Avenue, Suite 900, New York, NY 10016).

27. In the index for the *C. V.* he is identified as Major Nasir.

28. *M. V.*, p. 668. This arrangement was a short-lived expediency. The demilitarized zone remained a source of trouble for several years. The Israelis frequently accused the Syrians of taking advantage of the murky compromise by attacking Israeli civilians. The Syrians became increasingly agitated. The Israelis frequently reiterated the lament that land was too precious not to be more extensively cultivated. They brought heavy earth-moving machinery into the zone and sent in increasing numbers of people, exceeding the original intent of the agreement to allow only civilians who had previously lived in the territory included in the zone. In the 1950s the demilitarized zone, including the Sea of Galilee, became the theater for one of the more violent confrontations following the armistices which, as Bunche had put it, were "finally to liquidate . . . the military phase of the Palestine conflict." The Israelis moved troops and heavy fighting equipment into the zone in such numbers that the United States, with John Foster Dulles as Eisenhower's secretary of state, moved for Security Council action against Israel: see Security Council Resolution No. 93 (1951), May 18, 1951, in *UN Res.*, 133.

29. An exception may be the negotiations with Transjordan. But those negotiations—and the substantive evasions of the final agreement—were largely attributable to the secret talks involving Abdallah's personal representatives and the Israeli counterpart team, of which Moshe Dayan was probably the dominant figure. In those secret talks, of which Bunche was not informed for a long time because of an understanding between England and the United States, the complicated discussions of the Jerusalem problem took place. They should not have been reserved for such bilateral discussions because the partition recommendation had set the city apart for some form of international control. The Trusteeship Council of the United Nations was to have appointed a governor who, in turn, would be responsible to it. He was not to be "a citizen of either State in Palestine" (*UN Resolutions*, p. 12).

30. The apparent disparity in dates is explainable by the fact that Bunche was in New York. His message was transmitted to Tel Aviv at 10:51 P.M., July 13, which would have been July 14 in Israel. A copy was handed to the U.S. delega-

tion at the UN, and from there it was sent to Washington, also on the thirteenth (see *FRUS* 6 [1949], p.1255, n. 1).

31. (*FRUS* 6 [1949], p. 1242.) In a sense, Articles 39–42 of the UN Charter form a whole, stating the Security Council might "decide what measures shall be taken to maintain or restore international peace and security" if it had determined "the existence of any threat to the peace, breach of peace, or act of aggression."

10. Entr'acte

1. General Assembly Resolution No. 2672C of December 8, 1970, "*Declares* that full respect for the inalienable rights of the people of Palestine is an indispensable element in the establishment of a just and lasting peace in the Middle East." For a more complete chronological record of the evolution to recognition of the national character of the Palestinians, see Hadawi, *Bitter Harvest*, 262ff.

2. The complete text of the memorandum is found in Khalidi, *From Haven to Conquest*, 208ff.

3. I would like to discuss briefly the phrase "American and Jewish support" because of its frequent usage in discussions of U.S.-Israeli relations. Without intending any sinister implication, it appears to assign Jews a separate value system in a situation in which decisions affect the common interests of all Americans without distinctions of racial, religious, or ethnic distinctions. As in all political problems, Americans are free, as individual citizens, to hold different opinions about U.S.-Israeli relations. To single out Jews incorrectly implies they are directed by their Jewishness, so that as a group their political decisions about Israel are automatically motivated by visibly different criteria from the motivations of other Americans. This concedes a major argument to the Zionist ideological claim that all Jews are, as Herzl claimed, "one people," meaning they share a common transnational nationality and that, as Jews, they accept extraterritorial nationality ties to the Israeli state. I strongly advance the opinion that if confronted with some such interpretation of the phrase, most American Jews would resent and reject such a distinction in the context of secular American life.

4. *New York Times*, March 23, 1989.

5. Flapan, *Birth of Israel*, 12.

6. Shlaim, *Collusion*, 173. Shlaim's entire chapter 6, "The Torturous Road to War," is probably the best, most-detailed record in English of Israeli military initiatives and Arab disunity and inability to agree on any defense during April and May 1948. Israel's counterpart existed in the form of Irgun and Sternist military actions between the November 1947 date of the UN partition recommendation and May 15, 1948.

7. Ibid., 236ff.

8. John and Hadawi, *Palestine Diary*, 375, 376–77.

9. See appendixes 8, 9-A, 9-B in Khalidi, *From Haven to Conquest*, 858–71.

Culling data from a wide variety of sources, Khalidi has integrated in minute detail the available military resources at various stages of the conflict from January to May 15, 1948.

10. Khouri, *Arab/Israeli Dilemma*, 15.

11. For a detailed exposition of these provisions, see *UN Res.*, 6, 12–14.

12. Ibid., 7–8.

13. Flapan, *Birth of Israel*, 8.

14. Ibid., 31.

15. Khouri, *Arab/Israeli Dilemma*, "The Palestine Question Before the United Nations," 53–67, for a good overview of the actions and motives of the major powers.

16. Laqueur, *History of Zionism*, 575.

17. Khouri, *Arab/Israeli Dilemma*, 50–51; see also Hurewitz, *Struggle for Palestine*, 306–7.

18. Khouri, *Arab/Israeli Dilemma*, 50.

19. Ibid., 77; Safran, *Embattled Ally*, 38.

20. There is much confusion, even bitter controversy, over the legitimacy of the procedures used to poll the preferences of the Jewish displaced persons for resettlement after the war. Some evidence, not entirely undisputed, lends credence to the following. Against considerable British but less French opposition and at the instigation of the Jewish Agency–World Zionist Organization, the United States persuaded the occupying powers in Germany to agree to some separate D.P. camps for Jews. Jewish Agency personnel were in actual strategic, administrative positions in these camps. French and Soviet concerns with the D.P. problem were considerably less than those of Britain and the United States. The British believed that pressure to permit the majority of Jews to go to Palestine was part of a larger plan to exacerbate an already festering problem in that country.

In the United States, political concerns about the threat, real or imagined, of a Jewish vote complicated Washington's uncertain efforts to alleviate Britain's political distress over Palestine and to frustrate the USSR's ambition to exploit the explosive Palestine situation to wedge its influence into the Middle East. Ugly rumors of anti-Semitism among British personnel as part of the UNRRA (United Nations Relief and Rehabilitation Administration) bureaucracy in the camps filled the American press. Stories of the Jewish Agency running underground railroads for Jews using devious and circuitous routes to Palestine were rife. Many argued that a flood of Jewish immigrants would increase Arab anti-British actions, and this added to the growing popular sentiment in Great Britain to rid itself of responsibility for the future of Palestine. Charges were made, not without some evidence, that Jewish Agency operatives in the exclusive Jewish camps were bribing Jews with extra rations of clothes, food, and improved shelter to vote for emigration to Palestine.

For one of the few, perhaps more authoritative accounts of this period and activities in the Jewish camps, see Lieutenant-General Sir Frederick Morgan, *Peace and War: A Soldier's Life* (London: Hodder & Stoughton, 1961). Morgan had been Eisenhower's chief of staff in the Allied forces in 1944–45 and chief of UNRRA in Germany, 1945–46. An extensive excerpt from Morgan's book pertaining specifically to the problem of Jewish D.P.s and Zionist activities may be found in Khalidi, *Haven to Conquest*, 527–52. The thrust of Morgan's opinions may be gathered from a few explicit sentences: "The admirably organized Zionist command was employing any and every means of forcing immigration into the country [Palestine] irrespective of the hardship and suffering of the immigrants, few of whom seemed to have any spontaneous enthusiasm for the Zionist cause. . . . Except for a few ardent devotees with the light of fanaticism in their eyes I was never able to discover any great enthusiasm for the cause among the many to whom I spoke. In the camps all were subject to ingenious and ceaseless propaganda" (533).

Morgan's reports were received with less than appreciation by the Zionists. Responding to pressures from the United States and Britain, he was virtually forced to resign his UNRRA post.

21. Truman, *Memoirs*, 2:135ff.

22. Khouri, *Arab/Israeli Dilemma*, 33; Safran, *Embattled Ally*, 39.

23. Truman, *Memoirs*, 2:140. For a more detailed account of Truman's personal displeasure with Zionist lobbying at this time, see Tivnan, *The Lobby*, 24–25.

24. Safran, *Embattled Ally*, 29ff, esp. 41. Author's comment: Interestingly, the Israeli peace formula in 1989 was approximately a duplicate of the 1946 Arab formula with the majority and minority roles reversed. The Zionists rejected the Arab proposal then. The PLO and presumably the majority of the Palestinians in the occupied territories rejected the Israeli position in 1989.

11. Epilogue

1. The essay has since been published in the 1989 edition of the *Palestine Yearbook of International Law*, vol. 5, available at Al-Shaybani Society of International Law, Lt. P.O. Box 4247, Nicosia, Cyprus.

2. See Israel Shahak, "A History of the Concept of 'Transfer' in Zionism," *Journal of Palestine Studies* 18, no. 3 (Spring 1989): 22–37.

3. For the slightly abridged text of Arafat's statement, see *Jerusalem*, published by the Palestine Committee for Non-Governmental [UN] Organizations, December 1988, 4–9.

BIBLIOGRAPHY

Abdallah, King of Jordan. Foreword by King Hussein. *My Memoirs Completed.* London: Longman, 1951.

Badi, Joseph, ed. *Fundamental Laws of the State of Israel.* New York: Twayne Publishers, 1961.

Barbour, Nevill. *Nisi Dominus.* London: George G. Harrap & Co., 1946.

Begin, Menachem. *The Revolt.* Rev. ed. New York: Nash Publishing, 1977.

Ben-Gurion, David. *Rebirth and Destiny of Israel.* New York: Philosophical Library, 1954.

Berger, Elmer. "Pentagon Papers—1947." New York: AJAZ.

————. "The United States/Israeli Axis: Peace-Seekers or Rejectionists?" New York: AJAZ, 1986.

Bernadotte, Count Folke. *To Jerusalem.* Translated by Joan Bulman. London: Hodder and Stoughton, 1951.

Cattan, Henry. *The Palestine Question.* London: Croom Helm, 1988.

————. *Palestine and International Law.* London: Longman Group Limited, 1973.

Chomsky, Noam. *Pirates & Emperors.* New York: Claremont Research & Publications, 1986.

Cohen, Michael J. *Truman and Israel.* Berkeley: University of California Press, 1990.

Collins, Larry, and Dominique Lapierre. *O Jerusalem.* New York: Simon & Schuster, 1972.

de Reynier, Jacques. "Deir Yasin." In *From Haven to Conquest,* edited by Walid Khalidi. Beirut: Institute for Palestine Studies, 1971.

Encyclopedia of Zionism and Israel. New York: Herzl Press, McGraw-Hill, 1971.

Findley, Paul. *They Dare to Speak Out.* Westport, Conn.: Lawrence Hill & Co., 1985.

Flapan, Simha. *The Birth of Israel: Myths and Realities.* New York: Pantheon Books, 1987.

Goldmann, Nahum. *The Autobiography of Nahum Goldmann: Sixty Years of Jewish Life.* Translated by Helen Sebba. New York: Holt, Rinehart & Winston, 1969.

Hadawi, Sami. *Bitter Harvest, Palestine, 1914-1979.* New York: Caravan Books, 1979.

Hirst, David. *The Gun and the Olive Branch.* London: Futura, McDonald & Co., 1983.

Hurewitz, J. C. *Diplomacy in the Near and Middle East.* Vol. 2. Princeton, N.J.: D. Van Nostrand, 1956.

————. *The Struggle for Palestine.* New York: Norton, 1950.

Hutchison, E. H. *Violent Truce.* New York: Devin-Adair, 1956.

Isaacs, Stephen D. *Jews and American Politics.* New York: Doubleday & Co., 1974.

Jastrow, Morris. *Zionism and the Future of Palestine.* New York: Macmillan, 1919.

Jeffries, J. M. N. *Palestine: The Reality.* London: Longmans, Green & Co., 1939.

Jiryis, Sabri. *The Arabs in Israel.* Beirut: Institute for Palestine Studies, 1969. Reprint. London, New York: Monthly Review Press, 1976.

John, Robert, and Sami Hadawi. *The Palestine Diary.* Vol. 2, *1945-1948.* Beirut: Palestine Research Center, 1956.

Khalidi, Walid, ed. *From Haven to Conquest.* Beirut: Institute for Palestine Studies, 1971.

Khouri, Fred J. *The Arab/Israeli Dilemma.* Syracuse: Syracuse University Press, 1968.

Kimche, Jon. "Deir Yasin and Jaffa." In *From Haven to Conquest,* ed. Walid Khalidi. Beirut: Institute for Palestine Studies, 1971.

Kolsky, Thomas. *Jews Against Zionism.* Philadelphia: Temple University Press, 1990.

Kramer, Arnold. *The Forgotten Friendship: Israel and the Soviet Bloc 1947-1953.* Urbana and Chicago: University of Illinois Press, 1974.

Laqueur, Walter. *A History of Zionism.* New York: Schocken Books, 1976.

Lilienthal, Alfred. *The Zionist Connection.* New York: Dodd, Mead, & Co., 1978.

Lorch, Netanel. "Plan Dalet." In *From Haven to Conquest*, ed. Walid Khalidi. Beirut: Institute for Palestine Studies, 1971.

Louis, William Roger, and Robert W. Stookey, eds. *The End of the Palestine Mandate*. Austin: University of Texas Press, 1986.

Lustick, Ian. *Arabs in the Jewish State*. Austin: University of Texas Press, 1980.

Mallison, W. Thomas, and Sally V. Mallison. *The Palestine Problem in International Law and World Order*. Essex: Longman House, 1968.

Mardour, Monya M. *Haganah*. Foreword by David Ben-Gurion. New York: The New American Library, 1957.

Morgan, Frederick. *Peace and War: A Soldier's Life*. London: Hodder & Stoughton, 1961.

Morris, Benny. *The Birth of the Palestinian Refugee Problem, 1947–1949*. Cambridge: Cambridge University Press, 1987.

Patai, Raphael, ed. *Encyclopedia of Zionism and Israel*. 2 vols. New York: Herzl Press/McGraw-Hill, 1971.

Pentagon Papers, The. New York: Bantam Books, 1971. Originally appeared in the *New York Times*, written by Neil Sheehan et al., edited by Gerald Gold, Allan M. Siegal, and Samuel Abt.

Rabin, Yitzhak. *The Rabin Memoirs*. Boston: Little, Brown & Co., 1979.

Rosenthal, Yemina, ed. *Documents on Foreign Policy of Israel*. Vol. 3, *Armistice Negotiations with the Arab States, December 1948–July 1949*. Jerusalem: The Government Printer, 1982.

Rubenberg, Cheryl. *Israel and the American National Interest*. Urbana and Chicago: University of Illinois Press, 1986.

Safran, Nadav. *From War to War*. Indianapolis: Bobbs-Merrill, 1969.

———. *Israel: The Embattled Ally*. Cambridge: Harvard University Press, Belknap Press, 1981.

Shahak, Israel. "A History of the Concept of 'Transfer' in Zionism." *Journal of Palestine Studies* 18, no. 3 (Spring 1989): 22–37.

Shlaim, Avi. "Hosni Za'im and the Plan to Resettle Palestine Refugees in Syria." *Journal of Palestine Studies* 60, no. 4 (Summer 1986): 68–79.

———. *Collusion Across the Jordan*. New York: Columbia University Press, 1988.

Tannous, Izzat. *The Palestinians*. New York: I. G. T. Company, 1988.

Taylor, Allan R. *Prelude to Israel*. Beirut: Institute for Palestine Studies, 1970.

Tekiner, Roselle. "Jewish Nationality Status as the Basis for Institutionalized Racial Discrimination in Israel." *American-Arab Affairs* 17 (Summer 1986): 79–98.

Tillman, Seth P. *The United States in the Middle East*. Bloomington: Indiana University Press, 1982.

Tivnan, Edward. *The Lobby: Jewish Political Power and American Foreign Policy.* New York: Simon and Schuster, 1987.

Truman, Harry S. *Memoirs by Harry S. Truman.* 2 vols. New York: Doubleday, 1956.

United Nations. *The Origins and Evolution of the Palestine Problem.* Part 2, *1947–1977. New York, 1979.*

————. *United Nations Resolutions on Palestine.* Edited by George J. Tomeh. Beirut: The Institute for Palestine Studies, 1975.

United States of America Department of State. *Foreign Relations of the United States* 5, Part 1 (1947); 5, Part 2 (1948); 6 (1949). Washington, DC: Government Printing Office, 1971–77.

van Horn, Carl. *Soldiering for Peace.* New York: David McKay Co., 1966.

Weizman, Chaim. *Trial and Error.* Illus. ed. London: Harper & Brothers, 1949.

Wilson, Evan M. *Decision on Palestine.* Stanford: Hoover Institution Press, 1979.

INDEX

Abdallah, king of Transjordan, 48, 160,
186, 254n.5; and Arab Hashemite
Kingdom, 49, 92; British support for,
227; Israel and, 48-49, 56, 79, 82,
91-99, 102-4, 106-8, 110-13, 116-18,
120, 122, 129-37, 155, 168, 188, 192,
225, 226, 235, 251n.26, 252-53n.2,
254-56n.8, 257-58n.15, 260n.22,
263n.28, 267n.29. *See also* Arab
Legion; Greater Syria, Abdallah's
dream of; Negev; Transjordan
Abraham (bibl.), 266n.23
Acheson, Dean, 258n.16, 265n.19; and
Egypt-Israel negotiations, 61-63,
67-71, 78, 250n.22; and Israel recognition, 46, 249n.12; and Rusk, 118;
and Sharett, 262n.26; and Syria-
Israel negotiations, 158-63, 179-84,
192, 216, 217; and Transjordan-Israel
negotiations, 108, 114, 115, 120,
142-43, 257-58n.15; Truman note
defended by, 265-66n.20
Acre, 29
Airfields, Palestine, 251n.25

Akaba. *See* Aqaba
Al-Auja. *See* Auja
Allenby, Edmund, 221
Al-Saty, Shaukat, 93-94
Al-Tall, Abdullah, 48, 91-98, 105, 122,
129, 132, 135-36
American Jews, 268n.3; and Arafat,
240; political clout of, 186, 263n.4
(*see also* United States, Zionist pres-
sures on); and Zionism, 17 (*see also*
Jews, anti-Zionist)
American University (Beirut), 16
Anglo-French Convention (1920), 169-70
Anglo-Jordanian Treaty of Alliance, 99
Aqaba (town): British forces at, 100,
106, 128-29, 130; as Israel's goal, 45,
56, 63, 88, 95, 100; Israelis in, 100-
101, 102, 104, 106
Aqaba, Gulf of, 11, 14, 75, 98, 100
Arab-American Affairs, 224
Araba Valley, 98, 100, 101-2
Arab Hashemite Kingdom, 49, 92
Arab Higher Committee, 6, 26, 48, 92;
UN appeal to, 168

Egypt; Galilee; Galilee, Sea of; Gaza Strip; Golan Heights; Haifa; Hebron; Huleh, Lake; Israel; Jaffa; Jerusalem; Negev; Partition, Palestinian; Palestine mandate, British; Palestinians; Tel Aviv; Transjordan; West Bank; Zionism
Palestine, mediator in, 249–50n.17
Palestine, State of, 223, 239
Palestine Conciliation Commission (PCC), 45, 49–51, 53–55, 71, 75, 131, 139, 141, 187, 191, 216, 218, 257n.11; failure of, 206, 262n.26; and Jerusalem problem, 265n.19; and Lausanne Conference/Protocols, 108, 154, 182–83; mandate of, 249–50n.17, 256–57n.10; and refugee problem, 142, 158, 160, 186; and territorial disputes, 109, 175. *See also* Ethridge, Mark; Lausanne Conference
Palestine Jewish Colonization Association (PICA), 171
Palestine Liberation Organization (PLO), 223, 238, 239, 259n.17, 270n.24. *See also* Arafat, Yassir
Palestine mandate, British, 5, 6, 28, 109, 143, 171, 231, 244n.5; illegal immigration into, 25; Irgun vs., 244n.5 (*see also* King David Hotel, bombing of); termination of, 5, 16, 22, 24–26, 31, 225, 264n.9; Zionists during, 37, 266n.21
Palestine National Council, 239
Palestinians, 36, 37, 81, 189, 219, 220–24, 256n.8; Abdallah's plans for (*see* Abdallah, king of Transjordan, and Jericho Conference); in Arab Liberation Army, 244n.5; Arab states and, 226, 229; Biltmore Program and, 15; champions of, 16, 17; homeless (*see* Refugees, Palestinian); liquidation planned for, 252n.2; and partition, 4–5, 8; resistance of, 20, 25–32, 33, 247n.1 (*see also* Intifada); U.S. abandonment of, 117; Zionists vs., 252–53n.2. *See also* Palestine

Liberation Organization; Refugees, Palestinian
Palmach, 24, 27, 28, 246n.9 (*bottom*)
Paris Peace Conference (1919), 1, 221; Zionist input to, 10–14, 21, 32, 145, 150, 155, 167, 228, 237, 252n.30
Partition, Palestinian, 39, 187, 188, 217; Arab states and, 44, 226–27, 243n.2; cartological aspects of, 229; Israel and, 49, 63–64, 151, 167–68, 184, 189, 190–91, 230, 243n.2, 264n.8, 265n.20; major powers and, 231–34; and minority rights, 230; UN and, 4–5, 7, 18, 20–21, 22, 24–27, 31, 178, 220, 230, 244–45n.5, 246n.1, 4, 247n.1, 254n.5, 255, 261n.25, 265–66n.20, 268n.6; Zionists and, 22, 25, 29, 33
Patterson, Jefferson, 70–71, 72, 251n.25
PCC. *See* Palestine Counciliation Commission
Peace, territory for, 34, 247n.3
Peel Commission, 20
Pentagon Papers, 1–2
Peres, Shimon, 246n.13
PLO. *See* Palestine Liberation Organization
Potash, Dead Sea, 95, 254n.6
Potsdam Conference, 233
Power, Thomas, 106–7
Prisoners of war, 95, 251n.25
Provisional Government of Israel (PGI), 47, 49
Publications, Zionist, 22

Qastal, 28, 29
Qawuqji, Fawzi, 31
Qazaza, 29

Rabin, Yitzhak, 266n.22
Rafael, Gideon, 202
Rafah, 39
Rahim (Eg. ambassador), 46
Ramleh (Ramle), 7, 91, 93, 95, 186, 244n.5
Ras en-Nakura, 83, 86

Library of Congress Cataloging-in-Publication Data

Berger, Elmer, 1908–
   Peace for Palestine: first lost opportunity / Elmer Berger.
     p. cm.
   Includes bibliographical references (p.   ) and index.
   ISBN 0-8130-1207-4 (alk. paper)
    1. Israel-Arab War. 1948-1949—Armistices—Sources. 2. United
Nations—Palestine—History—Sources. 3. United States—Foreign
relations—Middle East—Sources. 4. Middle East—Foreign relations—
United States—Sources. 5. United States—Foreign
relations—1945-1953—Sources.   I. Title.
DS126.98.B46   1993   92-45726
956.04'2—dc20   CIP